ASSERTIVE INITIATIVE (A.I)

... the light that darkness cannot comprehend!

"light shineth in darkness and...
darkness comprehended >katalambánō
(assertive initiative) < *not*"
(John 1:5)

TOBE MOMAH M.D.

ISBN 978-1-957582-81-8 (paperback)
ISBN 978-1-957582-80-1 (eBook)

Printed in the United States of America

TABLE OF CONTENTS

DEDICATION

I dedicate this book to my father, late General (Dr). Sam Momah. After Seventy seven years on the earth, he transitioned to eternity on July 29, 2020. He taught me the need to be assertive and focused, no matter whose ox was gored along the way. He embarked on several initiatives without popular support, but today those same initiatives are the pillars of family, fortune, and freedom for those involved.

He believed in doing things well the first time, or not doing them at all! In affirmation of that conviction, he once told the officers and soldiers under his Engineering brigade command *I don't need all hands on deck; I only need clean hands on deck!* He taught me excellence, emotional intelligence, and willingness to embrace change when it became inevitable.

He was a consummate lover of humanity and a hero to all he came across. He breached protocols, upturned *status-quos*, paved uncharted paths, and was willing to walk the road alone - if necessary – to attain his goal. Fondly called *the lone ranger* by his peers, he lived by his convictions in a world that has since jettisoned theirs. Adieu Daddy, and thanks for the life lessons - like *Assertive Initiative* – that you taught me.

ACKNOWLEDGEMENTS

God inspired this book. He gave the words and allowed me to put them in print. It, however, would not have been possible without some invaluable assets along the journey who saw value in it and spurred me on. More than anyone else, my wife of eighteen years, Rita, provided a setting that encouraged and sharpened me to write. She had battled a lack of assertiveness, in life and ministry, and allowed me use her as a sounding board for several insights highlighted here.

My Church, Miracle Temple Evangelistic Church, Jackson Mississippi, and my pastors, Bishop and first lady Kenneth and Dorothy Preston, gave me a limitless platform to teach on this subject over a period of two years. Their encouragement enabled me to keep adding to the material until it became a reality. I, also, want to thank members of the ministry I superintend, Faith and Power Ministries, for their support and loyalty during this adventure. Their prayers and concerted efforts throughout the writing of this book was extra-ordinary.

My parents, late General (Dr.) and Mrs. Momah encouraged my writing to no end. From enrolling me in a computer school program, and paying for all my further education home and abroad, they have inspired me again and again to always go for my dreams and keep hope alive. They, alongside my siblings - Amaka, Ada, Emeka and Nkem and their spouses - have supported me in more ways than one and my heart overflows with appreciation to them.

Finally, I want to thank the body of Christ. They have embraced this gospel message of *assertive initiative* and afforded me the opportunity, via in person preaching, livestream media, radio and/or television to air the principles I have elucidated in this book. I trust that what you have made happen to me God will make happen for you multiple times over, in Jesus name! Amen.

PREFACE

In 2018, while preaching in Belzoni, Mississippi the Holy Spirit revealed the words on Jesus in John 1:5 to me in a new way. It reads *light shines in darkness and the darkness comprehended it not* (John 1:5), but the Holy Spirit emphasis was on the need for believers to begin stepping into environments and watching darkness disappear without challenge.

In that encounter, the Holy Spirit emphasized God's purpose for putting the church on the earth. He said God sent us to destroy devils (1 John 3:8), and to "…*aile*…(the) *sea, that thou fleddest,* (and)… *Jordan, that*…(it) *wast driven back?*" (Psalm 114:5) because of His presence (Psalm 114:7).

On the contrary, and in reality, many believers struggle to overcome the darkness. **The Church is not called to struggle with the darkness, but to subdue the darkness** (Genesis 1:28). The secret to subduing the enemy, however, is the light of God. The Church's lack of knowledge on what makes the light shine is the reason for her ignominy and oblivion.

The word *comprehend* in the phrase *darkness cannot comprehend* is a Greek word *Katalambano* and it means *Assertive Initiative* (A.I). Where Assertive Initiative (A.I) is lacking, darkness dominates but where an A.I attitude is present light shines that no amount of darkness can prevail over.

The solution to an insipid Church is assertiveness in whatever we initiate. God has called the Church to overcome the darkness, and not be overcome by it. He wants her to be a victor, not the victim, but it starts by dispelling the darkness through an assertive initiative mindset.

Tobe Momah
Madison, MS
December 2021

FOREWORD

There is a *process* for every *product*, a *how* for every *what*. Until we engage the right processes, products remain elusive; we labor the labor of the foolish which wearies them, "*because they do not know how to go to the city*" (Ecclesiastes10:15). Believers often overlook this fact in their quest to receive the promises of God, fulfill their ministry or to become all they've been ordained to be. An instant mindset ingrained by the world fortifies this neglect of divine processes.

In **Assertive Initiative**, Dr. Momah unveils the life of light – light that darkness can neither comprehend nor apprehend, and the process by which that light produces positive change. This life is unlike a *thermometer* (simply measuring and conforming to its environment) but is like a *thermostat* (imposing its own temperature wherever it is found). Dr. Momah unpacks the necessity of light in a dark world, the kind of light that will conquer the darkness, and how to receive and burn with that light. The sources of that light and the keys to shining are also discussed.

With multifaceted darkness engulfing the world, one wonders why a church of over two billion believers cannot set the world ablaze – quite unlike the early church of whom it was written that they, in their few numbers, "*turned the world upside down*" (Acts 17:6). How come there is so much darkness with so many "lights" and churches? Dr. Momah believes the missing ingredient is the *katalambano* factor – the blazing life of unquenchable light that routs darkness. This life is not passive but possesses an aggressive initiative that leaves darkness helpless before its blistering rays.

Indeed, there is nothing passive about light. The sun is 93 million miles away from earth. From our perspective it looks quiet, neat and nice, but in reality it is like billions of nuclear bombs going off! It has a surface temperature of $10,000^0$ F and solar flares some of which extend for thousands of miles from its surface. The early church was like the sun – erupting here and there, unstoppable, impossible to silence. They were everything but placid; they didn't sit around waiting for something to happen: they made things happen by *initiating* ministry and *asserting* the truths about Christ, even before the powerful religious and political figures of their time. As Smith Wigglesworth famously said, *"The only reason there is an Acts of the Apostles was because the apostles acted."*

The only hope for the triumphant life and the fulfillment of God's purpose in our time is light, *true* light. For that light to burn brightly, we must supply fuel for the fire, and then stoke that fire by the means clearly set forth in this book. Assertive initiative must become our default setting. I warmly recommend this book.

Dr. Ferdinand Nweke
General Coordinator, Eternity Ministries
Africa Coordinator, Global Great Commission Network

I want you to restrain the darkness over the city of Jackson, Mississippi!

- God's word to Tobe Momah
on moving to Jackson,
MS in December 2016

PART I

Between Assertive Initiative and Artificial Intelligence

- *Katalambano*
- Acuity of Assertive Initiative
- Law of Beginnings
- Sources of Light
- Purpose of Light
- Benefits of Light
- Bane of Brightness

If you can discover His light,
you will develop His life!

\- TOBE MOMAH M.D.

CHAPTER ONE

KATALAMBANÓ

"All things were made by him; and without him was not any thing made that was made. In him was life; and the life was the light of men. And the light shineth in darkness; and the darkness comprehended it not" (John 1:3-5).

In John 1:5, the Bible says *"…the light shineth in darkness; and the darkness comprehended it not."* The word *comprehendeth* is the Greek word *Katalambano* and it means Assertive Initiative (A.I). The ability of light to shine is, therefore, predicated on its ability to *Katalambano*, and for darkness not to.

Katalambánō is derived from two Greek words *Kata* and *Lambano*. *Katá* means down and *lambánō* means to aggressively take hold of exactly, with assertiveness and decisive initiative. It means to take ownership, have eager self-interest, make something one's own, seize, apprehend, come upon, or possess.[1]

That same word, *Katalambano*, is used in Ephesians 3:18 for *comprehend*. In that chapter, Paul prays the Ephesian Church *"… be strengthened with might by his Spirit in the inner man; (and) that Christ…dwell in…hearts by faith; that ye, being rooted and grounded in love, may be able to comprehend with all saints what is the breadth, and length, and depth, and height; and to know the love of Christ, which passeth knowledge, that ye might be filled with all the fullness of God"* (Eph 3:16-19).

Katalambano or Assertive Initiative is the last step to knowing the love of God and attaining the fullness of God bodily. When Assertive Initiative is common place in the Church, the glory of His fullness will be manifest in her midst. The Sun, for example, never struggles to shine. It wakes up every morning, knowing that it is going to overcome whatever dark clouds come against it because it knows what it is and how much heat it contains.

That is the *Katalambano* spirit! It is at the heart of the champion mindset, and is genuine, original and not borrowed or artificial. It is undeterrable, unwavering, and focused on **starting well to finish strong**. No wonder the sun is likened in Psalm 19:5-6 as "*...a bridegroom coming out of his chamber, and* (that) *rejoiceth as a strong man to run a race* (whose) *going forth is from the end of the heaven, and his circuit unto the ends of it: and there is nothing hid from the heat thereof.*"

THE ABUNDANCE OF LIGHT

There is currently a lot of talk about artificial intelligence in medicine, manufacturing, and military circles. The current buzz is all about remote precision surgery, tele health, *Siri*, *Watson*, Google clouds, robotic assembly lines, *Da Vinci* surgical technology, and deployment of drones in medical, military, and other such sundry theatres.

Tomorrow's soldier may not fight on the shores of Normady, France but will use *Nintenedo-like* equipment to bombard enemies. Tomorrow's automotive engineers may not manufacture cars on an assembly line like Henry Ford did, but will design cars from the comfort of their homes for automated production. In similar fashion, doctors of the future may never see an operating room, but will use remote surgery to operate on patients.

The artificial intelligence market is projected to reach $270 billion by 2027,[2] and has an anticipated growth rate of more than 100% per year.[2] These staggering numbers, notwithstanding, the greatest A.I. of our time will not be *artificial intelligence*, as often touted, but *Assertive Initiative!* **The world is not going to rotate on artificial intelligence, but on the axis of believers who have an assertive initiative (A.I) mindset.**

The Psalmist said, "*...he sent out his arrows, and scattered them; and he shot out **lightnings**, and discomfited them. Then the channels of waters were seen, and the foundations of the world were discovered at thy rebuke, O Lord, at the blast of the breath of thy nostrils. He sent from above, he took me, he drew me out of many waters* (and) *delivered me from my strong enemy, and from them which hated me...*" (Psalm 18:14-17).

If an individual wants to slaughter his or her enemies, he or she must go with an abundance of light! It is better to go with **lightnings'** than with just light, as even the Bible says, "*...one shall chase a thousand and two ten thousand*" (Leviticus 26:8). Even though artificial intelligence is the toast of many today, and rollicking with finances, Assertive Initiatives that bring added light to combat evil will be the foundation for future conquests and the kindler to triumphing in life.

THE LIGHT EFFECT

If your light is not dispel ling the darkness, you need to check what kind of light you're shining. The Bible says *in him was life; and the life was the light of men* (John 1:4). The dearth of the life of God in the Church stems from the lack of an assertive initiative mindset that shortchanges the light the Church should otherwise be shining.

Light naturally disperses darkness. No one puts on a light bulb, and wonders if darkness disappears. It just does! It (light) paralyzes darkness, and jump starts a breakthrough without satanic permission. The benefit of light is that it destroys darkness, no matter how thick, wide spread or long it has been around. It is, therefore, the shortest way to a breakthrough and a definite solution to darkness and its attendant challenges.

Sin is synonymous with darkness. In Ephesians 5:11-13, the Bible says "*...have no fellowship with the unfruitful works of darkness, but rather reprove them. For it is a shame even to speak of those things* *which are done of them in secret…All things that are reproved are made manifest by the light: for whatsoever doth make manifest is light."*

If you want darkness to flee, place light there. It is the power of light that instantly annuls darkness. Many have "…*treasures of darkness, and hidden riches of secret places…*" (Isaiah 45:3) that are unrivalled but yet unrevealed because their light is covered. It takes a "…*Sun of righteousness aris*(ing) *with healing in his wings…, *(to) *go forth, and *(make you) *grow up as calves of the stall* (so that) *ye shall tread down the wicked…"* (Malachi 4:2-3).

BEGINNING WITH BENIN

I was scheduled to see the Late Archbishop Benson Idahosa in his office at Miracle Temple Church Benin, Nigeria by 11 am. As a medical student at the University of Nigeria, Enugu Campus (UNEC) and Vice-President of the Christian Union UNEC fellowship I had reached out to him with an invitation to minister at our *Total Healing Crusade 1998*, and he had graciously invited me to discuss our plans.

I was scheduled to be in Benin, Edo State by 11am on that Thursday, March 12th 1998 and by 9am I was still in Enugu. Due to my late start, I arrived Benin about 12 noon and immediately noticed a flurry of activities in the Archbishop's office. I saw the State Security service personnel policing his office, and the nearby faith Mediplex hospital filled with blaring ambulances and rampaging medical personnel.

On the advice of the Archbishop's personal secretary, who had earlier apologized for his absence due to unforeseen circumstances, I returned to Enugu, Nigeria after re-scheduling my appointment. On the next day, I was with my father (who was visiting from Abuja, Nigeria) and became crest fallen when I saw the front pages of the National dailies announcing the sudden death of Archbishop Benson Idahosa.

My Dad immediately noticed my change of demeanor and asked what my relationship with the Archbishop was. I was tight lipped, however, because no one knew I had travelled to Benin the day before. I, therefore, rode the rest of the road trip with my Dad non-plussed and straight faced even though within me I was burdened.

Even though I was sad the archbishop had died, I felt sadder that I missed the passing of an Elijah of my time by my lack of assertive initiative. Out of that encounter, I learned to be more *assertively initiating* on tasks and developed a mentality that promoted promptness, timeliness, and conviction in commencement no matter the odds.

Prayer Point: Baptize me with spirit for *Assertive Initiatives*, O Lord, in Jesus name!

1. James Strong (2010). *The new Strong's Exhaustive Concordance of the Bible.* Thomas Nelson (Page 235).
2. Artificial Intelligence Market to Reach USD 266.92 Billion by 2027; Increasing AI Technology Users to Spur Market Growth: *Fortune Business Insights.* May 7, 2021.

The more you discover, the more you recover and the more you recover, the quicker you fulfill your destiny

...DR. DANIEL OLUKOYA
(GENERAL OVERSEER, MOUNTAIN
OF FIRE AND MIRACLES MINISTRIES
INTERNATIONAL WORLDWIDE)

CHAPTER TWO

ACUITY OF
ASSERTIVE INITIATIVE

"Arise, shine; for thy light is come, and the glory of the Lord is risen upon thee. For, behold, the darkness shall cover the earth, and gross darkness the people: but the Lord shall arise upon thee, and his glory shall be seen upon thee. And the Gentiles shall come to thy light, and kings to the brightness of thy rising" (Isaiah 60:1-3).

In John 8:12, Jesus threw down the gauntlet for His Church. He said, *"…I am the light of the world: he that followeth me shall not walk in darkness, but shall have the light of life."* The light the modern day Church is shining is not the same light Jesus shone while here on earth, and neither is it the light of life He bequeathed to her.

The life that Jesus came to give was the light that shines, and the darkness could not stop it. Light is supposed to change the environment and the reason Jesus left the Church here is so her light will change the world around her. That explains why, in Matthew 5:14, Jesus described the Church as *"…the light of the world* (and) *a city that is set on an hill* (that) *cannot be hid."*

When the children of Israel left Egypt, they left at the Begininning of Months and with a high hand. In Number 33:3-4, the Bible says "...*they departed from Rameses in the first month, on the fifteenth day of the first month; on the morrow after the passover the children of Israel went out with an* **high hand** *in the sight of all the Egyptians. For the Egyptians buried all their firstborn, which the Lord* had smitten among them: upon their gods also the *Lord* executed judgments."

The word *high hand* is the Hebrew word *ramah* and it means to go up like an erupting volcano. The last days Church is a picture of Israel leaving Egypt (1 Corinthians 10:8-11), and it is epitomized by an assertiveness akin to an erupting volcano. When the Church moves into *His high handedness*, it will release His marvels for "...*according to the days of thy coming out of the land of Egypt will He (God) shew unto* (us)...*marvellous things*" (Micah 7:15).

ARISE AND SHINE

In Isaiah 60:1-2, the Bible says "*arise, shine; for thy light is come, and the glory of the Lord* is risen upon thee. For, behold, the darkness shall cover the earth, and gross darkness the people: but the *Lord* shall arise upon thee, and his glory shall be seen upon thee and the Gentiles shall come to thy light, and kings to the brightness of thy rising."

The word *arise* as used in Isaiah 60:1, is from the original Hebrew word *Qum* and it means to *stand up, uphold,* or *be clearer.* If your light is not clear, or still blurry, you will struggle to shine in life. **A man who has a perceptive spirit, will live a profitable life**. The wise man said, "*through wisdom is an house builded; and by understanding it is established and by knowledge shall the chambers be filled with all precious and pleasant riches*" (Proverbs 24:3-4).

In Judges 5:16, Barak and Deborah chastised the Reubenites who, while the Army of Israel chased the Midianites, had "...*great thoughts of heart,* (and)... *abodest... among the sheepfolds, to hear the bleatings of the flocks for* (in) *the divisions of Reuben there were great searchings of heart.*" Those who sit on the crossroads, instead of being active participators, never shine in life!

No wonder Reuben's epitapth, at his death, reflected this attribute. In Genesis 49:4, his father (Jacob) had said about him *"unstable as water, thou shall not excel…"* and years later Moses had prayed *"let Reuben live, and not die; and let not his men be few"* (Deuteronomy 33:6). His demise came from his lack of decisiveness, and his failings from foolish choices like sleeping with his father's concubine (see Genesis 35:22).

The late Evangelist, Reinhard Bonnke (1940 – 2019), repeatedly chided *those who forever seek the will of God as been over run by those who do it.* Everyone has their season of visitation, and one second off timing can result in mistakes to the mission. Just like the Israelites left Egypt with a high hand (Numbers 33:3-4), so must these generation of believers do same if they are to enter their promised land and overcome their enemies.

FIRST RIPE

The first ripe fruit is the acceptable offering God instituted for the Israelites. He said, *"…whatsoever is **first ripe** in the land, which they shall bring unto the Lord, shall be thine; every one that is clean in thine house shall eat of it"* (Numbers 18:13). He does not want over-ripe or under-ripe fruits, but first ripe fruits! There is a season for every blessing, and failure to offer a first ripe sacrifice is the *sine-qua-non* for an unacceptable sacrifice or in modern day parlance a frustrated future.

For example, in Acts 10, Peter refused to take the opportunity to arise and kill the unclean animals God asked him to kill and eat (Acts 10:13). As a result, his ministry was limited to the Jews, and according to Paul *"…the gospel of the circumcision was* (committed) *unto Peter"* (Galatians 2:7) while the gospel of the uncircumcised was committed to him (Paul).

Timing is imperative for offerings! When opportunity meets preparation, success is inevitable. When presumption meets ill preparedness, however, misfortune and calamity are inevitable. It took Israel not knowing the time of their visitation, in Luke 19:44, to throw them into a gulag of bondage for thousands of years. A first ripe fruit is optimally prepared fruit, and such fruit delivers the greatest benefits when eaten first-ripe.

In Micah 7:1-4, the Lord said to Israel "...*my soul desired the first ripe fruit. The good man is perished out of the earth: and there is none upright among men: they all lie in wait for blood; they hunt every man his brother with a net. That they may do evil with both hands earnestly, the prince asketh, and the judge asketh for a reward; and the great man, he uttereth his mischievous desire: so they wrap it up. The best of them is as a brier: the most upright is sharper than a thorn hedge: the day of thy watchmen and thy visitation cometh; now shall be their perplexity.*"

God's visitation, in the above scripture, coincided with the time He desired the first ripe fruit! It (first ripe) is another word for *due season* (Psalm 145:15), *fully come* (Acts 2:1), and *day of his shewing* (Luke 1:80). It is, according to Jesus, "...*when the fruit is brought forth,* (and) **immediately** *he putteth in the sickle, because the harvest is come*" (Mark 4:30). The last days are harvest days for the Church (James 5:7-9), and unnecessary delay in putting forth the sickle to gather the harvest may turn first ripe fruit to rotten fruit and thus jeopardize the harvest.

RAPID RESPONSE IN RAYMOND

A pastor in Raymond, Mississippi was referred by his Son-in-law to my medical office for treatment of newly diagnosed renal cell carcinoma. He had pastored for more than twenty years, and was eating dinner when he suddenly blacked out. He was rushed to the hospital and on investigation was found to have a mass on his left kidney.

He was referred to a urologist for urgent excision biopsy but because this pastor had no medical insurance, his treatment was unnecessarily delayed till he could show evidence of capability to pay. I saw him in my office and educated him on the urgency of the situation and referred him to a cardiologist for medical clearance, and within a few weeks he has undergone a right sided nephrectomy.

The miracle was that the excised kidney had cancer, but it was limited to that excised kidney. Today, this pastor is back to pastoring and attributes his quick and rapid referral to the surgeon as the reason he survived the onslaught of renal cancer. Delay truly can be dangerous and being stationary a cause of staccato living.

Prayer Point: Shadow of death assigned against my star, expire in the name of Jesus.

If you know the end from the beginning, it is a lot easier to walk in divine direction.

\- DR. JESSE DUPLANTIS
JESSE DUPLANTIS MINISTRIES
DESTREHAM, LOUISIANA

CHAPTER THREE

THE LAW OF BEGINNINGS

"A glorious high throne from the beginning is the place of our sanctuary" (Jeremiah 17:12).

God wants the Church to start well, not just end well! He is a God of great beginnings and even better endings, and wants the Church to initiate assertively in order to paralyze satanic enemies on our journey through life. In Proverbs 8:22-23, the wise man said *"the Lord possessed me in the beginning of his way, before his works of old. I was set up from everlasting, from the beginning, or ever the earth was."*

It was in the beginning that God possessed the believer, and established his or her journey! Before the journey starts God has already earmarked the path to follow that would bring the allotted blessings upon His people...if they would take it. It shows, therefore, that there is an emphasis on beginnings in God's timetable of doing things.

In Jeremiah 17:12, the Bible says *"a glorious high throne from the beginning is the place of our sanctuary"* and in Numbers 10:10, the prophet Moses said *"...in the beginnings of your months, ye shall blow with the trumpets over your burnt offerings, and over the sacrifices of your peace offerings that they may be to you for a memorial before your God..."* (Numbers 10:10).

When Jesus began his ministry, he did not choose an inconsequential or lack luster platform to do so. Rather, he chose a wedding feast in Cana of Galilee to launch His ministry. He turned water into wine, at the request of his hosts who had run ou of wine (John 2:1-10), and as a result *"this **beginning of miracles** did Jesus in Cana of Galilee, and manifested forth his glory, and his disciples believed on him"* (John 2:11).

Jesus knew the power of a good beginning, and chose to start strong. This miracle at Cana of Galilee was instrumental in preparing his disciples for the faith journey that awaited them and called them to a higher realm of glory. **God always starts well, in order to finish well.** In Paul's epistle to the Church in Phillipi, he said *"…He which hath **begun a good work** in you will perform it until the day of Jesus Christ"* (Philippians 1:6).

God starts His good work well, not tardily, or tenuously. As a result, He always completes what He starts with zest, zeal, and zero tolerance for failure. When the Church starts with an assertive manner in her initiatives and knows who she is, no demon or devil can stop her!

Commanded Light!

Life is not a product of luck, but a law from the beginning that if obeyed will bring its attendant abundant blessings (see John 10:10). In Numbers 23:19-20, Balaam speaking as a prophet of God said *"God is not a man, that he should lie; neither the son of man, that he should repent: hath he said, and shall he not do it? or hath he spoken, and shall he not make it good? Behold, I have received commandment to bless: and he hath blessed; and I cannot reverse it."*

There is an **irreversible blessing**, and only via **commands**, not constant changes to one's speech can one access it. The commanded light shines from the beginning and no amount of darkness can deny it from shining. The will of God is for the light shone by the Church to be a commanded, not compared, or considered light.

In 2 Corinthians 4:6, the Aposte Paul said "...*God, who* **commanded the light to shine** *out of darkness, hath shined in our hearts, to give the light of the knowledge of the glory of God in the face of Jesus Christ.*" The lack of a commanding or assertive nature towards light has robbed the Church of her glory severally, and is contrary to Bible patterns.

For example, in Ephesians 5:13-14 the Bible says "...*all things that are reproved are made manifest by the light: for whatsoever doth make manifest is light. Wherefore he saith, awake thou that sleepest, and arise from the dead, and Christ shall give thee light.*" When light is present, there is no need for a middle man between God and man. It (light) directs His vengeance, and the power of His light rebukes His enemeies openly.

The commanded light shines with force, and carries an immediate reproving! It does not concede to intimidation, but immediately directs judgement for the most high God and judge of all the earth. The greatness of our God is in the brightness of his shining. Let the Church take off the veil of timidity and wavering, and begin to shine His light assertively. When she (the Church) does, judgement will begin for her in earnest.

GLOBAL IMPACT

There are a people of global impact spoken of by the prophet Isaiah. He says, in Isaiah 18:3, that "*all ye inhabitants of the world, and dwellers on the earth, see ye, when he lifteth up an ensign on the mountains; and when he bloweth a trumpet, hear ye*" (Isaiah 18:3).

These ones lift up an ensign, or a banner, and make a sound the world must hear! These ones are a "...*people terrible from their beginning...*" (Isaiah 18:2), and who move with assertive initiative as they go forward. In Isaiah 18:4, God describes the aftermath of this.

He says, "...*the Lord* said unto me, I will take my rest, and I will consider in my dwelling place like a clear heat upon herbs, and like a cloud of dew in the heat of harvest." When there is light that is clean, and heat that is clear from a believer, his ascent (like a cloud of dew) cannot be muddied or muddled! Neither can it be mimicked or mocked.

You can change your world by changing your will! Be assertive, not ambivalent and watch the world rise to celebrate God's glory in your life. For example, in Exodus 40:2-3, God established the need for assertive initiative in establishing the presence of the Lord over the land. It says, "*...on the first day of the first month shalt thou set up the tabernacle of the tent of the congregation. And thou shalt put therein the ark of the testimony, and cover the ark with the vail.*"

THE PRAYER THAT SAVED HUDSON TAYLOR

At fifteen years of age, Hudson Taylor was a stranger to Christ. He says, "*often I had tried to make myself a Christian and failing, of course, in such efforts, I began at last to think that for some reason or other I could not be saved.*"

Discouragement caused him to drift to infidelity and waywardness. One day, when his mother was visiting about seventy or eighty miles from home, she went to a room determined to pray for her only son until he was born into the heavenly family. For hours she laid hold of the mighty arm of power which surrounds every imperiled soul. And there she remained till she received evidence in her spirit that her son was converted.

In the meantime, while Taylor Hudson's mother travailed in prayer for his soul, his attention was drawn to a little tract in the home library, and the words "The *finished work of Christ,*" especially impressed him. "*What was finished?*" He questioned; and thus he answered: "*A full and perfect atonement and satisfaction for sin; the debt was paid by the Substitute; Christ died for our sins, and not for ours only, but also for the sins of the whole world.*"

Then came the thought, '*If the whole work was finished and the whole debt paid, what is there left for me to do?*' And with this dawned the joyful conviction, as light flashed into his soul by the Holy Spirit, that there was nothing in the world to be done but to fall down on one's knees, and, accept this Savior and His salvation, and to praise

Him forever more. Being brought up in such a circle and saved under such circumstances, it was natural that from the commencement of Hudson Taylor's spiritual life, he would view prayer as transacting business with God, whether on one's own behalf or on behalf of those for whom one sought His blessing.

He went on to found the China Inland Mission. A Briton, he gave up everything to pursue his God given dream of being a missionary to China. At the end of his life sojourn, in 1905, the China Inland Mission he founded had two hundred and five mission stations, eight hundred missionaries, and over one hundred and twenty-five thousand Chinese Christians.

All this would not have been possible if Hudson Taylor's mother had not stopped, and sought God for his soul when he was fifteen years of age, as prompted by the Holy Ghost. Many of life's opportunities are bypassed by people too speedy or unspiritual to connect with the God of the universe.

Prayer: Lord, I refuse to be moved from the beginnings of the Godhead Biblically.

Light shines Brighter from within, than on reflection!

- TOBE MOMAH M.D.

CHAPTER FOUR

SOURCES OF LIGHT

*"For with thee is the fountain of life: in thy **light** shall we see **light**"* (Psalm 36:9).

Darkness has no power to stop or stand against the light from God! The true light is the only panaces to the devil's wiles. Many, unfortunantely, attempt to fight demonic darkness with a false light. In John 1:9, Apostle John writes that *"Jesus was the **true Light,** which lighteth every man that cometh into the world"*

Stop using a false light to fight demons and devils! Instead, use the true light who is Jesus Christ. He said, in John 8:12, that *"...I am the light of the world: he that followeth me shall not walk in darkness, but shall have the light of life."* He added, in John 9:5, that *"as long as I am in the world, I am the light of the world."*

The number one source of light is Jesus Christ! No one or thing can shine brighter than the source itself. In 1 John 2:8-10, Apostle John states that *"...because the darkness is past, and the **true light** now shineth, he that saith he is in the light, and hateth his brother, is in darkness even until now* (but) *he that loveth his brother abideth in the light, and there is none occasion of stumbling in him."*

There is no excuse for false lights anymore because *"...of His fulness have all we received, and grace for grace. For the law was given by Moses, but grace and truth came by Jesus Christ"* (John 1:16-17).

Darkness does not play lip-service but answers strictly to the true light. It does not answer to logic or linguistics but to the light of God's word, which is Jesus Christ (John 1:1).

SEEING THE SUN

In Ecclesiastes 7:11, the wise man said *"wisdom is good with an inheritance: and by it there is profit to them that see the sun."* Many believers, and even unbelievers, see the light of God's word but few perceive it for what it is – the true light that shatters darkness. The reason for this, according to Ecclesiastes 7:11, is the lack of wisdom.

Wisdom without insight is unprofitable! It takes seeing the sun, or spiritual insight, to tap into the benefits of that light. Wisdom is doing what you know, and while many hear and few see wisdom, the real tragedy is not doing with this spiritual armementerium of true light what the believer should do with it. Worse still is having these weapons, and not knowing how to apply them.

These ones follow the crowd, and atimes even do the instructions, but they lack understanding of what or why they are doing what they are doing. For example, in Daniel 10:7, Daniel said *"I...alone saw the vision: for the men that were with me saw not the vision; but a great quaking fell upon them, so that they fled to hide themselves."*

Those who, like Daniel, see the sun gain insight beyond the light others can see. They see the light, and by its brightness build the life reserved for them by God. They know what to do and when to do it, and as a result, their profiting is demonstrated to all. That is why, in 1 Timothy 4:15, Apostle Paul said *"meditate upon these things* (Word of God); *give thyself wholly to them; that thy profiting may appear to all."*

SEVEN STANDARD-BEARERS (OF LIGHT)

1. **Scriptures**: The Word of God is an invaluable resource for true light. In Psalms 119:130, the Psalmist said *"the entrance of thy words giveth light; it giveth understanding unto the simple."* Without the scriptures, life is sparsely

furnished (2 Timothy 3:16) and bereft of the garment of light (Psalm 104:2). In Isaiah 51:4, God said *"Hearken unto me, my people; and give ear unto me, O my nation: for a law shall proceed from me, and I will make my judgment to rest for a light of the people."*

2. **Speech:** How you speak determines what amount of light you manifest! In Isaiah 8:20, the prophet Isaiah said *"... if they speak not according to this word, it is because there is no light in them."* It was words that divulged and delivered the people of God from strangers in their closed places. In Psalm 18:44-45, the Psalmist said *"as soon as they hear of me, they shall obey me: the strangers shall submit themselves unto me. The strangers shall fade away, and be afraid out of their close places."*

3. **Spirit of faith:** In John 12:46, Jesus said *"I am come a light into the world, that whosoever believeth on me should not abide in darkness"* and in John 12:35-36, He said *"...a little while is the light with you. Walk while ye have the light, lest darkness come upon you: for he that walketh in darkness knoweth not whither he goeth. **While ye have light, believe in the light, that ye may be the children of light.**"* Without faith, there is no light, and without belief there is no brightness.

4. **Submission:** In John 8:12, Jesus said *"...I am the light of the world: he that **followeth** me shall not walk in darkness, but shall have the light of life."* Following connotes surrender, and because *"...in* (His)...*light shall we see light"* (Psalm 36:9), believers must first be fully submitted to the Lordship of Jesus Christ to keep thriving in His light.

5. **Sure word of prophecy:** In 2 Peter 1:19-21, the Apostle Peter said *"we have also a more sure word of prophecy; whereunto ye do well that ye take heed, as unto a light that shineth in a dark place, until the day dawn, and the day star arise in your hearts: Knowing this first, that no prophecy of the scripture is of any private interpretation. For the prophecy came not in old time by the will of man: but holy men of God*

spake as they were moved by the Holy Ghost." The prophetic can birth light for direction. Don't ignore it; rather, take heed to it!

6.   **Son of God**: Jesus is the surest source of true light. In John 9:4-5, He said *"I must work the works of him that sent me, while it is day: the night cometh, when no man can work. As long as I am in the world, I am the light of the world."* He went on to add, in John 12:46, that *"I am come a light into the world, that whosoever believeth on me should not abide in darkness."*

7.   **Sign of the Times**: There must be a propenderance of true light, in the last days, to fight evil and the darkness attacking the awakened Church. In Ephesians 5:14-16, Apostle Paul said *"awake thou that sleepest, and arise from the dead, and Christ shall give thee light...Redeeming the time, because the days are evil."* The non-plussed believer, however, who is not interested in spiritual things will miss that light because it requires locating, living, and loving the Light to shine in the last days. In Romans 13:11-13, Apostle Paul teaches *"...that, knowing the time, that now it is high time to awake out of sleep for now is our salvation nearer than when we believed. The night is far spent, the **day is at hand:** let us therefore cast off the works of darkness, and let us put on the armour of light. Let us walk honestly, as in the day; not in rioting and drunkenness...."*

THE SHENANIGANS OF SIN

Bishop Emmah Isong is a foremost Evangelistic and apostolic leader in the Nigerian evangelical community. He was visiting the city of Enugu, Nigeria where I was a student of Medicine and Surgery, and I persuaded him to visit our medical campus and preach a word at our Wednesday evening meeting. He was, however, scheduled to preach a city wide crusade the following day (Thursday) and I volunteered to be part of the crusade organizing committee.

At these organizing committee meetings were a man and woman who were head of the crusade committee and prayer co-ordinator respectively. They were from out of the state, and together they co-ordinated the pasting of posters, prayers, and mobilizing of pastors for the crusade.

The Wednesday evening meeting at the medical campus was standing room only. It is still talked about by those who were there as Bishop Emmah Isong gave words of knowledge that forever delivered respondents, and blessed the community on campus tremendously.

The community crusade, however, never got off the ground. Notwithstanding, the prayer, publicity and pastors mobilized for the crusade in Ngwo park, Enugu the crowds were spartan and there were few or no signs and wonders manifest. The word of the Lord was preached, but there was no evidence it was mixed with faith by the attendees.

More than ten years, later, I saw Bishop Emmah Isong in Abuja, Nigeria at my father's hotel (Crystal Palace Hotel, Abuja), and he revealed to me why the crusade failed. According to him, there were wrong sexual relationships going on during the crusade between the crusade leaders.

Apparently, though both of them were married, the female prayer co-ordinator and the male crusade co-ordinator were having an affair at the hotel they both stayed in. Their sexual escapades were brought to the knowledge of Bishop Emmah Isong after the crusade, and he distanced himself from further acquaintance with them.

Nothing shines when the true source of light – God - is not available. The light that cannot stop shining is God himself! He will shine where ever the Word of God, the Holy Spirit and God the father are giving opportunity to rule and rein. Where they are constrained, curtailed, or culled darkness is inevitable as was amply shown at this crusade organized by Emmah Isong crusades.

Prayer: Baptize me with your Light, O God, in Jesus name!

*You cannot live in Purposelessness
and expect Lightedness!*
- TOBE MOMAH M.D.

CHAPTER FIVE

PURPOSE OF LIGHT

"Which in his times he shall shew, who is the blessed and only Potentate, the King of kings, and Lord of lords; Who only hath immortality, **dwelling in the light** *which no man can approach unto; whom no man hath seen, nor can see: to whom be honour and power everlasting"* (1 Timothy 6:15-16).

The purpose of light is to fulfill destiny! When God made man, He fashioned them to be *"...a flame of fire"* (Hebrews 1:7) and designated *"...His ministers a flaming fire"* (Psalm 104:4). To get to that fiery point, however, light is essential! In Isaiah 10:17, the prophet states that *"...the light of Israel shall be for a fire, and his Holy One for a flame: and it shall burn and devour his thorns and his briers in one day."*

The root cause of darkness is lack of purpose! In Proverbs 4:18-19, the wise man states that *"...the path of the just is as the shining light, that shineth more and more unto the perfect day* (but) *the way of the wicked is as darkness: they know not at what they stumble."* For light to shine incrementally, the knowledge of purpose and one's application to that purpose are essential.

James, the younger brother of Jesus, had observed Him for a large part of his ministry. He knew how purposeful Jesus was, especially following their determination to get him to go up to Jerusalem prematurely (John 7:1-5). As a result, he counsel led the Church to "*draw nigh to God, and* (let) *him draw nigh to you* (and so) *cleanse your hands, ye sinners; and purify your hearts, ye double minded*" (James 4:8).

The dearth of purpose is why so many live uninspired and tepid lives. When Jesus came to the earth, He had a clear sense of purpose. He said, in Luke 12:49, that "*I am come to send fire on the earth; and what will I, if it be already kindled?*" The destruction of the devil was the chief purpose of Jesus life on earth (1 John 3:8), and why he told Pilate, "*...to this end was I born, and for this cause came I into the world, that I should bear witness unto the truth*" (John 18:37).

GOD'S GOAL IS THE GOODNESS OF GOD

The soul that has not known God's goodness lives in darkness. It takes your soul tasting goodness to become a light to the world. Until your soul tastes the goodness of God, your light will remain in darkness and you can't unravel the mystery of demonic darkness. It takes contacting the goodness of God, in the soul to defeat darkness in the spirit realm.

One of the cardinal purposes of light is to get the goodness of God into the soul. In Eccl 6:3-4, the wise man said "*if a man beget an hundred children, and live many years, so that the days of his years be many, and **his soul be not filled with good**, and also that he have no burial; I say, that an untimely birth is better than he. For he cometh in with vanity, and **departeth in darkness**, and his name shall be covered with darkness. Moreover he hath not seen the sun, nor known any thing....*"

When God made man, He planted him in a garden with the intention to make him "*...be fruitful, and multiply, and replenish the earth, and subdue it: and have dominion over...*" all creature on it (Genesis 1:28). When man rebelled, however, by eating the forbidden fruit in the garden of Eden (Genesis 2:6), their sterling destiny became chequered and crestfallen.

In 1 Thess 5:4-8, Apostle Paul states that "...*ye, brethren, are not in darkness, that that day should overtake you as a thief. Ye are all the children of light, and the children of the day:* **we are not of the night, nor of darkness.** *Therefore let us not sleep, as do others; but let us watch and be sober. For they that sleep sleep in the night; and they that be drunken are drunken in the night. But let us, who are of the day, be sober, putting on the breastplate of faith and love; and for an helmet, the hope of salvation.*"

Where ever there is faith, love, hope, and salvation light must be present, according to 1 Thessalonians 5:4-8. The goodness of God is revealed deliberately by light, for as the Psalmist said "*the heavens declare the glory of God, and the firmament sheweth his handywork. Day unto day uttereth speech, and night unto night showeth knowledge (for there is no speech nor language, where their voice is not heard*" (Psalm 19:1-3).

GOD WILL SHOW YOU HIS FACE, NOT HIS BACK!

When you have the anointing of the face of God, it causes your face to shine! In Psalm 34:5, the Bible says "*they looked unto Him, and were lightened: and their faces were not ashamed.*" The secret to a life of shining is to behold His face...not His back!

In 2 Corinthians 3:18, the Bible says "*...we all, with open face beholding as in a glass the glory of the Lord, are changed into the same image from glory to glory, even as by the Spirit of the Lord.*"

If, instead, you face God's back an east wind that brings calamity will be your lot! This east wind, according to the Bible, connotes destruction and adversity (as shown in Hosea 13:15, Ezekiel 19:10-12).

If God turns His face towards you, and not His back, transformation must take place. In Jeremiah 18:17, God says "*I will scatter them as with an east wind before the enemy; I will shew them the back, and not the face, in the day of their calamity.*"

CALLED TO CONQUER, NOT COWER!

When I arrived the United States of America (USA) in 2005, I had come straight from the Ethiopian mission field of Gimbie, Western Wellagoa. I called a few of my clasmates and family to intimate them of my arrival, and to my dismay they mostly replied that *I return to the United Kingdom if I plan to practice clinical medicine.*

They based their premise on my average scores in the United States clinical exam training sessions, and my past records while a medical student in Nigeria. I had, however, heard God state to me clearly in 2003 to unequivocally *go down to New York City, and base the headquarters of my ministry there.*

To add to their chagrin, I had no United States clinical experience and was only in the United Staes on a Visitor's visa. To repair this mild indiscretion, a visit to an immigration lawyer was arranged, and he told me that based on my current status, he could get me married to an American (for a certain sum of money), utilize me as a science teacher in a high school, dissolve the marriage after maybe ten years, and then after obtaining my American citizenship start trying again for Medical residency positions.

I immediately rejected his and my relative's counsel in this regard. The learned legal counsel looked at me with pity, and advised me to return when I was ready and had come to the end of my attempts at seeking US Citizenship and getting into a medical residency.

More than sixteen years later, I am on the edge of obtaining my US citizenship. It was a painstaking and lengthy process, that involved bringing my wife over from Nigeria, obtaining three different work permits to work in rural areas of America, but meanwhile still rising up the ladder of academic medicine in America. That immigration lawyer, on the other hand, has had FBI charges levelled against him and his associates for falsifying applicant's immigration claims and as a result has had his office downsized recently.

Prayer: Transform my life O Lord, by showing me your face, in Jesus name!

If you look at the Sun, you
don't see the Clouds!

- TOBE MOMAH M.D.

CHAPTER SIX

BENEFITS OF LIGHT

*"that ye may be blameless and harmless, the sons of God, without rebuke, in the midst of a crooked and perverse nation, among whom ye **shine as lights** in the world; Holding forth the word of life; that I may rejoice in the day of Christ, that I have not run in vain, neither laboured in vain"* (Phil 2:15-16).

Those who are guided by the Lord of lights will avoid the repercussions and remonstrations of darkness. In Luke 6:39-40, Jesus spoke a parable asking *"…can the blind lead the blind? shall they not both fall into the ditch? The disciple is not above his master: but every one that is perfect shall be as his master."*

Light is not a trivial addendum in God's armemeterium for the Church, but a key tool in the last day Champions' armor. It is why Apostle Paul advocates for it as a key component of the soldier's armor in the last days. He says, in Romans 13:11-12, that *"…now it is high time to awake out of sleep: for now is our salvation nearer than when we believed* (as) *the night is far spent,* (and) *the day is at hand: let us therefore cast off the works of darkness, and let us put on the **armour of light**."*

The greatest armor are not the most expensive, or elaborate, but the most effective at destroying enemy fire. **Light is an arch-destroyer**

of darkness; it detonates darkness leaving it with no room for escape. For example, in Job 38:24 the Lord God asked Job, "*by what way is the light parted, which scattereth the east wind upon the earth?*"

The east wind, in Biblical times, was notorious for portending evil and destruction (see Jonah 4:8, and Hosea 13:15), but when light comes against it, it scatters. **Beyond every great battle is a strong mantle**, and the mantle for this hour is the light of God's word and His presence (Ephesians 5:17-22 and Romans 13:12). Those who stand fully clothed with His armor of light will watch their enemies bow, and be destoyed summarily.

THE CHILDREN OF THE LIGHT

Before we explore the benefits of light, it is important to establish that the Church are children of the light. Our father is the Father of lights (James 1:17), and we are joint heirs (Romans 8:17) with the light of the world - Jesus Christ - the Son of God (John 8:12 and John 9:5).

In 1 Thessalonians 5:5, Apostle Paul calls the Church "*...the children of light, and the children of the day* (who are)...*not of the night, nor of darkness.*" Jesus further re-iterates this thought, in John 12:36, when He tells his disciples that "*...while ye have light, believe in the light, that ye may be the **children of light**.*"

Chldren are inherent reflections of their parents. There can be no children of light without the father of lights (James 1:17), and every grounded life begins from a gutted light. In Ephesians 5:8, apostle Paul says "*...ye* (who) *were sometimes darkness, but now are ye light* in the Lord (so) *walk as children of light.*"

When God created the greater and lesser lights, in Genesis 1, they were each to shine or radiate light in their spheres of influence. These were those with the "*...the glory of the celestial...the glory of the terrestrial...glory of the sun, and another glory of the moon, and another glory of the stars: for one star differeth from another star in glory*" (1 Cor 15:40-41).

Differing lights shine at differing levels, but nonetheless are created by the father of lights to give light for their time and sphere of influence. These lights include "...*great lights:*(such as) *the sun to rule by day:* ...(and) *the moon and stars to rule by night:...*" (Psalm 136:7-9). You are a child of the light: Find what and where you are called to rule and shine right there!

THE POWER OF LIGHT

Light is a veritable weapon in God's armory (Romans 13:12), and He has given the believer access to it. It gives several benefits to the Church including

1. **Direction:** Without Light, direction is duplicious. In Isaiah 58:10-11, the prophet Isaiah said "...*thy light* (shall) *rise in obscurity, and thy darkness be as the noonday: And the Lord shall* **guide thee continually***, and satisfy thy soul in drought, and make fat thy bones: and thou shalt be like a watered garden, and like a spring of water, whose waters fail not.*" Light is a precipitator for direction! Without it, catastrophe and calamity on the journey are inevitable.

2. **Distinction:** Until you begin to walk in the light of God's word, shining and distinction are suspect and short-changed. In Job 29:3-6, Job testified of the days "*when His candle shined upon my head, and when by His light (He) walked through darkness* (and) *the secret of God was upon* (his) *tabernacle* (for) *...the Almighty was yet with me,* (and) *when I washed my steps with butter,...the rock poured me out rivers of oil*" (Job 29:3-6). That rock portends impossibilities, and the oil an anointing for the impossible that made Job the richest man in his tme, and one universally celebrated for philantrophy, perception, and power (Job 29:7-20). This enviable position was, however, predicated on the light he saw as a youth (see Job 29:3).

3. **Due Season:** Light provokes a believer's due season. It is God's divine instrument to divulge what is appropriate and when to appropriate it. In Luke 12:35-38, Jesus said *"let your loins be girded about, and your **lights burning** and ye yourselves like unto men that wait for their lord, when he will return from the wedding; that when he cometh and knocketh, they may open unto him immediately...Who then is that faithful and wise steward, whom his lord shall make ruler over his household, to give them their portion of meat in **due season?"** Your attention to light enables you to give meat in due season to those who need it.

4. **Desires granted:** Millions of desires stay hung up on the shelves of heaven because the Church are ignorant of Kingdom requirements for granted desires (Hosea 4:6). In Psalm 44:2-3, the Psalmist said *"how thou didst drive out the heathen with thy hand, and plantedst them; how thou didst afflict the people, and cast them out. For they got not the land in possession by their own sword, neither did their own arm save them: but thy right hand, and thine arm, and **the light of thy countenance**, because thou hadst a favour unto them."*

5. **Depths of God:** It is the *"the entrance of* (His) *words* (that) *giveth light* (and) *giveth understanding unto the simple"* (Psalm 119:130). The simple are the un enlightened! When light comes, the depths of God are revealed and the difference between foolishness and wisdom become starkly visible. In Ecclesiastes 2:13, the wise man said *"...I saw that **wisdom excelleth folly**, as far as **light excelleth darkness**."*

6. **Deliverance:** One of the cardinal tenets of light is that it births deliverance. In Acts 13:47, God unveiled the power of light through the life of Paul. He told this former murderer, arsonist, and liar that *"...I have set thee to be **a light of the Gentiles**, that thou shouldest be for **salvation** unto the ends of the earth."* It takes light to shake the powers of this world (see Psalm 136:7-9). The Psalmist elaborates further by saying, *"...light my candle* (so) *the LORD my God*

will enlighten my darkness (and I can)...*run through a troop and...leap over a wall*" (Psalm 18: 28-29).

7. **Darkness destroyer:** No matter how dark the mist may be, light shatters the cover of darkness (John 1:4-5) and raises his glory upon a people. That is why Jesus is called "...*a light to lighten the Gentiles, and the glory of thy people Israel*" (Luke 2:32). When the Apostle Peter recalled the appearance of Moses and Elijah, alongside Jesus, on the mount of transfiguration he said "...*this voice which came from heaven we heard, when we were with him in the holy mount...(and so) have a more sure word of prophecy whereunto ye do well that ye take heed, as unto a light that shineth in a dark place...*" (2 Peter 1:18-19).

THE POWER OF PERCEPTION

My wife had finished her Masters in Public health and was excited to join the labor market. She had not worked for the last three years and wanted to start something she felt could enable her earn some money. She applied to several companies, and the feelers from the job market looked promising.

On a particular night, however, I had a dream where I saw her teaching on a classroom board. I discussed my dream with her and recommended she apply to the doctoral degree program in public health at the Jackson State University, Jackson Mississippi.

Even though our home in West Monroe, Lousiana was about two hours from Jackson, Mississippi she applied and five years later graduated with a doctorate in public health.

She is currently working in HIV Education at the Mississippi department of health, and feels more fulfilled in her career. She is a product of the perception given to yours truly that enabled her to go in the appropriate direction for her life. May you never miss His light in Jesus name.

Prayer: Father, let your light shine upon my ways in Jesus name!

Bright Light Exposes the Weakness of Darkness

...Dr. Daniel Olukoya
(General Overseer, Mountain of Fire and Miracles Ministries International Worldwide)

CHAPTER SEVEN

BANE OF BRIGHTNESS

*"...if our gospel be hid, it is hid to them that are lost: In whom the god of this world hath **blinded** the minds of them which believe not, lest the **light** of the glorious gospel of Christ, who is the image of God, should **shine** unto them"* (2 Cor 4:4).

God wants to demonstrate His glory through the Church. That is why he is coming for a glorious Church (Ephesians 5:25), and not a garbage or gloomy Church. The *Assertive Initiative* kind of light you received when you came to Jesus (Matthew 5:14) is this kind of light. This light shines in the darkness, and simultaneously destroys devils and glorifies God.

In Luke 2:31-32, Simeon said *"...thou hast prepared* (Jesus) *before the face of all people* (as a)...**light to lighten** *the Gentiles, and the glory of thy people Israel."* When light comes, dominion is entrenched and glory is released. In Numbers 24:16-19, God said a star shall shine out of Jacob, and the result will be dominion over their enemies.

He said to Israel *"...there shall come a **Star** out of Jacob, and a Sceptre shall rise out of Israel, and shall smite the corners of Moab, and destroy all the children of Sheth. And Edom shall be a possession, Seir also shall be a possession for his enemies; and Israel shall do valiantly. Out of*

Jacob shall come he that shall have dominion, and shall destroy him that remaineth of the city" (Numbers 24:16-19).

It (light) produces valiant strength and wealth. The word *valiant* as used in Numbers 24:18 is the Hebrew word *Chayil* and it means efficiency, excellence, and wealth. Light delivers you from satanic enemies and gives you strength that manifests for all to see. It makes glory to rise upon oneself (Isaiah 60:1), and "*...the Gentiles* (to) *come to thy light, and kings to the brightness of thy rising*" (Isaiah 60:3).

The Flight of Light

The enemy of shining is satan, and the bane of brightness is belial! Described as the god of this world, in 2 Corinthians 4:4, his purpose is to "*...blind the minds of them which believe not, lest the light of the glorious gospel of Christ, who is the image of God, should shine unto them*" (2 Corinthians 4:4).

Balaam, for example, could not see the angel of the Lord with a sword drawn in his hand because the light of the Gospel had fled from him. He is described by Peter as one who had "*...forsaken the right way, and...gone astray...*(because he)*...loved the wages of unrighteousness but was rebuked for his iniquity: the dumb ass speaking with man's voice forbad the madness of the prophet*" (2 Peter 2:15-16).

His ass saw the angel (thankfully) and "*...fell down under Balaam and Balaam's anger was kindled, and he smote the ass with a staff*" (Numbers 22:27). His covetousness, avarice, and desire for filthy lucre had blinded him from the light of God, and until the angel told him in Numbers 22:32 that "*...I went out to withstand thee, because thy way is perverse before me*" he thought the ass was been indignant and insubordinate to him and had hit him thrice (see Numbers 22:23, 25, 27).

The believer must beware of the *flight of light* caused by the lusts of the flesh and love for the world! In Exodus 23:8, the Bible says "*... thou shalt take no gift: for the gift blindeth the wise, and perverteth the words of the righteous.*" This flight of light eventually blinded Balaam, and led to his fall. In Jude 1:11, Jude warns against "*...the error of*

Balaam…" and in Revelation 2:14, he is described as he *"…who taught Balac to cast a stumbling block before the children of Israel, to eat things sacrificed unto idols, and to commit fornication."*

LET THERE BE LIGHT

It takes spiritual, not physical, light to destroy darkness! This light is Jesus Christ, the Son of God. He said *"…I am the light of the world"* (John 9:5), and in John 12:24 added that *"I am come a light into the world, that whosoever believeth on me should not abide in darkness."*

When *"…the earth was without form, and void and darkness was upon the face of the deep…"* (Genesis 1:2), it took the Word of God to turn darkness into light. According to the writer of Hebrews, God *"…in these last days spoke unto us by his Son, whom he hath appointed heir of all things, by whom also he made the worlds"* (Hebrews 1:3).

No matter how deeply entrenched the darkness may be, that darkness can be dissipated by Jesus Christ, who is also called the Word of God in John 1:1. The only barrier to His light is a willful refusal of the light! That is why Jesus said, *"…this is the condemnation, that light is come into the world, and men loved darkness rather than light, because their deeds were evil. For every one that doeth evil hateth the light, neither cometh to the light, lest his deeds should be reproved."* (John 3:17-20).

When God spoke in Genesis 1:5, He *"…called the light Day, and the darkness he called Night…."* This, however, did not signify the manifesting of the Sun, moon, or stars to the world. In fact, it was only in Gen 1:14-15, that God spoke saying *"…let there be lights in the firmament of the heaven to divide the day from the night; and let them be for signs, and for seasons, and for days, and years: And let them be for lights in the firmament of the heaven to give light upon the earth: and it was so."*

This physical light was represented by the stars, suns, and moon, while the spiritual light is represented by the Word of God. The former were *"…to rule over the day and over the night, and to divide the light from the darkness…"* (Genesis 1:18), while the latter were not just to separate the light from darkness, but to **shatter the darkness** (John 1:5).

Bishop Olutayo and Blurred Opinions

I was visiting from the United States in 2016, and was worshipping at the Durumi location of the Dunamis International Gospel Center, Abuja Nigeria. After the service, I went to discuss with the senior pastor – Dr (Pastor) Paul Enenche - and along the line a conversation about a recent Church affair came up.

Apparently, a few years before our conversation a brother-in-law to Bishop David Oyedepo (Presiding Bishop of Living Faith Church, worldwide) named Bishop Dayo Olutayo had left the Living Faith Church he pastored in Abuja, Nigeria in an un savory manner. He had gone on to start his own Church in the same city, and there were a lot of undercurrents following this action. Since I was in town, I decided to get my erstwhile pastor's thoughts on what had happened.

After asking his opinion on the *church split* incident involving Bishops Oyedepo and Olutayo, Dr. Paul Enenche quickly brushed my question aside and changed the topic. Rather than disparage any party, or take sides, he moved on to other more edifying topics.

It was not a surprise, therefore, to hear how God went on to elevate Dr. Paul Enenche. He is acknowledged internationally as having the largest Church auditorium in the world at his headquarters facilitiy. It is called *Glory dome,* and from that platform he has seen his ministry impact millions around the world.

Many trouble themselves and defile others because of the root of bitterness in them (Hebrews 12:14-15). Instead of speaking words that defile, the apostle Paul counsels the believer to *"let your speech be always with grace, seasoned with salt, that ye may know how ye ought to answer every man"* (Colossians 4:6).

Prayer point: Baptize me with the Spirit of life in Christ Jesus that shatters darkness!

PART II

Dangers of Darkness

- Death
- Disease
- Disliked
- Down
- Doubt
- Dimness
- Depression

*The only way you are going to
make a headway in life, is when
God is at the head of your life!*

- TOBE MOMAH M.D.

CHAPTER EIGHT

DEATH

*"...when he **dieth** he shall carry nothing away: his glory shall not descend after him. Though while he lived he blessed his soul: and men will praise thee, when thou doest well to thyself. He shall go to the generation of his fathers; **they shall never see light**"* (Psalm 49:16-19).

The only reason for struggling in a particular area is because there is a lack of light in that particular area. That lack of light quickly deteriorates into dishonor and death. In Psalm 49:19-20, the Bible says *"He shall go to the generation of his fathers; they shall never see light* (and this) *man that is in honor, and understandeth not, is like the beasts that perish."*

The only reason why violence, destruction, anarchy and oppression persist is because of darkness! The minute the light shines is the minute their power ends. In Psalm 74:20, the Bible says *"have respect unto the covenant: for the dark places of the earth are full of the habitations of cruelty."* The word used for *cruelty*, in the original Hebrew, is *chamac* and it means damage, falsehood, injustice, oppression, unrighteousness, or violence.

The Church has been placed here on earth, as the lights of the world, to save a world savaged by perdition, perfidy, poverty, pain, penury, and loss of Godly principles for living. In Acts 13:47, Paul and Barnabas told the Jews in Antioch that *"...the Lord commanded us, saying, I have set thee to be a light of the Gentiles, that thou shouldest be for salvation unto the ends of the earth."*

The Church are *"...the light of the world* (and) *a city...set on an hill* (that)*...cannot be hid* (but rather) *give light unto all that are in the house"* (Matthew 5:14-15). Jesus therefore counsel led the Church to *"let your light so shine before men, that they may see your good works, and glorify your Father which is in heaven"* (Matthew 5:14-16). When light shines, the life of God births forth (John 1:5) but where Darkness exists death is near!

THE SHADOWS OF DEATH

The Bible, in Psalm 107:10-12, describes those whom darkness has pervaded and led to the very shadows of death. It says that these ones *"...sit in darkness and in the shadow of death, being bound in affliction and iron because they rebelled against the words of God, and contemned the counsel of the most High. Therefore he brought down their heart with labor; they fell down, and there was none to help."*

These ones are those who work without inspiration, and labor without result. They give *"...the labor of the foolish* (that) *wearieth every one of them because* (they)*...knoweth not how to go to the city"* (Ecclesiastes 10:15). These folks are working with labor, but without result because they are in darkness. When you're living in darkness, everything is hard. There is nothing that comes through easily for that individual, and as a result life is a perpetual struggle.

The chief characteristic of these dying ones in the shadow of death is that they sit in darkness! Until *"...they cried unto the Lord in their trouble, and he saved them out of their distresses"* (Psalm 107:13) they remained afflicted. The minute they cried out for help, however, *"He brought them out of darkness and the shadow of death, and brake their bands in sunder"* (Psalm 107:14).

A last day highway, called the highway of holiness, will be a bastion of brightness and the springboard for security for those days. In Isaiah 35:8-9, God says *"...an highway shall be there, and a way, and it shall be called The way of holiness; the unclean shall not pass over it; but it shall be for those: the wayfaring men, though fools, shall not err therein. No lion shall be there, nor any ravenous beast shall go up thereon, it shall not be found there; but the redeemed shall walk there."*

Ravenous beasts and lions know not to go where the redeemed dwell and God lives. One of the chief causes of premature and needless death are people living under the burden of labor because they are in the wrong place, doing the wrong thing, and for the wrong reasons. Like Jonah, they preach unwillingly, and in an attempt to run away from the call of God end up in the belly of the fish (Jonah 1:1-17). Get the light of God, and you will get life and avoid death! That is why John the Baptist said, *"In him was life; and the life was the light of men"* (John 1:4).

KEPT FROM KILLINGS

The devil is a serial killer, and he makes no apology for it. He is, according to Jesus, determined *"...to steal, and to kill, and to destroy..."* (John 10:10a) but thank God, Jesus has *"...come that they might have life, and that they might have it more abundantly"* (John 10:10b).

Where darkness pervades, death is near but when light shines life spreads! The arbiter for a life filled with death is light. In Psalm 13:3, the Psalmist prayed *"consider and hear me, O Lord my God: lighten mine eyes, lest I sleep the sleep of death."*

The only waters that fail are those from the streams of a light that is covered in darkness. In Isaiah 58:10-11, the Lord says if you and I *"...satisfy the afflicted soul; then shall thy light rise in obscurity, and thy darkness be as the noon day: And the Lord shall guide thee continually, and satisfy thy soul in drought...."*

When God spoke to Israel, in Job 33:14-18, he warned them to take heed to His word in order to avoid a deathly existence. He repeats His often quoted refrain about darkness been a prelude to death and the need to hearken to His word (or the light of the gospel) as its arbiter.

He said, "...*God speaketh once, yea twice, yet man perceiveth it not. In a dream, in a vision of the night, when deep sleep falleth upon men, in slumberings upon the bed; Then he openeth the ears of men, and sealeth their instruction that he may withdraw man from his purpose, and hide pride from man. **He keepeth back his soul from the pit, and his life from perishing by the sword.**"*

As the age comes to an end, the psychopathic blood-sucking revelry of hell will only get worse (Revelations 12:12). As a result, the Church must put on the armor of light if she is to ward off adversaries and be kept from satanic hatchet men. In accordance with these objectives, Paul adjures the Church that "...*the night is far spent,* (and) *the day is at hand* (so) ***let us therefore cast off the works of darkness, and...put on the armor of light*"** (Romans 13:12).

JERRY SAVELLE'S HEALING

Jerry Savelle is an international teacher and preacher of the gospel who has circled the globe with Kenneth Copeland, Kenneth Hagin, and Oral Roberts preaching the gospel. He is the president of Jerry Savelle ministries, and founder of the Heritage of Faith Christian center Church in Texas and Australia.

In 2015, while undergoing a routine carotid endarterectomy procedure for an incidentally discovered carotid plaque stenosis he developed a cerebrovascular accident with attendant paralysis of the right half of his body. Apart from the paralysis, his understanding was left rudimentary, and his speech primitive. His family were told by his doctors that he would remain a vegetable, and never preach again.

He was prayed for on several occasions by his friends, and family, and Jesse Duplantis recalls praying on one occasion for him only for Jerry Savelle to burst out in tongues. After a prolonged stay in hospital, that bordered on months, and several futile attempts in rehab to get his physical function restored, Jerry went home to be cared for by his wife, children, and grandchildren.

A few days after his return home, he pointed his left hand in the direction of the garage and his granddaughter (Rachel) led him to his collection of rare automobiles and motor bikes and turned them all on. After they were turned on, and then turned off, by his granddaughter he stretched forth his right hand demanding the key to his favorite Harley Davidson 1942 Motor bike by saying *Rachel give me the key.*

Rachel nearly ran out of the garage! Her granddad had not spoken for months and was supposed to be unable to move the right side of his body. Jerry Savelle was not done, however. He moved towards the Harley-Davidson motor bike and standing on his once impaired right leg started the motor bike. Before anyone else could intervene, Jerry was praising God in his understanding and has not stopped since.

Today, Jerry Savelle is completely healed, with no residual weakness or impairment of speech or memory. He has regained full ability to remember scriptures and events, and his preaching is better than ever. The devil wanted to take him out, but the light of the glorious gospel shone through him and set him free. Halleluyah!

Prayer: I will not die but live to declare the goodness of the Lord in the land of the living, in Jesus name!

A man or woman that has a living God does not fight his or her own battles!

– Rev. (Dr). Uma Ukpai
Evangelist/President Uma Ukpai
Evangelistic association, Nigeria.

CHAPTER NINE

DISEASE

"But unto you that fear my name shall the Sun of righteousness arise with healing in his wings; and ye shall go forth, and grow up as calves of the stall" (Malachi 4:2).

The reason why people are afflicted is because they forget! In Psalm 103:2-5, the Bible says *"bless the Lord, O my soul, and **forget** not all his benefits: who forgiveth all thine iniquities; who healeth all thy diseases; who redeemeth thy life from destruction; who crowneth thee with lovingkindness and tender mercies; who satisfieth thy mouth with good things; so that thy youth is renewed like the eagle's."*

The words you allow to settle into your life will determine the healing of your body. In Isaiah 6:9-10, the Lord said *"...Hear ye indeed, but understand not; and see ye indeed, but perceive not. Make the heart of this people fat, and make their ears heavy, and shut their eyes; lest they see with their eyes, and hear with their ears, and understand with their heart, and **convert, and be healed**."*

When a believer rejects God's words and builds on the words from their environment they end up in darkness, disease, and desolation. The devil uses affliction – including infirmities, pain, disease, and sickness - to blind believers from their God given vision for their life.

In Isaiah 8:20-22, the Lord says "...*if they speak not according to this word, it is because* **there is no light in them**. *And they shall pass through it, hardly bestead and hungry: and it shall come to pass, that when they shall be hungry, they shall fret themselves, and curse their king and their God, and look upward. And they shall look unto the earth; and behold trouble and* **darkness**, *dimness of anguish; and they shall be driven to* **darkness**.*"*

EATING IN DARKNESS

Darkness is a doomsday prognosticator, and when you eat in the dark, it is a sign of wasting, and vanity that will eventually cause sorrow and sickness. In Ecclesiastes 5:16-17, the Bible says "...*this also is a sore evil, that in all points as he came, so shall he go: and what profit hath he that hath labored for the wind? All his days also he* **eateth in darkness**, *and he hath much sorrow and wrath with his* **sickness**.*"*

When you eat in the dark, you are taking food from others who are in the dark. A life that is wasted, and beset with sorrow and sickness, is hinged on evil associations. **Those who eat in the dark receive from others who are also in the dark,** and it is a signpost to their future of desolation and destruction.

In Revelation 2:14-16, the Church of Ephesus was accused by God of "...*eat*(ing) ***things*** *sacrificed unto idols,...commit*(ting) *fornication* (and)...*hold*(ing) *the doctrine of the Nicolaitanes, which thing I hate. Repent; or else I will come unto thee quickly, and will fight against them with the sword of my mouth.*"

The Church of Thyatira was in similar dire straits as the Church of Ephesus. In Revelation 2:20-23, the Lord said, "... I have a few things against thee, because thou *sufferest that woman Jezebel, which calleth herself a prophetess, to teach and to seduce my servants to commit fornication, and to* **eat** *things sacrificed unto idols. Behold, I will cast her into a bed, and them that commit adultery with her into great tribulation, except they repent of their deeds and I will kill her children with* **death***;....*"

Death and destruction follows the eating of demonic food items, and anytime you eat from the dark - and in the dark - it is a recipe for disease propagation. Jesus triumphed over darkness because He came to "...*work the works of him that sent me, while it is day:* (for) *the night cometh, when no man can work* (and) *as long as* (Jesus is)...*in the world,* (He is the)...*the light of the world"* (John 9:4-5).

ENLIGHTENED EYES

When your eyes are enlightened, your energy levels are restored and your health is quickened. In 1 Samuel 14:27, the Bible says Jonathan "...*put forth the end of the rod that was in his hand, and dipped it in an honeycomb, and put his hand to his mouth and his eyes were enlightened.*" When you ignore the secrets of God, however, anguish, disease and destruction become your lot, but when the light shines it births healing.

Paul prayed for the Church in Ephesus, that "...*the Father of glory, may give unto you the spirit of wisdom and revelation in the knowledge of him* (with) **the eyes of your understanding being enlightened**; *that ye may know what is the hope of his calling, and what the riches of the glory of his inheritance in the saints, and what is the exceeding greatness of his power to us-ward who believe, according to the working of his mighty power"* (Ephesians 1:16-19).

When your eyes are enlightened, the exceeding greatness of His power is made manifest in your life. The power of healing rises when those who fear the Lord speak the word often to each other. It was when those who "...*feared the Lord* spake often one to another (that) *the Lord* hearkened, and heard it" (Malachi 3:16), and "...*the Sun of righteousness arose with healing in his wings;*...(so they can)...*go forth, and grow up as calves of the stall"* (Malachi 4:2).

Calves in biblical times were yokeless calves. These species were unique, in the sense that they cannot be shackled, stopped, straight jacketed, or seized. In 1 Samuel 6:7, the Bible makes it clear that only upon the "...*two milch kine, on which there hath come* **no yoke,** (can)... *the kine* (be tied)...*to the cart,*...." It is only upon an unyoked calf that the sun of righteousness lights upon, with healing in His wings. No sickness or infirmity can limit them, and no disease can stop them.

Not A Second Short nor a Dollar delayed!

Mrs. P was a mercurial member of the St Paul's Church of God in Christ, Jackson MS. An associate professor at the Jackson State University (JSU), she served as leader of several youth groups and was always ready – alongside her husband – to support any programs or projects for the sake of the kingdom of God.

On many occasions, she had given over and above what was the norm to accommodate exigencies that came along. She was a virtuous woman of God to the public, but one thing had burdened her for decades in the private and she could not bear to live with it anymore.

This acclaimed woman of substance and steel, who had risen to the top in her chosen profession and was considered a model to others in the Church, harbored unforgiveness towards another professor in JSU for some vitriolic attacks that professor had thrown at her in the past.

As the COVID-19 pandemic hammered home, and shut down institutions across the world, Mrs. P felt it necessary to call this professor and apologize to her and ask for forgiveness. With a sense of urgency, she picked up the phone, called the professor and explained her ill feelings towards her, and asked for her forgiveness.

The professor was stunned, and take aback. She had sat on Mrs. P's promotion, sent attackers after her with lies and derogatory statements that were false and yet Mrs. P was apologizing to her! She accepted the apology, albeit hesitantly, and called for a truce. She promised to reach out for a physical meeting when COVID-19 *shelter in place* orders were eased.

That was, however, never to be. Mrs. P died suddenly a week after the rapprochement with the professor leaving behind a husband and two children. She also left behind a devastated Church community, and a JSU community that heard her story of reconciliation and marveled at the timing.

She was not a second short, or a dollar delayed! She rose in obedience to the promptings of the Holy Spirit, and made peace with her erstwhile *public enemy No. 1*. That one act decided her destiny, and ensured her an eternity with the saints. If she had not, the repercussions may have been eternal and the consequences all consuming.

Prayer: I choose to live in the light of the life of Christ, in Jesus name!

The only dust that should hang around you is star dust!

- TOBE MOMAH M.D.

CHAPTER TEN

DISLIKED

"...*they got not the land in possession by their own sword, neither did their own arm save them: but thy right hand, and thine arm, and the* **light** *of thy countenance, because thou hadst a favor unto them*" (Psalm 44:3).

God did not call you to be masked, marred or masqueraded by the enemy! He said, in Matthew 5:14-16, that "*ye are the light of the world. A city that is set on an hill cannot be hid. Neither do men light a candle, and put it under a bushel, but on a candlestick; and it giveth light unto all that are in the house. Let your light so shine before men, that they may see your good works, and glorify your Father which is in heaven.*"

He did not call you a village or a town, but a city! He elevated you to the highest heights, and as you accomplish your purpose of being a light to the world don't demote yourself by denying his light and embracing falsehoods. The scripture does not call you the dustheap of society, but a destiny hewer for lives untold. He calls you "*...a chosen generation, a royal priesthood, an holy nation, a peculiar people; that ye should shew forth the praises of him who hath called you out of darkness into his marvelous light*" (1 Peter 2:9).

When the Word of God enters a believer's life, light shines forth. In Psalm 119:130, the Bible says "*the entrance of thy words giveth light; it giveth understanding unto the simple.*" When the light rises upon individuals, their rising financially, physically, and spiritually is un hindered! That is why God said, "*let them shout for joy, and be glad, that favor my righteous cause: yea, let them say continually, Let the Lord* be magnified, which hath pleasure in the prosperity of his servant" (Psalm 35:27).

When you choose favor, prosperity is inevitable. Favor is, however, predicated on the anointing of light. In Psalm 44:3, the Psalmist says "*...they got not the land in possession by their own sword, neither did their own arm save them: but thy right hand, and thine arm, and the light of thy countenance, because thou hadst a favour unto them.*"

In Isaiah 60:10-11, He adds that "*...the sons of strangers shall build up thy walls, and their kings shall minister unto thee: for in my wrath I smote thee, but **in my favor have I had mercy on thee**. Therefore thy gates shall be open continually; they shall not be shut day nor night; that men may bring unto thee the forces of the Gentiles, and that their kings may be brought.*"

Before that happens, however, His light must rise upon you. These ones are those "*...the Lord shall arise upon..., and his glory shall be seen upon...and the Gentiles shall come to thy light, and kings to the brightness of thy rising*" (Isaiah 60:2-3). They are those whom God will favor (Isaiah 60:10) for it takes **His risen light to rise in life.**

MISSION, NOT MISSING, MENTALITY!

In Luke 15:8-9, Jesus tells the parable of the woman who lost one coin. He said, "*...what woman having ten pieces of silver, if she lose one piece, doth not light a candle, and sweep the house, and seek diligently till she find it? And when she hath found it, she calleth her friends and her neighbors together, saying, Rejoice with me; for I have found the piece which I had lost.*"

This woman's silver coins were all the same, but that notwithstanding, this woman went out of her way to look for the one coin that was lost. If that woman had refused to look for her missing coin, that coin would have remained missing forever. The reason why some gifts are discovered, and others relegated to plunder, is because someone went after the hidden gift with light while others miscued theirs.

Darkness is the cannon fodder for dislike! Though she had 90% success rate, this woman (in Luke 15) still wanted 100% level. She went in with her light to recover what was lost and changed the **darkness of dislike** to the **light of love**. In Psalm 44:3, God told the Israelites that "...*they got not the land in possession by their own sword, neither did their own arm save them: but thy right hand, and thine arm, and the **light of thy countenance**, because thou **hadst a favor** unto them."*

The light of God's countenance births favor, and gives an individual what they normally would not have gotten. The last day Church is a favor-laden Church. In Proverbs 15:16, the Bible says "*in the light of the king's countenance is life; and his favor is as a cloud of the latter rain."* The latter rain clouds, that give the Church supernatural favor, are swirling all around her and if she chooses to operate in the light of His countenance, there will be no obstacle too tall or enemy too great she cannot overcome.

DANIEL: DESTINED FOR DISTINCTION

Too many of God's people are living in dislike because they have not discovered their destiny! After been castrated and made a eunuch, "...*God...brought Daniel into favor and tender love with the prince of the eunuchs"* (Daniel 1:9). From that time forward, Daniel's upward trajectory was unstoppable.

The oil of favor will only work where the milk of God's word is embraced! Daniel was a capital executor of the Word of God, and as a result Favor was released in his life. He told the head Eunuch, before been encompassed with God's favor, that he had "...*purposed in his heart that he would not defile himself with the portion of the king's meat, nor with the wine which he drank: therefore he requested of the prince of the eunuchs that he might not defile himself"* (Daniel 1:8).

In Isaiah 27:11, the secret of divine favor is revealed. It says, they are "...*a people of **no understanding**; therefore he that made them will not have mercy on them, and he that formed them will shew them **no favor**."*

One of the greatest dangers of darkness is dislike, or lack of favor, and only a lover of understanding will dispel its tentacles.

In Proverbs 3:1-4, the Bible says *"My son, forget not my law; but let thine heart keep my commandments: For length of days, and long life, and peace, shall they add to thee. Let not mercy and truth forsake thee: bind them about thy neck; write them upon the table of thine heart: So shalt thou find **favor** and good understanding in the **sight of God** and man."*

That law is God's *"...word, (and the)...lamp unto my feet, and a light unto my path"* (Psalm 119:105). Every time an individual walks in obedience to God's word, the favor of God and the light of life shines upon him or her. In Proverbs 8:34-35, the Lord said *"blessed is the man that heareth me, watching daily at my gates, waiting at the posts of my doors. For whoso findeth me findeth life, and shall obtain **favor** of the Lord."*

AWUZIE AND 2ND MB

I had sounded out my medical school classmates on my readiness to report any culprits and stop the repetitive crass exam malpractice that had become the norm in our medical school. I was, therefore, not totally surprised when a day before the anatomy exam in 2016, two classmates strode into my study room with a sense of perplexity and an anomy of confusion.

They quickly exchanged pleasantries, and told me the exam for the next day had leaked. They revealed the site where our classmates were purchasing the exam papers for more than $70:00, and their fears of a widespread after effect on those who didn't get their hands on the leaked paper (as only a set number could graduate to the next class).

The stakes were high, and the die was cast. They looked me in the eye, and said they could not afford the asking price for the question papers (which was $20 cheaper than the questions and answer bundle) and I was their only hope. They wished me the best, but asked me not to mention their names (and to date I haven't).

I called my Father, who gave me one of his military attaches (named Warrant Officer Adiele), in an undercover operation. At about 7pm that Sunday evening we headed to the *conclave* where the future of innocent medical students were been traded and torn apart by greedy professors.

The then head of Anatomy, Dr. Awuzie, was behind the sale of these exam papers (using his Engineering undergrad son as a proxy), and under cover I bought the $50:00 version and hid it in my closet until morning (without prying at the questions).

I engaged the Christian Union University of Nigeria, Enugu Campus (UNEC) Organizing Secretary, Armstrong Odeta (now a pastor in Sapele, Nigeria), to drive me down to the Provost of the college of Medicine's home by 5am the next morning. It was a Monday, and his adorable wife was startled to see me at their door so early. He had not woken up, but on been awakened was even more startled to be told (by yours truly) that *the exam for that morning had leaked and here is a copy to prove it.*

The anatomy exam was in two parts, including Essay and multiple choice questions. Instead of starting by 8am, as scheduled, the multiple choice took off at 9am. Before that, a flurry of activities including unprecedented traffic in and out of the Provost's office, occurred. At the end of the first part of the exam (multi-choice), however, it looked like I would stand on the wrong side of history as many of my classmates were seen celebrating as they had gotten a peek of these same questions the night before.

For the essay questions, however, I was the one laughing last as the Provost had caused another lecturer in the department to change the Anatomy essay questions. The final exam was, thereafter, scored without any input from the multiple choice questions but based solely on the essay section. I had stood on the right side of history, and was vindicated!

Dr Awuzie and his sons were livid. They threatened my life, and promised they would never allow me to graduate as a medical doctor. I got messages from different lecturers (in and out of the Anatomy department) telling me I was a marked man and had better withdraw because I was penciled down to fail the repeat Anatomy exam (which I had failed on my first attempt).

Undeterred and unwavering, I employed enormous spiritual and academic arsenal into this battle for my future. I studied as hard as I could, and prayed even harder! On the day of the release of the exam result, I was celebrating my pass in anatomy when the Dean of the pre-clinical school (Dr. Mordi) approached me and said *Never report a lecturer again. You were the reason the 30 minutes meeting turned into a 4 hour debate between the Dean, Faculty of Medicine and Dr. Awuzie on whether you should pass or fail.*

I was flabbergasted, and overwhelmed. The dean, Dr Umerah, was a revered radiologist and a father figure to many in the medical community. I had never met him personally, but he stood up for me (in the Dean's meeting) and insisted I pass Anatomy (even though the Head of department – Dr. Awuzie - thought to the contrary) which was unprecedented. It was divine favor, and today I am a medical doctor as a result.

Dr Awuzie, on the other hand, went on to be investigated by future administrations of the College of Medicine and was dismissed by the University after a thorough investigation into his activities by the Professor Udeh led panel of inquiry (2000). That incident is etched in the memoirs of my University, and it single handedly broke the back of the longest serving exam racketeering scheme in the University of Nigeria. Praise God and Glory to his name alone.

Prayer: Make me Heaven's favorite through the instrumentality of Heaven's Word in Jesus name.

*Stars are never placed on
the floor, but in the sky!*

- Tobe Momah M.D.

CHAPTER ELEVEN

DOWN

*"Ye are the **light** of the world. A city that is set on an hill cannot be hid. Neither do men light a candle, and put it under a bushel, but on a candlestick; and it giveth light unto all that are in the house. Let your light so **shine** before men, that they may see your good works, and **glorify** your Father which is in heaven"* (Matthew 5:14-16).

You and I are called to be a *"...city set on a hill...that cannot be hid..."* (Matthew 5:14). It means therefore that the Church cannot be hid, because she is destined for the topmost top. She is *"...the light of the world"* (Matthew 5:14-16), but it takes **looking up at His light, to avert going down in life**.

In Matthew 5:15-16, the Bible says *"neither do men light a candle, and put it under a bushel, but on a candlestick; and it giveth light unto all that are in the house. Let your light so shine before men, that they may see your good works, and glorify your Father which is in heaven."*

Again, in Isaiah 52:11-13, the Bible says *"depart ye, depart ye, go ye out from thence, touch no unclean thing; go ye out of the midst of her; be ye clean, that bear the vessels of the Lord. For ye shall not go out with haste, nor go by flight: for the Lord* will go before you; and the God of Israel will be your reward. *Behold, my servant shall deal prudently, he shall be exalted and extolled, and be **very high**."*

Your prudence makes for your promotion, and your visage of light is your stage for unending victory. When Obed-Edom kept the Ark of God for 90 days, he did not go down but rather became so rich that even King David took notice of his prosperity (2 Samuel 6:11-12)!

His secret was the light of God's presence! He loved, embraced, and carried the light of God's presence wherever he went. You are not called to be the tail, or below but the head and above only (see Deuteronomy 28:13).

As a result of heavenly light, the highest heights are the Church's birthright. No wonder He is called *"the Lord...(who)...bringeth down to the grave, and bringeth up. The Lord (who) maketh poor, and maketh rich: ...(who)...bringeth low, and lifteth up...(who)...raiseth up the poor out of the dust, and lifteth up the beggar from the dunghill, to set them among princes, and to make them inherit the throne of glory: for the pillars of the earth are the Lord's, and he hath set the world upon them. He will keep the feet of his saints, and the wicked shall **be silent in darkness**; for by strength shall no man prevail"* (1 Samuel 2:7-9). **Those silent in darkness stay down, but those lighted will be forever lifted!**

URIAH: THE LORD IS MY LIGHT

Uriah the Hittite was supposed to be an outcast in Israel, because he was a descendant of Heth (2 Samuel 11:3), whose genealogy Noah had cursed (Genesis 9:25 and 10:25). He, instead, beat the racial, cultural and spiritual odds to become one of the thirty mighty men of David (1 Chronicles 11:41). He was a core loyalist of the King, and went on to marry the King's counsellor's (Ahitophel) granddaughter (2 Samuel 11:3, 23:34). In addition, he refused to engage in sexual relationship with his wife while the Ark and the army of Israel were sitting under the tents of war.

Uriah rose to become one of only thirty mighty men in an Israeli army of hundreds of thousands. His name meant the ***Lord is my Light*** and his actions bellied his name. He told David *"the ark, and Israel, and Judah, abide in tents; and my lord Joab, and the servants of my* *lord, are encamped in the open fields; shall I then go into mine house, to eat and to drink, and to lie with my wife? as thou livest, and as thy soul liveth, I will not do this thing"* (2 Samuel 11:11). **Only a foolish warrior goes to war without the presence of God.**

Uriah was made drunk, in 2 Samuel 11:13, by King David. Even though Uriah was inebriated, and his emotions, memory and physical senses were altered, his spirit was impenetrable to alcohol. He had an attitude of warfare, that was ingrained into his spirit, notwithstanding his surrounding circumstances. He was akin to the soldier described by Paul in 2 Timothy 2:3-4, who *"…endure(d) hardness, as a good soldier of Jesus Christ* (for) *no man…that warreth entangleth himself with the affairs of this life; that he may please him who hath chosen him to be a soldier."*

Uriah was such a good general that when David asked Joab to place him at the front of the worst war offensive (2 Samuel 11:16), it did not evoke any uproars from the rest of the Israeli army. He rose to the pinnacle of his career, because he was not a man-pleaser but a God-pleaser. In Ephesians 6:5-8, the Bible says *"servants, be obedient to them that are your masters according to the flesh, with fear and trembling, in singleness of your heart, as unto Christ; Not with eyeservice, as menpleasers; but as the servants of Christ, doing the will of God from the heart; With good will doing service, as to the Lord, and not to men: Knowing that whatsoever good thing any man doeth, the same shall he receive of the Lord, whether he be bond or free."*

THE DAWN OF THE DEW!

The dew is otherwise called *Night Mist*, and it means spiritual and watering rain in the night season. This dew changes everything! In Psalm 133:1-3, the Psalmist says *"…how good and how pleasant it is for brethren to dwell together in unity! It is like the precious ointment upon the head, that ran down upon the beard, even Aaron's beard: that went down to the skirts of his garments; As the **dew** of Hermon, and as the **dew that descended upon the mountains of Zion**: for there the Lord **commanded the blessing**, even life for evermore."*

The *commanded blessing* is irrevocable where the dew is available. Every time you want to rise, you must **get rid of the dust** and **embrace the dew**. Without moisture, there can't be fruitfulness as the dew is the basic ingredient for the blessing. To the contrary, dust connotes emptiness. In Isaiah 52:1-2, the Bible says "*awake, awake; put on thy strength, O Zion; put on thy beautiful garments, O Jerusalem, the holy city: for henceforth there shall no more come into thee the uncircumcised and the unclean. Shake thyself from the dust; arise, and sit down, O Jerusalem: loose thyself from the bands of thy neck, O captive daughter of Zion.*"

The key to getting awake, and putting on beautiful garments, is shaking the dust off one's life! A Christian will never walk in beauty or strength until dust and darkness are banished from their lives. In Ephesians 5:7-17, the Bible says "*...now are ye light in the Lord* (so) *walk as children of light: ...and have no fellowship with the unfruitful works of darkness, but rather reprove them. For it is a shame even to speak of those things which are done of them in secret. But all things that are reproved are made manifest by the light: for **whatsoever doth make manifest is light**. Wherefore he saith, Awake thou that sleepest, and arise from the **dead**, and **Christ shall give thee light**.*"

These scriptures are a last day scripture, and when the Church sleeps in the dust instead of in the dew, they are "*...fools,* (un aware) *the days are evil*" (Ephesians 5:15). They must, to the contrary, "*...be ye not unwise, but understanding what the will of the Lord is*" (Ephesians 5:16).

Dust can be dangerous, while dew is the key to one's deliverance! When God wanted to pronounce the blessings upon Israel, He said "*there is none like unto the God of Jeshurun, who rideth upon the heaven in thy help, and in his excellency on the sky. The eternal God is thy refuge, and underneath are the everlasting arms: and he shall thrust out the enemy from before thee; and shall say, Destroy them. Israel then shall dwell in safety alone: the fountain of Jacob shall be upon a land of corn and wine; also his **heavens shall drop down dew**" (Deuteronomy 33:26-28).

The dew of heaven is what resurrects the impossible. It says, in the book of Job 14:7-9, "*...there is hope of a tree, if it be cut down,* *that it will sprout again, and that the tender branch thereof will not cease. Though the root thereof wax old in the earth, and the stock thereof die in the ground; Yet through **the scent of water** it will bud, and bring forth boughs like a plant.*"The scent of water is akin to the dew, and it makes the impossible possible.

The **difficult times are times for dew therapy**, not the dust. In Job 29:19-20, Job attributed his *wealthiest in the east* status to the power of the dew. He said, "*my root was spread out by the waters, and the dew lay all night upon my branch. My glory was fresh in me, and my bow was renewed in my hand.*" Disregarding the dew of the Holy Spirit is tantamount to refusing His lifting and promotion in life. It is that light, emanating from the dew, that guarantees increase and success. Without it, doom, destruction and desolation are inevitable!

CLEMENT OKOLO: CALLED OUT, CHASED OUT, AND NOW THE CROWNED ONE!

Clement Okolo was the Head of department at the Pathology department of the College of Medicine, University of Ibadan and Deputy Chief Medical Administration Committee (CMAC) in charge of finance and budget, when he faced the most blatant and audacious threat to his life.

He had single-handedly stopped the non-academic medical staff's running of labs in the University College Hospital (UCH) and it was ruffling some feathers. He was accused by them of stopping a conduit through which the hospital was losing millions, and as a result those involved were threatening his life and that of his family.

He was not a stranger to challenges, but this was of a new sort. He had endured a string of failures in medical school, and was once on the cusp of being thrown out of medical school until God intervened and gave him victory. He was expected (at UCH) to cower, throw in the towel and run for cover as several before him had done, but instead he stood up and fought this enemy called corruption to a standstill.

As a result, his promotions were delayed, and he had to re-locate from Nigeria to safeguard the life of his family. He was also the pastor of a local parish of the Redeemed Christian Church of God (RCCG), and sought prayers while in hiding for preservation, protection, and prosperity.

A year later, God has truly turned Clement and his family's captivity. He is now the Dean of the Basic sciences program at a leading private University's Medical school, a full professor of anatomical pathology and absolved of any blame by a panel of enquiry into his activities in the department of pathology by the supervising Ministry.

No man can truly serve God and stay down! He is too good to fail and specializes in turning captivities and re-writing one's story. He is the story changer, covenant keeper, life lifter, captivity-turner, multiple blesser, who gives excess mercy and supernatural strength to overcome any and every battle one may face.

Prayer: Lord, make me inherit my throne of glory, in Jesus name!

Faith is a leap into the light,
not a step into the darkness

– BONNKE, REINHARD (1940-2019)
EVANGELIST, CHRIST FOR ALL NATIONS

CHAPTER TWELVE

DOUBT

*"Who is among you that feareth the Lord, that obeyeth the voice of his servant, that walketh in darkness, and hath no light? let him **trust** in the name of the Lord, and stay upon his God. Behold, all ye that kindle a fire, that compass yourselves about with sparks: walk in the **light** of your fire, and in the sparks that ye have kindled..."* (Isaiah 50:10-11).

The Church is accommodating evil by her indecisiveness, and lack of sure footedness. An old English adage says, *hit the iron while it is hot* while an American adage says *pick and stick.* These two adages encourage decisiveness and assertiveness, which go contrary to some of the Church's languid and *laissez-faire* attitude. Umbrage, rather than a sense of understanding, is what is required to counter this lack of assertiveness in the modern day Church.

A similar situation played out, in John 9:4-5, when the disciples debated the genesis or exegesis of the blind man's precarious health condition. Instead of doing something about it, the disciples debated, dilly-daallied and doubted God's word over the individual (Exodus 15:26). Jesus, to the contrary, told them *"I must work the works of him that sent me, while it is day: the night cometh, when no man can work. As long as I am in the world, I am the light of the world."*

Instead of joining the debate, as so many in the Church today are wont to do, Jesus charged them to be the light where ever they found themselves if they want darkness to flee. The hesitancy, double mindedness, wavering, and halting in the Church has paralyzed her from shining this light to a dark and dying world.

As a sign of His assertiveness, Jesus "...*spat on the ground, and made clay of the spittle, and...anointed the eyes of the blind man with the clay, and said unto him, Go, wash in the pool of Siloam, (which is by interpretation, Sent.) He went his way therefore, and washed, and came seeing*" (John 9:6-7).

WHEN THE DAY BECOMES DARK

When God wants to destroy a people he makes the day dark. It is the absence of day that signals the beginning of captivity and judgement. The absence of light keeps people in bondage, and one of the greatest abettors of doubt that brings unending judgement is darkness.

In Ezekiel 30:18-19, the Lord God said "*at Tehaphnehes also the day shall be darkened, when I shall break there the yokes of Egypt: and the pomp of her strength shall cease in her: as for her, a cloud shall cover her, and her daughters shall go into captivity. Thus will I execute judgments in Egypt: and they shall know that I am the Lord.*"

Beware when a cloud or darkness covers your glory. It means your strength is gone (Ezekiel 30:18), and judgement is not far off. It signals a dearth of your strength in God (aka doubt), and is why, in Ephesians 5:13-14, Paul adjures the Ephesian Church to know that "...*all things that are reproved are made manifest by the light: for whatsoever doth make manifest is light. Wherefore he saith, Awake thou that sleepest, and arise from the dead, and Christ shall give thee light.*"

In Biblical stereotypes, strength and awakening connotes increasing faith in God. In Isaiah 51:9 and 52:1, the Prophet said "*awake, awake, put on thy strength...*" because it (strength) is measured by faith. In Romans 4:19-20, Paul said that Abraham "...*being not weak in faith,...considered not his own body now dead, when he was about an hundred years old, neither yet the deadness of Sarah's womb* (and)... *staggered not at the promise of God through unbelief; but was **strong in faith**, giving glory to God."*

In the last days, one of the greatest tests for the Church will be the test for light by faith. In 1 Thessalonians 5:4-8, Paul warns believers saying "*...ye brethren are not in darkness, that that day should overtake you as a thief. Ye are all the children of **light**, and the children of the day: we are not of the night, nor of darkness. Therefore let us not sleep, as do others; but let us watch and be sober. For they that sleep sleep in the night; and they that be drunken are drunken in the night. But let us, who are of the day, be sober, putting on the **breastplate of faith** and love; and for an helmet, the hope of salvation."*

BY STRENGTH SHALL NO MAN PREVAIL!

In 1 Samuel 2:9, Hannah prayed saying God "*...will keep the feet of his saints, and the wicked shall be silent in darkness; for by strength shall no man prevail.*" The word used for **prevail**, in the above verse, is the Hebrew word *Gabar* and it means to be strong, mighty, valiant, and exceed expectations.

In a nutshell, she stated that to prevail or triumph in life is not dependent on human effort, capacity, wealth, or force but by faith in God. The word used for **strength** in 1 Samuel 2:9 is the Hebrew word *Kowach*, and it means firmness or vigor. This strength results in failure, but faith and victory become manifest when divine strength avails.

In 1 John 5:4-5, the Bible says "*...whatsoever is born of God overcometh the world: and this is the victory that overcometh the world, even our faith* (for) *who is he that overcometh the world, but he that believeth that Jesus is the Son of God?*" Some remain silent in the darkness, trusting in their strength, but all to no avail.

Without light, strength to prevail is impossible! It is "*...the entrance of* (His)...*words* (that) *give light...*" (Psalm 119:130), and until the Word comes "*faith* (that) *cometh by hearing, and hearing by the word of God*" (Romans 10:17) is null and void. **Those who want to**

prevail in life must get out of darkness, because darkness stimulates doubt not faith.

ZOO IN JACKSON

My wife and I drove from Monroe, Louisiana to see the animals in the Zoo in Jackson, Mississippi. It was a two hour drive, and even though Monroe had a Zoo we were desirous to see other animals that were not present in our locale at the bigger Jackson Zoo.

On arrival, we made our intentions known to the lady at the gate of the Zoo. Rather than excitedly allow us entry, after paying the requisite fees, she retorted *"why did you come here when you have a Zoo in Monroe?"* We explained our desire to be entertained by the sight of Giraffes, lions and Elephants that were absent in Monroe but present in Jackson.

Her next words doused all our expectations. She said the Giraffes were hidden, and may not come out, the lions were sick, and the Elephants would be a rare sighting if seen at all. She said it would be a waste of our time, and we might as well return to our locale.

My wife and I were shocked at her lack luster attitude, and returned to Monroe and have not been to the Jackson Zoo since! Even though we have since moved to Jackson, there still remains no desire to return to the Jackson Zoo. The first cut, like they say, is the deepest and the languid and listless words of that lady at the gate has ruined any thoughts of our ever going to the Jackson Zoo.

Prayer: May I never have a better yesterday, and let my path shine brighter and brighter unto a perfect day, in Jesus name.

When you live in darkness,
the only light you can have is truth!

- TOBE MOMAH M.D.

CHAPTER THIRTEEN

DIMNESS

"Yet a little while is the light with you. Walk while ye have the light, lest darkness come upon you: for he that walketh in darkness knoweth not whither he goeth. While ye have light, believe in the light, that ye may be the children of light" (John 12:35-36).

There is a hidden darkness, otherwise called dimness, in the realm of the spirit where the proud end up. God describes it in Job 40:12-13. He says, *"look on every one that is proud, and bring him low; and tread down the wicked in their place. Hide them in the dust together; and bind their faces in secret."*

One of the worst things about pride is the aloofness, and aloneness, these ones find themselves in. Rather than ask for guidance, in humility, they stymie in darkness and fall over themselves. No wonder Jesus advised his disciples to **"let them alone** (for) *they be blind leaders of the blind. And if the blind lead the blind, both shall fall into the ditch"* (Matthew 15:14).

The strategy for surviving the last days is meekness, not pride. Meekness gives you light, while pride brings dimness. In Psalm 25:9, the Psalmist says *"the meek will he guide in judgment (for)...the meek will he teach his way."* He adds, in Psalm 22:6, *"the meek shall eat and be satisfied: they shall praise the Lord that seek him: your heart shall live for ever."*

THE MISTAKE OF THE CHURCH

One of the greatest mistakes of the Church is believing the theorem that if I remain in my corner, the devil will leave me alone. That analogy is contrary to God's commands. Apostle Paul told King Agrippa, while talking about the death and resurrection of Jesus Christ, that *"…the king knoweth of these things, before whom also I speak freely: for I am persuaded that **none of these things are hidden** from him; for this thing was not done in a corner"* (Acts 26:26).

Jesus called believers *"the light of the world* (and) *a city that is set on an hill that cannot be hid* (for) *neither do men light a candle, and put it under a bushel, but on a candlestick; and it giveth light unto all that are in the house"* (Matthew 5:14-15). He therefore adjured the Church to *"let your light so shine before men, that they may see your good works, and glorify your Father which is in heaven"* (Matthew 5:16).

The light of the world is Jesus Christ (John 9:5), and He reflects His light on those who follow him, not those who hide in a corner. That is why Jesus told his disciples *"I am the light of the world: he that followeth me shall not walk in darkness, but shall have the light of life"* (John 8:12). He then urges them to take another step in reflecting His light by believing in Him. He said, in John 12:36, *"while ye have light, believe in the light, that ye may be the children of light."*

His will for the Church is not dimness, but shining. He calls the Church *glorious* in Ephesians 5:27, and states that the *"the path of the just is as the shining light, that shineth more and more unto the perfect day"* (Proverbs 4:18). Without light, dimness of vision is inevitable but with light, greatness is a *fait accompli*. That is why Jesus goes further, in John 12:46, to say *"I am come a light into the world, that whosoever believeth on me should not abide in darkness."*

RESTRAIN, NOT REPEAT, THE DARKNESS!

Too many repeat the darkness of their times, instead of restraining it. God told Eli, "...*I will judge* (your*) house for ever for the iniquity which he knoweth; because his sons made themselves vile, and he restrained them not*" (1 Samuel 3:13). Instead of restraining them for their acts of darkness, however, Eli repeated their darkness to them (1 Samuel 2:22-25) but it was all to no avail.

The word used for **restrain** is the word *Kahah* which means to *darken, be dim, fail, or be faint*. It means the only remedy to darkness is to put it in the dark! It meant removing their privilege, power, and proprietary rights as priests in Israel, but instead Eli "...*honored* (his) *sons above* (God), to *make* (them)*selves fat with the chiefest of all the offerings of Israel my people*" (1 Samuel 2:29). Stop moaning about the darkness in your community, and instead put it out by shining the light!

When my wife and I moved to Jackson, Mississippi in December 2016, God gave us a charge saying "*restrain the darkness over the city of Jackson, Mississippi.*" Since that word came forth, we have faithfully stayed in prayer, praise and prophecy over our City (on the second Fridays of every month) and have seen a transformation of our City and His glory released over Jackson Metropolis.

LAND OF GIMBIE

My wife and I arrived in Gimbie, West Wollega in North West Ethiopia in October 2004. We had arrived to serve as missionary laboratory personnel and missionary doctor respectively, and after six months of short stay missions there, a light that still shines bright till today was ignited.

While in Gimbie, Ethiopia, my wife and I conducted weekly Holy Ghost Night vigils (on Friday nights), preached in several local Churches, visited and fed prisoners in the prison, developed a standard operating procedure (S.O.P) work book for the lab and treated several patients at the host Adventist hospital.

The prelude to our trip was, however, tenuous. My wife had just come out of the hospital, and I had just successfully finished my Master's course at the London School of Hygiene and Tropical Medicine (LSHTM), University of London and was expected by family and friends to join the medical workforce in the United Kingdom.

God, however, had a different opinion. He laid it on my heart, after reading an LSHTM advert for a Missionary doctor in Gimbie, Ethiopia to travel there even though there were no financial salaries attached to the job. I wanted clarity, and decided to attend a T.D Jakes meeting in London, UK in order to seek His vision for my life.

At the meeting, I obtained assurance of His direction and stepped out assured of God's provision and protection. I returned home, and told my wife to get ready to travel to Ethiopia the next week. The cocksureness I reflected, shocked my wife but on return from Ethiopia six months later, God miraculously gave me a place to train as a Surgeon in the Brooklyn Hospital, New York.

The rest, as they say, is history. I finished two years of General Surgery, and started Family Medicine on the stellar recommendations of my Surgery colleagues. I graduated top of my class in my residency program, and became Medical Director of the largest community health center in Louisiana.

Today, I am a faculty and an Associate professor at a United States Medical school. My assertive initiative to go to Gimbie in 2004, is partly the reason I am where I am today! It took a trip to Gimbie to open doors in New York, and an assertiveness to birth His abundance.

Prayer: Where ever I stand, I decree darkness flees in Jesus name!

*It is better to light one candle
than to curse the darkness.*

- FATHER JAMES KELLER (1900 – 1977)

CHAPTER FOURTEEN

DEPRESSION

*"The **light** of the eyes **rejoiceth** the heart: and a good report maketh the bones fat"* (Proverbs 15:30).

A melancholic or malevolent mindset is not what God made a believer's mind to be. He made their minds to be exactly like the mind of Christ. The apostle Paul told the Corinthian Church that *"…we have the mind of Christ"* (1 Corinthians 2:16), and in 2 Timothy 1:7, he told Timothy that *"…God hath not given us the spirit of fear; but of power, and of love, and of a sound mind."*

Don't let depression stop your dreams and impale your destiny. **A colorless life starts with a clouded mind!** Refuse the bait of envy and grumbling and live in the mind of Christ permanently. The word of God counsels the church in this regard; It says *"keep thy heart with all diligence; for out of it are the issues of life"* (Proverbs 4:23).

Before the Israelites rose to defend themselves against the draconian laws of Haman (Esther 9:1-6), Mordecai had been lifted from the palace gates to become the prime minister over the whole realm of 127 nations. After his elevation, the Bible says the *"…Jews had **light**, and **gladness**, and **joy**, and **honor**"* (Esther 9:16).

Where light is available, rejoicing in required and celebration compulsory! That is why, in Colossians 1:10-12, apostle Paul describes the Church as *"…being fruitful in every good work, and increasing in* *the knowledge of God* (and so is) *strengthened with all might, according to his glorious power, unto all patience and longsuffering with joyfulness; Giving thanks unto the Father, which hath made us meet to be partakers of the inheritance of the saints in light."*

THE MYSTERY OF THE JUNIPER TREE

In 1 Kings 19:4, a fearful prophet Elijah was running from the rampaging Queen Jezebel and sat under a juniper tree. It says, Elijah *"...went a day's journey into the wilderness, and came and sat down under a juniper tree: and he requested for himself that he might die; and said, It is enough; now, O Lord, take away my life; for I am not better than my fathers."*

Though Elijah was hungry and haunted at the onset of his journey to Beersheba, his emotions snowballed into severe depression and suicidal ideation while under the juniper tree. The juniper tree, which is a broom like tree in Israel with sparse coning among its leaves, has flexible small leaves and grows to about three to twelve feet tall. It offers a promise of cover from the sun but because to its thin leaves, it gives very poor protection from the sun.

The juniper tree represents an environment that is full of promise but without performance and one that offers camouflage but no cover or color. It represents emptiness and could manifest subtly as severe depression. The believer that overcomes depression must rid him or herself of what Jude called *"...clouds...without water, carried about of winds; trees whose fruit wither, without fruit, twice dead, plucked up by the roots...wandering stars, to whom is reserved the **blackness of darkness** for ever"* (Jude 1:12-13).

The blackness of darkness connotes severe depression, and it is the product of an empty environment. A juniper-tree sounds a death knell to life and ministry, as it did to the ministry of Elijah. Soon after being under the Juniper tree, God told Elijah, *"...Elisha...shall thou anoint to be prophet in thy room"* (1 Kings 19:16). A believer that covers him or herself with emptiness dies in depression, but he or she who stands on the substance of God's word births delight. Get rid of negativity in your environment and you will develop notable excellence.

To be Solitary is to Be Suicidal!

The burden to achieve more, accompanied by increased isolation, has caused more burn out, depression and suicide than the feared terror plots and assassination attempts in the corridors of wealth and power. The wise man, Solomon, concurred with this analogy. He said, in Proverbs 29:15 that, "…*a child left to himself bringeth his mother to shame.*"

Elijah's greatest burden in ministry was his solitariness. When asked by God why he was hiding in a cave from Jezebel, he answered "*I have been very jealous for the Lord God of hosts: because the children of Israel have forsaken thy covenant, thrown down thine altars, and slain thy prophets with the sword; and I, even I only, am left; and they seek my life, to take it away*" (1 Kings 19:14).

He went from Beersheba alone, having left his servant there (1 Kings 19:3). There in the throes of solitariness, the dark veil of suicide became more glaring. Even though Israel had at least a hundred other prophets, Elijah stayed perennially isolated. A recent study by the Harvard risk management forum reported that medical professionals who were depersonalized (or solitary) with their patients ended up having poor communication skills and a higher risk of burnout, exhaustion and depression.

No man or woman is an island to him or herself. When God said "*it is not good that the man should be alone; I will make an help meet for him*" (Genesis 2:18), it meant solitariness is not good. A nine-year study on life expectancy showed that men who were divorced were 37% more likely to die than men who remained married. It has also been shown that social isolation contributes to increased mortality in those who are bereaved, divorced or never married. These socially isolated ones have an 82% higher risk of dying from heart disease, compared with those who have strong interpersonal relationships.[2]

Betrayal, guilt or shame are fertile ground for depression. Judas fell prey to it and died from it because he refused to forgive himself and lived in isolation. Acts 1:20 says, describing Judas environs, *"let his habitation be desolate, and let no man dwell therein...."* This rabid isolationism brought untold shame that precipitated his suicide.

Peter, on the other hand, survived depression's scourge by taking heed to Jesus counsel to feed His sheep (John 21:15-17). He maintained open channels of communication with the brethren such that when he returned to fishing, they followed suite (John 21:3). He eventually became a leader in the early church, and spearheaded the expansion of the gospel to the Gentiles. He refused to allow his past shame determine his future success and, by so doing, he overcame depression.

THE APOSTLE OF ALWAYS JOY

Pastor (Dr) Joy Dara is the pastor of the largest church in central Louisiana. He arrived America in 1980 as an undergraduate student, and had to sleep on classroom floors because of limited resources. As a Christian, however, he believed in always being joyful regardless of the circumstance. His philosophy of life stems from James 1:2-4 which says, *"...count it all joy when ye fall into divers temptations. Knowing this, that the trying of your faith works patience. But let patience have her perfect work, that ye may be perfect and entire wanting nothing."*

He excelled in his classroom studies and went on to obtain a Doctor of Jurisprudence (JD) degree from Southern University, Baton Rouge, Louisiana, and Masters of Law degree from the University of Arkansas, Fayetteville, after his Bachelor of Arts degree from California Baptist University, Riverside, California. As a minister, he served under different denominational leaders as worship leader and assistant pastor and after settling into secular life as an attorney, he was invited by a local church in Pineville to serve as their pastor.

This church (Zion Hill Baptist Church Pineville, Louisiana) was not growing and had lost two pastors to the cold hands of death, in quick sucession. The church board that interviewed him pointedly asked him, *"Do you still want the job knowing the previous two occupants died suddenly?"* In his ebullient and unassuming manner, Joy Dara said that he was not afraid of death; and if given the position, he would cause that spirit of death to depart from the church.

He took the position as senior pastor and in less than ten years the church increased by leaps and bounds. The congregation built a state of the art facility that seats over a thousand people, anchored a statewide television program called *Always Joy* and attracted respect from the community with their innovative programs designed to empower the local population. Dr. Joy Dara also currently oversees hundreds of inter-denominational ministers and his influence is felt across race, denomination and age. No wonder he is fondly called the apostle of always Joy!

Prayer: Make me an instrument of your peace on earth, O Lord, in Jesus name.

PART III

The Light That Lightens

- Perceptive Light
- Persuaded Light
- Pure Light
- Purposeful Light
- Prophetic Light
- Passionate Light
- Persistent Light

When the Shepherd loses his or her voice, the sheep lose their vision!

- TOBE MOMAH M.D.

CHAPTER FIFTEEN

PERCEPTIVE LIGHT

*"Nevertheless when it shall turn to the Lord, the vail shall be taken away. Now the Lord is that Spirit: and where the Spirit of the Lord is, there is liberty. But we all, with open face beholding as in a glass the glory of the Lord, are changed into the same image from **glory** to **glory**, even as by the Spirit of the Lord"* (2 Cor 3:16-18).

Many of us are struggling because of the lack of light. There's a light that if ignored by the Church, will birth struggling. The light that lightens is all you need to bring you out of that situation. In Hosea 4:6, the Bible says *"my people are destroyed for lack of knowledge: because thou hast rejected knowledge, I will also reject thee..."* (Hosea 4:6).

God said *"my people"* are destroyed not because they don't go to church, or they don't partake in praise and worship, but because they lack knowledge. They did not have *"...eyes of...understanding...(to be) enlightened...(so) that* (they) *may know what is the hope of...(their) calling, and what the riches of the glory of his inheritance in the saints and...the exceeding greatness of his power to us-ward who believe,..."* (Ephesians 1:18-20).

In the midst of a dark and dying world, the light that lightens creates a formerly unrevealed and unsurmountable pathway to progress and power. One of the lights that lighten the load of life is the perceptive light. The word *perceptive* is defined as the act of seeing with a sense of awareness, comprehension or an understanding of something beyond the ordinary.

Where there is perception, prosperity is inevitable. The wise man said, in Proverbs 21:16, that *"the man that wandereth out of the way of understanding shall remain in the congregation of the dead."* If, on the other hand, they *"...find wisdom, and...get understanding,* (they will get) *the merchandise...better than the merchandise of silver,* (with)... *the gain thereof* (more) *than fine gold* (for) *she is more precious than rubies and all the things thou canst desire are not to be compared unto her. Length of days is in her right hand; and in her left hand riches and honor"* (Proverbs 3:13-16).

TIME TO TURN!

In Deuteronomy 1:6-8, the Lord spoke to Israel saying *"...ye have dwelt long enough in this mount,* **turn you**, *and take your journey, and go to the mount of the Amorites, and unto all the places nigh thereunto, in the plain, in the hills, and in the vale, and in the south, and by the sea side, to the land of the Canaanites, and unto Lebanon, unto the great river, the river Euphrates.* (for) *behold, I have set the land before you: go in and possess the land which the Lord* sware unto your fathers, Abraham, Isaac, and Jacob...."

Until Israel turned, they could not take possession of their promised land! They had *"...slain Sihon the king of the Amorites, which dwelt in Heshbon, and Og the king of Bashan, which dwelt at Astaroth in Edrei"* (Deuteronomy 1:4), seen God come down in Mount Horeb, and heard His voice (Deuteronomy 1:19), and experienced the miracle of provision and preservation in the wilderness but still were outside their promised land because they walked in the wrong direction.

The proof of divine perception is divine provision! When Israel turned, Moses prophesied to them that *"the Lord* God of your fathers (will) *make you a thousand times so many more as ye are, and bless you, as he hath promised you"* (Deuteronomy 1:11). The promised land opens up when there is a change in direction, not by a wish or a claim!

In 2 Corinthians 3:16-18, apostle Paul adjures the Church to turn if they want to change their story to glory. He said, "*...when it shall turn to the Lord, the vail shall be taken away. Now the Lord is that Spirit: and where the Spirit of the Lord is, there is liberty. But we all, with open face beholding as in a glass the glory of the Lord, are changed into the same image from glory to glory, even as by the Spirit of the Lord.*"

Until the veil or covering cast is removed, with a waiting upon Him to save (Isaiah 25:7-9), perception is impossible. It is why, in Psalm 80: 17-19, the Psalmist said "*let thy hand be upon the man of thy right hand, upon the son of man whom thou madest strong for thyself. So will not we go back from thee: quicken us, and we will call upon thy name. Turn us again, O Lord God of hosts, cause thy face to shine; and we shall be saved.*"

GENERATIONAL LIGHTS

The eye that is evil, will birth a body that is full of darkness, but the eye that is good will bring forth light. In Luke 11:34-35, Jesus said "*the light of the body is the eye: therefore when thine eye is single, thy whole body also is full of light; but when thine eye is evil, thy body also is full of darkness. Take heed therefore that the light which is in thee be not darkness.*"

The word *evil*, as used in Luke 11:34, is the Greek word *poneros* and it means malignant, hurtful, or degeneracy. If you have an eye that is malignant, or that is evil, the whole body is full of darkness. In Psalm 49:16-20, the Bible talks of a wealthy man who lives his life on earth without perception of who he was on the earth.

He had "*...the glory of his house...increased* (but)*...when he dieth he shall carry nothing away* (for) *his glory shall not descend after him though while he lived he blessed his soul,...he shall go to the generation of his fathers; they shall never see **light** (for) man that is in honor, and understandeth not, is like the beasts that perish.*"

He died bereft of understanding, and as a result his generation had no light! His lack of light brought untold hardship to his generations following. To the contrary, when the eye is single, "*...thy* *whole body therefore be full of light, having no part dark, the whole shall be full of light, as when the bright shining of a candle doth give thee light"* (Luke 11:36). That is why Jesus cautioned believers to be careful or perceptive in order to *"take heed therefore that the light which is in thee be not darkness"* (Luke 11:35).

The perceptibility of a believer will enshroud his generations in unassailable light. The Bible says *"…in thy light shall we see light"* (Psalm 36:9) and in Isaiah 9:8, prophet Isaiah adds *"the Lord sent a word into Jacob, and it hath lighted upon Israel."* **Your perception is the mother of generational lightings.** In Psalms 77:18 and 97:4, the prophet said *"…the lightnings lightened the world…"* because one's light can change that of coming generations.

It is time for you to become a generational light! You can become a colossus who changes hs community. You can lift your lineage by giving heed to the Light of God. **It is not enough to just be a light; make yourself a generational light!**

A certain preacher, named Jonathan Edwards, lived between 1703 and 1758. He left a legacy of revival services from the second great awakening, and family members who went on to become Vice-president of the USA, university presidents, preachers, newspaper editors, business men, and other men and women of means and other rare feats.

Those who watch, in the last days, will be celebrated and blessed by the Master (Luke 12:36) but those who lack perception and *"… looketh not for him, and at an hour when he is not aware…will* (He) *cut…in sunder, and will appoint him his portion with the unbelievers"* (Luke 12:46). Without insight, there will be no respite from life's afflictions. **It is those who find revelation that birth revolutions.** That is why Job said, in Job 17:4-5, that God *"…hast hid their heart from understanding: therefore shalt thou not exalt them. He that speaketh flattery to his friends, even the eyes of his children shall fail."*

HIV IN A MONROE LADY

I had a female patient, and when she was young she had gone to the Louisiana state penitentiary, Angola. While there she had undergone routine ante-natal tests because she was a few weeks pregnant. It was, however, in the prison that she found out she had HIV, and in those days (the mid-1980's) HIV was a death sentence.

People didn't survive it, and when you were pregnant, you had to take very toxic medication to prevent transmission of the virus to the baby. That medicine was *Zidovudine*, and because of its high risk potential to the baby, this patient opted to forgo anti-retroviral drugs in order to avoid any deleterious effects on the baby in her womb.

Within a year or two, she had finished her sentence, given birth to her baby, and moved to Monroe, Louisiana. It was another twenty years before I met her, however. By the time I saw her, she was suffering from a facial lesion - called herpes zoster - and in order to do a thorough evaluation I ordered a HIV test. She, by that time, had had a hysterectomy but had not mentioned to anyone that she had the HIV virus. She worked as a cook, and purposely chose to forego unemployment benefits that accrued to people with HIV, through the Ryan White grant, in order not to tell anyone she had the virus.

Her results returned as positive for HIV, and on her return visit I asked her *why haven't you taken any medicine till now?* Rather than answer, she asked me responsively *How did you find out?* I told her that it is a miracle that she has not taken any medicine for twenty years and she was still alive! It was then she told me her story, of how **perception of the supernatural changed her prognosis.**

She stated that she was praying in the Church, on one occasion, and Jesus appeared to her. She saw a vision of Him, and His face shone towards her. After that encounter, she believed she was healed of HIV and never mentioned it again to anyone.

Her vision was, however, more than just a vision. It was an encounter that catapulted her to her wealthy and healthy place. At the time I saw her, she had had three healthy children and had a freelance culinary business where she catered to different individual customers and Church meetings. She demonstrated the power of perception, and showed that what you see can take you to your healthy, and wealthy, place.

This power of perception is demonstrated in Exodus 15:25-26. In that scripture, Moses "...*cried unto the Lord; and the Lord* **shewed** *him a tree, which when he had cast into the waters, the waters were made sweet: there he made for them a statute and an ordinance, and there he proved them, and said, If thou wilt diligently hearken to the voice of the Lord thy God, and wilt do that which is right in his sight, and wilt give ear to his commandments, and keep all his statutes, I will put* **none of these diseases** *upon thee, which I have brought upon the Egyptians: for I am the Lord that healeth thee.*"

It does not take long if you remain strong

- TOBE MOMAH M.D.

CHAPTER SIXTEEN

PERSUADED LIGHT

*"...Jesus Christ, who hath abolished death, and hath brought life and immortality to **light** through the gospel: Whereunto I am appointed a preacher, and an apostle, and a teacher of the Gentiles....nevertheless I am not ashamed: for I know whom I have believed, and am **persuaded** that he is able to keep that which I have committed unto Him..."* (2 Tim 1:9-12).

To be persuaded means to have confidence, rely, agree or have firm foundations. It is when the foundations are out of course that darkness thrives. According to the Psalmist, *"...neither will they understand; they walk on in darkness: all the foundations of the earth are out of course. I have said, Ye are gods; and all of you are children of the most High. But ye shall die like men, and fall like one of the princes"* (Psalm 82:5-7).

Those, on the other hand, who are planted, rooted, and have foundations in God are persuaded individuals. These ones fill the world with fruit. In Isaiah 27:5-6, the Bible says *"let him take hold of my strength, that he may make peace with me; and he shall make peace with me. He shall cause them that come of Jacob to take **root**: Israel shall **blossom** and **bud**, and fill the face of the world with **fruit**."*

Like Paul, said in 2 Timothy 1:12, the believer must go beyond knowing, to believing, and then move to the point of persuasion to bring light to their generation. Many go into the wars of life, without this persuasion and come back casualties. The above scripture says, "...*I am not ashamed: for I know whom I have believed, and am persuaded that he is able to keep that which I have committed unto him against that day.*"

The word *persuaded*, as used in 2 Timothy 1:12, is the Greek word *peíthō* and it means obedience as a result of God's persuasion. Rather than act as arm-chair generals, who sit rather than act on His promises, the Church must put action to her faith (see James 2:17). As a medical student in Nigeria, I signed my books as *Professor Tobe Momah* even though twenty five years ago I looked the most unlikely to pursue an academic career in Medicine. Today, however, I am an associate professor at a University in Mississippi and on an upward trajectory for academic accomplishments.

FAITH FOR FRUITFULNESS

God states that if he can find people who take root, they will fill the earth with fruit (Isaiah 27:6). The whole world is truly our parish, as stated so eloquently by John Wesley (1703 – 1791). The Psalmist adds, in Psalm 92:13-14, that "*those that be planted in the house of the Lord* shall flourish in the courts of our God. They shall still bring forth fruit in old age; they shall be fat and flourishing.*"

If a man trusts in God, he or she will be blessed beyond measure. The Psalmist said, in Psalm 84:11-12, that "*the **Lord** God is a sun and shield (who)...will give grace and glory* (and) *no good thing will he withhold from them that walk uprightly* (for) *O Lord* of hosts, ***blessed is the man that trusteth in thee.*"

There can be no radiance of the sun for *status quo* believers, who refuse to go from knowing to believing to persuading (2 Timothy 1:12). Those who stay rooted cannot be blinded, but those who are unrooted will end up in the ditches of life. In Matthew 15:14-16, Jesus "*...answered and said, Every plant, which my heavenly Father hath* *not planted, shall be rooted up. Let them alone: they be blind leaders of the blind. And if the blind lead the blind, both shall fall into the ditch....*"

FAITH FOR THEIR FUTURE

Those who are children of the light, first believe or are persuaded before they see the light radiate on them. In John 12:36, Jesus told his disciples that "...*while ye have light,* **believe** *in the light, that ye may be the children of light.*" There are people who do not believe and yet want to be children of the light. They, instead, have "...*darkness come upon them for he that walketh in darkness knoweth not whither he goeth*" (John 12:35).

These ones have been blinded by the gods of this world and reside in the midst of gross darkness. Their focus is darkness, and their end destruction. Paul describes them in 2 Cor 4:4, saying "*if our gospel be hid, it is hid to them that are lost in whom the god of this world hath blinded the minds of them which* **believe not**, *lest the light of the glorious gospel of Christ, who is the image of God, should shine unto them.*"

You cannot have what you don't believe in! True shining is conceived in the womb of strength, not stumbling. Without faith, darkness and destruction will pervade one's life but with faith, victory and greatness are unparalleled. Apostle John, in 1 John 5:4, said "... *whatsoever is born of God overcometh the world: and this is the victory that overcometh the world, even our faith. Who is he that overcometh the world, but he that believeth that Jesus is the Son of God?*"

BOMA'S BONANZA

A high school classmate, Boma Tamuno, had a father who was the pre-eminent professor of history in Nigeria at the time. His mother was registrar at the University, while his siblings consisted of *crème de la crème* of the nation's doctors and lawyers. His parents, and siblings, wanted him to become a doctor and it seemed natural as Boma was an all-round brilliant student. He was exceptional in sports, eclectic in personae, top in academics, and astute at politics.

However, there was just one problem; all Boma talked about during the six years we spent together in high school was planes. He drew planes, recited their different speeds, and exhilarately recounted his cockpit experiences in them while travelling to and from his summer holidays. He knew almost everything about fighter planes, helicopters, passenger planes, and luxury jets, and so we were all shocked when he ended up in Medical school instead of flying school.

He spent eight years training to become a Medical doctor at the nation's premier University. On finishing, he enrolled in post-graduate training to become an anesthesiologist. By this time, he was in his mid-thirties, and at some point along the way he said to himself, *I'm tired and can't do this anymore.* He was frustrated with the practice of Medicine in Nigeria, and was looking for a way out.

Rather than migrate abroad to practice Medicine, as most of his colleagues were doing, Boma moved to South Africa and paid thousands of dollars to learn how to fly planes. He finished his course, and started flying helicopters in Nigeria. From Nigeria, he took another course that enabled him to fly planes in the United States of America and today he flies for one of the largest commercial airlines in America.

He is still a medical doctor, like me, but he was not *persuaded* about staying in that course for the rest of his life. He enjoys flying, and today he is a light to his world by taking people to and fro their destinations safely. He was persuaded about his dream of becoming a pilot, and was willing to take an unfamiliar detour to accomplish it. It (the desire to fly) ate him up until he could resist it no longer. The light that lightens your world is the persuaded light, and it is resolute, focused, and committed to fulfilling her call no matter what the cost may be.

Prayer: Father, birth in me an assertive and persuaded spirit, O God, in Jesus name!

The Light available to you
determines the speed of your journey!

- TOBE MOMAH M.D.

CHAPTER SEVENTEEN

PURE LIGHT

*"Blessed are the **pure** in heart: for they shall see God"*
(Matthew 5:8)

The first thing the devil does when you face a crisis is to stop your illumination. He knows there is no limit to those who are illuminated, and that purity gives one clear directions. He, therefore, seeks to impugn your purity. This is the same age-old strategy he employed against Israel when Balaam looked for a reason to curse them for King Balak.

Israel were the centerpiece of God's artistry, and Balaam, in Numbers 24:5-9, described them by saying *"how goodly are thy tents, O Jacob, and thy tabernacles, O Israel! As the valleys are they spread forth, as gardens by the river's side, as the trees of lign aloes which the Lord hath planted, and as cedar trees beside the waters....His king shall be higher than Agag, and his kingdom shall be exalted* (for)...*God brought him forth out of Egypt* (and)...*he hath as it were the strength of an unicorn: he shall eat up the nations his enemies, and shall break their bones, and pierce them through with his arrows. He couched, he lay down as a lion, and as a great lion...."*

In Numbers 23:21-23, Balaam further eulogized Israel. He said, God *"...hath not beheld iniquity in Jacob, neither hath he seen perverseness in Israel: the Lord his God is with him, and the shout of a* king is among them. *God brought them out of Egypt; he hath as it were the strength of an unicorn. Surely there is no enchantment against Jacob, neither is there any divination against Israel: according to this time it shall be said of Jacob and of Israel,* **What hath God wrought!**"

Unfortunately, by Numbers 25, Israel had been infiltrated by Moabitish women and a plague had broken out among them. It says, "*Israel abode in Shittim, and the people began to commit whoredom with the daughters of Moab. And they called the people unto the sacrifices of their gods: and the people did eat, and bowed down to their gods. And Israel joined himself unto Baalpeor: and the anger of the Lord* was *kindled against Israel*" (Numbers 25:1-3). That once sprawling expanse of vegetative glory and majestic strength became a plague infested cesspool of loose women and wayward leaders who needed to be slaughtered for the plague to be stayed (Numbers 25:4-9).

Purity will give you direction in your darkest days. No matter how dark your world might be, if your heart is pure before God, He will give you direction that will get you out of the darkness. The Bible says, "*there hath no temptation taken you but such as is common to man: but God is faithful, who will not suffer you to be tempted above that ye are able; but will with the temptation also make* **a way to escape***, that ye may be able to bear it*" (1 Cor 10:13).

THE RIDICULE OF REUBEN

The reason why an individual becomes double minded is because they live in sin. In James 4:8, Elder James warned the Church to "*draw nigh to God, and he will draw nigh to you. Cleanse your hands, ye sinners; and purify your hearts, ye double minded.*"

Double mindedness is not docility, or indecisiveness, but a sin that plugs up vision. After Reuben defiled his father's bed (Genesis 35:22), he ended up on the throes of death. He was cursed in Genesis 49:3-4 by Jacob who said "*Reuben, thou art my firstborn, my might, and the beginning of my strength, the excellency of dignity, and the excellency of power: Unstable as water, thou shalt not excel; because thou wentest up to thy father's bed; then defiledst thou it: he went up to my couch.*"

Eventually Moses had to pray in Deuteronomy 33:6 that *"Reuben live, and not die; and let not his men be few."* This man, who was reserved the blessings of the firstborn, died in ignominy. He left the tribe of Reuben depleted, and devoid of power and at the lowest ebb of its attainment among all Israel.

Even though he was the first born, and the exclusive custodian of double his father's strength, anointing and power (according to Deuteronomy 21:17), he died powerless and purposeless because he had failed in his responsibility as Jacob's firstborn to preserve and protect his father's bed from defilement.

Reuben went from first to last because he was unstable. A moment of pleasure cost him a lifetime of triumph, and his indecision the prize of the firstborn. In 1 Chronicles 5:1, the Bible says Reuben *"…was the firstborn but forasmuch as he defiled his father's bed his birthright was given unto the sons of Joseph"*. The birthright is beneficial but only if *buts* in your life are removed.

PURITY – THE PATHWAY TO SHINING

There are too many believers who stumble in the noonday from lack of purity. These one are described in Isaiah 59:9-12; it says *"… we wait for light, but behold obscurity; for brightness, but we walk in darkness. We grope for the wall like the blind, and we grope as if we had no eyes: we stumble at noon day as in the night; we are in desolate places as dead men. We roar all like bears, and mourn sore like doves: we look for judgment, but there is none; for salvation, but it is far off from us. For our transgressions are multiplied before thee, and our sins testify against us: for our transgressions are with us; and as for our iniquities, we know them;"*

Those who hold onto the past, let go of their future. According to Psalm 97:11 *"**light** is sown for the **righteous**, and gladness for the upright in heart."* Could it be that the light that is supposed to be shone by the Church has been dimmed by sin? Has sin plugged the shine of the Church and made our light less bright, so that the world is making a mockery of the gospel because of the Church?

This is contrary to the gospel which proclaims that "...*the path of the just is as the shining light, that shineth more and more unto the perfect day* (but) *the way of the wicked is as darkness...*" (Proverbs 4:18-19). **The pre requisite for the brightness of God is holiness.** No matter how dark one's circumstances are, holiness births prayer that culminates in favor which is enshrined in brightness.

In Job 11:15-17, Zophar told Job, "*if iniquity be in thine hand, put it far away, and let not wickedness dwell in thy tabernacles. For then shalt thou **lift up thy face without spot**; yea, **thou shalt be stedfast**, and shalt not fear: Because thou shalt forget thy misery, and remember it as waters that pass away: And thine age shall be clearer than the noonday: thou shalt **shine** forth, thou shalt be as the morning.*"

Brightness is the consummation of the Christian walk, and makes one the cynosure of all eyes. Holiness takes an individual from a face to face relationship with God, to one that is full of faith (or steadfast). Thereafter, they graduate to realms of favor, where the individual is as bright as the noonday sun and shines forth to his or her environment!

In Matthew 5:8, Jesus said "*blessed are the pure in heart: for they shall see God.*" If you see God, your direction is clear. When there is a lack of clarity, it may be because of a lack of purity. That is why, in Psalm 37:5-6, the Psalmist adjures believers to "*commit thy way unto the Lord; trust also in him; and he shall bring it to pass. And he shall **bring forth thy righteousness as the light**, and thy judgment as the noonday.*"

THE ECONET EXPERIMENT!

Strive Masiyiwa and his parents were run out of Zimbabwe – then named Rhodesia – by the Apartheid regime of Ian Smith in the 1970's. He went to high school in Scotland, and attended the University of Wales for a degree in Telecommunication Engineering. He returned to Zimbabwe in 1987, after apartheid ended, and with the nationalization of its public companies started working for the official Zimbabwe telecommunications company.

He got born again in the late 1980's, and began attending a Bible-believing Church in Harare, Zimbabwe where the the pastor believed in replicating himself amongst his youth. He organized seminars, and trained them in financial stewardship and entrepreneurship and kingdom of God investments. Today, those young men are leaders of society in Zimbabwe with three of them owning a private bank, and Strive (the fourth) owning a telecom conglomerate.

It started in 1995 when Strive received a vision to start the first Global Systems for Mobile (GSM) in Zimbabwe. He had successfully run a construction company for five years, and saw a niche in the telecom industry that he could take advantage of. He offered to go into a joint venture with the government of Zimbabwe, but the government flatly rejected his offer and told him it was illegal to set up a private telecommunications company in Zimbabwe.

For the next five years, he took the government of Zimbabwe to court and after a protracted court battle that involved a change in Supreme Court Judges, and a judgment delivered on Sunday to avert another change in Judges, Strive got the first private telecom license in Zimbabwe and launched ECONET Africa in Zimbabwe. He subsequently opened ECONET offices in Nigeria, Botswana, South Africa, Fiji, New Zealand, Canada, Papau New Guinea, and Lesetho and todays sits atop a business that is worth more than one billion dollars. He has developed a cell phone company that uses phones to transfer money, and he tells the story of how he had to refuse overtures to bribe government officials in Nigeria to start the company.

He kept to the Bible teachings he had been taught, and refused to compromise. He said, *I would rather lose knowing God was with me than winning and knowing God is not with me.* In 2006, he was run out of his investment in Nigeria, and for ten years entered a legal battle with the ECONET Nigeria board. At the end, he won the largest arbitration ever awarded to a company in Africa.

He attributes his success to a vision he had from a prayer partner years ago, and the constant inspiration he gets from the Word of God. He has had to live outside his home country for the past twenty years because of local political turmoil, but was recently listed in his adopted country of Great Britain as the first black billionaire in the United Kingdom.

Prayer: Make me a light to my generation, in Jesus name!

There can be no Sun for status quo believers!

\- Tobe Momah M.D.

CHAPTER EIGHTEEN

PURPOSEFUL LIGHT

*"The light of the body is the eye: therefore when thine eye is single, thy whole body also is full of light; but when thine eye is evil, thy body also is full of darkness. Take heed therefore that the light which is in thee be not darkness. If thy whole body therefore be **full of light**, having no part dark, the whole shall be **full of light**, as when the bright **shining** of a candle doth give thee **light**"* (Luke 11:34-36).

The light that lightens is the purposeful light. If you want the light that causes your journey through life to be light, you cannot have a purposeless life. **You cannot have a life that is without direction, if you want to shine!** To be purposeful is to have or show determination or resolve, with a definite aim and a strong desire to achieve it.

In Luke 12:35-36, Jesus said *"let your loins be girded about, and your lights burning; And ye yourselves like unto men that wait for their lord, when he will return from the wedding; that when he cometh and knocketh, they may open unto him immediately."* The loins of an individual means their understanding, and if an individual can find understanding for why he or she is here on earth their light will burn bright!

Jesus is coming back soon, and it is essential the Church are found where they are assigned by Him. If they are found in the wrong place, doing the wrong thing, they are not going to get the prize or the reward. He (Jesus) said, in Luke 12:37, "*blessed are those servants, whom the lord when he cometh shall find watching: verily I say unto you, that he shall gird himself, and make them to sit down to meat, and will come forth and serve them.*"

In 1 John 3:8, the Bible says "*...for this purpose the Son of God was manifested, that he might destroy the works of the devil.*" Jesus was always on purpose, and that is why his light shone so much the devil could not comprehend it (John 1:5). He lived His life on assignment, not assumptions. He refused to follow the crowd, who wanted to make him king (John 2:23-25), but instead died a shameful death on the cross to redeem humanity because He knew what He was here for (John 18:37).

The secret to a successful ministry is purpose. People whose light shines brighter may initially look like nothing is happening, but the more they pursue God's purpose the brighter their light shines! Jesus elaborated on this, in Luke 11:34-35, and said, "*the light of the body is the eye: therefore when thine eye is single, thy whole body also is full of light; but when thine eye is evil, thy body also is full of darkness. Take heed therefore that the light which is in thee be not darkness.*"

Your lack of purpose may be why your light is not dispelling the darkness. If you want to display the light that dispels darkness, maybe you need to get a single eye. The word *single* in the Greek is the word *haplos* and it means without a secret agenda, or an over complicated or easily distracted life. It means not to be divided in your focus, and keep your focus on the audience of one – the Lord God Almighty. If your eye is not single, however, you dim your light and are instead full of darkness (Luke 12:34).

PAUL'S ASSERTIVENESS VERSUS PETER'S ASSUMPTION (I)

When God called Paul, in Acts 9:15, He told him "*...he is a chosen vessel unto me, to bear my name before the Gentiles, and kings, and the children of Israel for I will shew him how great things he must suffer for my name's sake.*" God gave him clear instructions, with the emphasis of ministry to the gentiles.

After he received his sight, God made Paul's purpose clearer to him. In Galatians 1:15-17, he said "...*when it pleased God, who separated me from my mother's womb, and called me by his grace, to reveal his Son in me, that I might preach him among the heathen; immediately I conferred not with flesh and blood: Neither went I up to Jerusalem to them which were apostles before me; but I went into Arabia, and returned again unto Damascus.*"

That means Paul was a chosen vessel to bear God's name before the Gentiles, kings and the children of Israel, in that order. God emphasized this on the day he got saved, and in Galatians 2:7, he wrote "...*the gospel of the uncircumcision was committed unto me as the gospel of circumcision was onto Peter.*" It was no coincidence, therefore, that every time Paul landed in Jerusalem, they wanted to kill him but when he got to Asia ministry exploded so that in two years, Paul was able to reach the whole of Asia (Acts 19:10).

The lesson learnt here is that if anyone stays in their position of purpose, the light that dispels darkness shines. To the contrary, when you are off purpose you die prematurely with no light for your coming generations. In 1 Corinthians 9:25-27, Paul explained his vision for ministry. He said, "...*every man that striveth for the mastery is temperate in all things. Now they do it to obtain a corruptible crown; but we an incorruptible. I therefore so run, not as uncertainly; so fight I, not as one that beateth the air: But I keep under my body, and bring it into subjection: lest that by any means, when I have preached to others, I myself should be a castaway.*"

PAUL'S ASSERTIVENESS VERSUS PETER'S ASSUMPTION (II)

Paul said, in 1 Corinthians 9:25-27, that he lived life on purpose and refused to be distracted. One of the key reasons many fail is because they are easily distracted. If the enemy cannot get you off God's best, he will try to give you second best as a distraction. That is why Apostle Paul said, "*I press toward the mark for the prize of the high calling of God in Christ Jesus*" (Phil 3:14).

Peter, on the other hand, had a global ministry that he shuttered due to ill-conceived innuendos. God had told him, "...*rise, Peter; kill, and eat. But Peter said, Not so, Lord; for I have never eaten any thing that is common or unclean. And the voice spake unto him again the second time, What God hath cleansed, that call not thou common. This was done thrice: and the vessel was received up again into heaven"* (Acts 10:13-16).

Peter was the one with the mandate to build His church (Matthew 16:18), and the gates of hell not prevail against them. He was the leader of the early church, and the one God showed the revelation in Acts chapter 10 of a blanket opening from heaven and inviting the gentiles to the harvest. His Jewish old testament roots, however, made him reluctant and *"...while Peter doubted in himself what this vision which he had seen should mean..."* (Acts 10:17), he went to the house of Cornelius and as he was speaking, the Holy Spirit was poured out.

Peter was called to take the gospel to all the people, and not just the Jews. He narrowed himself down and became a leader of just the Jewish church which was contrary to God's commission to him in Acts 10:42-43 which says, God *"...commanded us to preach unto the people, and to testify that it is he which was ordained of God to be the Judge of quick and dead* (and) *to him give all the prophets witness, that through his name **whosoever** believeth in him shall receive remission of sins."*

You cannot live in propose less ness and expect lighted ness! If you want to see the light of God's word, you have to live on purpose. Simon Peter could have influenced a larger sphere of society if he was more assertive and less assumptive. He was rebuked by Paul, when the Presbytery visited from Jerusalem, because *"...when they were come, he* (Peter) *withdrew and separated himself, fearing them which were of the circumcision. And the other Jews dissembled likewise with him; insomuch that Barnabas also was carried away with their dissimulation"* (Gal 2:12-13).

ELVIS, WHITNEY, AND OTHERS...

Elvis Presley, as a teenager, learned to play the guitar in the East Tupelo Assembly of God church in Tupelo, Mississippi. On one occasion, he was reported to have gone to his choir master and music teacher at the local Assembly of God he attended to suggest a different tone and more African American rhythm to playing the guitar.

The Choir leader's response was no, and he reportedly said *we don't play it like that in the Assemblies of God church*. He soon relocated at 13 years of age to Memphis, Tennessee from where he went on to become a global icon with hundreds of millions of records sold and with an international following. Unfortunately, Elvis died suddenly in 1977, at 42 years of age, and never publicly returned to the Church.

Whitney Houston grew up in Newark, New Jersey, and was a member of New Hope Missionary Baptist Church choir alongside her mother who was the choir director. She rendered several solos, and was known for singing several awesome songs while in the Choir. When her mother allegedly had an affair with the pastor, however, Whitney shut out the Church, Choir and at Eighteen years of age moved out of the home she had been raised in.

She moved to Atlanta, and after her marriage to Bobby Brown, to California and starred in several movies and waxed some of the highest selling albums in history. Unfortunately she died in 2012, at the age of 48, and never returned publicly to the Church before her death. Both her and Elvis died prematurely, with their lights caught short in the early stages of their lives.

These two mega-stars were generational lights who were plagued down by a lack of purpose. They became Pop idols, instead of praise Instruments, and had they used their gifting for the purpose God had intended it their end may have been different. When the use of a thing is not known, abuse is inevitable. Elvis Presley was anointed to bring people to the knowledge of Jesus through his music, and so was Whitney Houston, but when they missed their purpose their gift became a gift for the secular entertainment industry.

Prayer: O God, show me my purpose on the earth in Jesus name!

Those who stay prophet less
remain profit less in life!

- Tobe Momah M.D.

CHAPTER NINETEEN

PROPHETIC LIGHT

*"We have also a more sure word of **prophecy**; whereunto ye do well that ye take heed, as unto **a light that shineth** in a dark place, until the day dawn, and the day star arise in your hearts"* (2 Peter 1:19).

Many believers are carrying a burden because they are not walking with the light that lightens. I believe life doesn't have to be as heavy a struggle if you apply the light that lightens. There is a light that when you capture it, your journey is smoother. For example, if you get in front of an 18 wheel truck that has maximum lights beaming your speed increases because that 18 wheel truck's lights gives you extra light. It helps you see further, and as a result you can avoid the road bumps, gallops and potholes on the way.

In Isaiah 9:8, the Bible says the *"Lord sent a word into Jacob and it had lighted upon Israel."* Jacob was the grandson of Abraham, and his father was Isaac. He became the founder of the nation of Israel and gave birth to twelve sons who today constitute the twelve tribes of Israel. God wanted to get a message to the whole of Israel, but chose to go through a man called Jacob. Without Jacob, they (Israel) would have remained in perpetual darkness, but thankfully a word came to Jacob that caused light to blossom across Israel. Atimes, the reason for darkness could be due to the absence of a man or woman who communicates prophetic truth to one's life.

This prophet may be imperfect, like Jacob was, but he or she is still a light source. Though a *slick-willy*, slanderer and a supplanter, God still chose to use Jacob to bring light to the people of Israel. Many don't have a prophetic light source, and yet expect their journey through life to be swift and smooth. That is impossible. The lack of a prophet over one's life relegates such a one to the backwaters of oblivion and ignominy. If Israel had ignored the word that came from God through Jacob, they would never have received light.

The Power of Prophetic Light!

Until there is a prophet, there will be a lack of profit! It takes the prophetic light to garner the profits of life. When Moses came on the scene in Egypt, Israel had been in bondage under Egyptian servitude for 430 years (Exodus 12:40). They had spent an extra 30 years (see Genesis 15:13) because they had no prophetic light. They were, as described in Deuteronomy 4:20, 1 Kings 8:51 and Jeremiah 11:4, living in an iron furnace and it was therefore no surprise they were enveloped in darkness.

The moment Moses showed up, however, Israel was released by an executive fiat from Pharaoh's iron grip. The reason was simply because light had come. In Hosea 12:13, the Bible says, "*by a prophet the Lord* brought Israel out of Egypt, and by a prophet was he preserved." **Your value multiplies when you are under the handling of a prophet**. You are no more wasted but wise; you are not pillaged but prosperous and instead of little, you become large!

There is power in a prophetic covering, and Apostle Paul acknowledged this in 1 Corinthians 14:1, where he said "*follow after charity, and desire spiritual gifts, but rather that ye may prophesy*." He emphasizes it further in 1 Corinthians 14:39, where he urges the Church in Corinth, to "...*covet to prophesy,....*"

In Psalm 74:9, a cry went out from the Psalmist saying "*we see not our signs: there is no more any prophet: neither is there among us any that knoweth how long.*" He lamented the demise of the nation, as a result, and cited Psalm 79:18,20 as evidence. He said, "*remember this, that the enemy hath reproached, O Lord, and that the foolish people have blasphemed thy name…Have respect unto the covenant: for **the dark places of the earth** are full of the habitations of cruelty.*"

When there is a dearth of the prophetic, darkness pervades the land! In 1 Samuel 3:1-3, the Bible says "*…the word of the Lord* was precious in those days (and) *there was no open vision and it came to pass at that time, when Eli was laid down in his place,* (that) *his eyes began to wax dim, that he could not see; and ere the lamp of God went out in the temple of the Lord, where the ark of God was,….*"

When the prophetic was absent in the temple, darkness became prevalent! In Jeremiah 23:11-12, a similar scenario played out because there were no true prophets' in the land. It says, "*…both prophet and priest are profane; yea, in my house have I found their wickedness, saith the Lord. Wherefore their way shall be unto them as slippery ways in the darkness: they shall be driven on, and fall therein: for I will bring evil upon them, even the year of their visitation, saith the Lord.*" The slippery road of darkness follows the prophet less, and they will fall on it.

The reason why the dark places of the earth are full of the habitations of cruelty is because there are no prophetic signage's available to this generation. Could you be the prophet in your house, Church or office? Could it be that the reason why darkness persists in your environment is because your light as the prophet has been dimmed? Instead, of speaking curses and confusion, speak the prophetic words of encouragement, edification, and comfort (1 Corinthians 14:3) from God's word into the atmosphere and that prophetic word will cause light to burst forth.

BRIGHT ARROWS

In John 5:33-35, Jesus spoke about John the Baptist saying, "*Ye sent unto John, and he bare witness unto the truth. But I receive not testimony from man: but these things I say, that ye might be saved. He was a burning and a **shining light**: and ye were willing for a season to rejoice* *in his light."* He stated that the reason John the Baptist was a burning and shining light was because He (Jesus) received the testimony about John from heaven, and not from the earth!

In Jeremiah 51:10-11, Jeremiah declared that arrows are a prophetic symbol, and a bright arrow indicates a light bearing arrow! He told the children of Israel to bring *"...forth* (their) *righteousness..., and...declare in Zion the work of the Lord* our God (and) *make **bright the**(**ir**) **arrows** gather the shields: the Lord* hath raised up the spirit of the kings of the Medes: for his device is against Babylon, to destroy it; because it is the vengeance of the *Lord, the vengeance of his temple."*

Your ability to win in life is determined by the brightness of your arrows. If you have bright arrows, you don't have to fight your battles by the strength of man because the prophetic will do it for you. In Psalm 127:4-5, God says that *"as arrows are in the hand of a mighty man; so are children of the youth. Happy is the man that hath his quiver full of them: they shall not be ashamed, but they shall speak with the enemies in the gate."*

The prophetic shines illumination where there was desolation and births manifestation. Paul talking to Timothy, his protégé, said *"neglect not the gift that is in thee, which was given thee by prophecy, with the laying on of the hands of the presbytery. Meditate upon these things; give thyself wholly to them; that thy profiting may appear to all."* (1 Timothy 4:14-15). **The level of profiting in one's life depends on how much of the cutting edge of prophecy one relies on or stirs up.**

The reason John was a burning and a shining light was because he (John) received instruction from Jesus, even though to the outside world Jesus was just his younger cousin. Familiarity can breed contempt, and if John had despised his young cousin's gifting, the world would never have heard John's voice. It was Jesus's prophetic utterance that made John the Baptist radiate and attract thousands to the wilderness. Without Jesus, he would have been like a reed in the wilderness with no results following (John 15:5).

In Acts 13:2, the prophetic word came forth saying *"...separate me Barnabas and Saul for the work whereunto I have called them"* and from that day the world heard Paul and Barnabas's voice. The reason why they did everything they did was because of the prophetic. If Barnabas and Paul had just seen the vision, and heard the prophetic word, but never received it they may never have fulfilled their destiny. There is a certain grace from the prophetic that causes the light to shine upon an individual.

Prophecy is called the "...*testimony of Jesus...*"(Revelation 19:10), and Jesus is called the Word of God (John 1:1). It is the preaching of the Word of God that gives the light that shows you the next step to take. Many of us are walking in circles because we lack that prophetic light. It takes the "...*voice which came from heaven...*(to give us a) *more sure word of prophecy; whereunto ye do well that ye take heed, as unto a light that shineth in a dark place, until the day dawn, and the day star arise in your hearts...*"(2 Peter 1:18-19).

A PROPHET IN THE HOUSE

Jesse Duplantis shares the story of how he was a dysfunctional youth. He never liked to do anything they told him to do, but razed cats, sold his brother's clothes, and drank alcohol liberally. Today he's preaching the gospel all around the world. He had a mother with a prophetic gift, and on one occasion while partying with his friends at the Mexican border his mother called the strip club, and told him God had shown her where they were and he better return home before she comes down there. He quickly returned to Louisiana, but that birthed his inquisition about the prophetic.

A few years later, his mother told the family she had to leave home at about 11 pm on a week night to go to the bridge connecting both sides of New Orleans. The family tried to discourage her but she insisted. To their amazement, she reported meeting a newly pregnant young girl on the side of the bridge who was about to jump thousands of feet to her death by suicide. After talking to her, and encouraging her, Jesse Duplantis's mother got her to go home and thus saved her life and that of her yet unborn baby. Jesse was awed by his Mother's prophetic gift, and years later when he met that lady (and her daughter) he called to remembrance the gift of his mother.

- 134 -

Some of the greatest prophets in an individual's life are those from his or her own home. It took one word from Jack Hayford, and Enoch Adeboye's mother's to change the direction of their lives. A parent is like a bow, and his or her children their arrows (according to Psalm 127:4-5), and how far they fly is dependent on the strength of their bow. If the arrows don't shoot far and wide, and if those arrows don't shoot high, it's not the fault of the arrow but the fault of the person who has the bow. They have, unwittingly, refused to let them fly.

In the case of Jack Hayford, his mother told him while he was running from the Lord that he would be a great preacher no matter how many years he tried to run away from it. Evenetally, Jack Hayford got saved, started King's University, became international president of Four Square Churches worldwide, and composed congregational favorites such as *Majesty*.

Ernest Adeboye, on the other hand, was the youngest son of his mother and she single handedly trained him from her trading proceeds. She was one of the wives in a polygamous setting, and after years of struggling to pay her son's school fees, he returned to the village to celebrate her. He was then a lecturer at the University of Lagos, and had come home with a car which astounded the community. He came with a gift to give the mother, and she declared prophetically that *when he calls one, ten will answer*. Today, as the convener of the world's largest religious gathering (the Holy Ghost Congress), her words have come true!

Prayer: Stir up my prophetic gift, O Lord, in Jesus name!

To be a Christian does not mean
to be religious in a particular way,
but to be the man Jesus creates us to be.
It is not the religious act that makes
the Christian, but participation in the
sufferings of God in the secular life

– BONHOEFFER, DIETRICH (1906 - 45)

CHAPTER TWENTY

PASSIONATE LIGHT

*"He was a **burning** and a **shining light:** and ye were willing for a season to rejoice in his **light**"* (John 5:35)

In Deuteronomy 28:47-48, God reprimanded the Israelites for depressed and dour dealings with Him. He said, *"because thou servedst not the Lord thy God with joyfulness, and with gladness of heart, for the abundance of all things; Therefore shalt thou serve thine enemies which the Lord shall send against thee, in hunger, and in thirst, and in nakedness, and in want of all things: and he shall put a yoke of iron upon thy neck, until he have destroyed thee."*

Rejoicing affects all things and so does revolting, albeit in a negative manner. When Paul was departing from the Thessalonian Church, he asked them to *"rejoice evermore, Pray without ceasing* (and) *in every thing give thanks* (so God can)*...sanctify them wholly and... their whole spirit and soul and body be preserved blameless unto the coming of the Lord Jesus Christ"* (1 Thessalonians 5:16-18,23).

A colorless life starts with a clouded mind, and in Proverbs 17:22 the wise man said *"a merry heart doeth good like a medicine: but a broken spirit drieth the bones."* The light that changes his or her environs must be passionate, not dour or dull. In Malachi 4:2-3, God says *"...unto you that fear my name shall the Sun of righteousness arise with healing in his wings; and ye **shall go forth**, and **grow up as calves** of the stall. And ye* *shall tread down the wicked; for they shall be ashes under the soles of your feet in the day that I shall do this, saith the Lord of hosts."*

No Changes!

One of the greatest causes of lack of light is a lack of desire for change. It is the intensity of your hunger that determines the gravity of your encounter with God and His word. In Matthew 5:6, Jesus said *"blessed are they which do hunger and thirst after righteousness: for they shall be filled."* There has been a dearth of light in the Church because of a lack of passion for God but it stems from a *no-change* life philosophy.

In Psalm 55:19, the Psalmist says "...*because they have **no changes**, therefore they fear not God.*" Just like the great telephone companies of yesteryears, including Nokia, Motorola, and Blackberry failure to make changes by adapting to technology (such as touch sensitive screen) led to their capitulation in the 1990's.

The same thing happened in the photo industry, where Kodak had long dominated with printed photos, unaware that phones with sharp photo pixels were the next great thing.

The **static Church is a stagnant Church**. A wise man once said that *if you fish out of a bath tub every week, you will only catch the same fish.* The only way to change the static is to spread your wings and fly on the everlasting arms of the Father. It is time to get off our lees, according to prophet Jeremiah, who challenged the Moabites to stop "...*being at ease from youth and* (do not) *settle on their lees* (lest)...*He* (God) *send unto him* (Moab) *wanderers that shall cause him to wander and empty his vessels"* (Jeremiah 48:11).

The worst wanderers and the emptiest entertainers are those who refuse to adapt to change. Getting off the lees means to shake off dregs that have settled in, and instead keep moving by the power of the Holy Spirit. Those who walk in bondage to fear have not allowed the dynamism of the Holy Spirit in their lives but have continued in business as usual. Routine is not righteousness and habit is not holiness. It is not right because you have always done it that way but because God says so.

DAYSPRING DYNAMO!

The Dayspring is the rising of sunlight, and represents the dawning of a new day. Its brightness is hinged on its daily breakthroughs, as it runs from east to west. The sun does not base its brightness on what clouds constitute a nuisance to its shining that day, but shines nonetheless. It follows its circuit, irrespective of the positioning of the clouds, because it **follows passion not positioning.**

In Psalm 19:4-6, the Psalmist describes "*their line* (as) *gone out through all the earth, and their words to the end of the world* (for) *in them hath he set a tabernacle for the sun, which is as a bridegroom coming out of his chamber, and rejoiceth as a strong man to run a race. His going forth is from the end of the heaven, and his circuit unto the ends of it: and there is nothing hid from the heat thereof.*"

Inertia causes implosion, but spontaneity births sweetness! In Proverbs 15:30, Solomon says "***the light of the eyes rejoiceth the heart:*** *and a good report makes the bones fat.*" When there is passion for God, light is released, and "*blessed is the people that know the joyful sound: they shall walk, O Lord, in* **the light of thy countenance**. *In thy name shall they rejoice all the day: and in thy righteousness shall they be exalted. For thou art the glory of their strength: and in thy favor our horn shall be exalted*" *(*Psalm 89:15-17).

The Psalmist prayed to the Lord, in Psalm 74:20-22, to "*have respect unto the covenant: for the dark places of the earth are full of the habitations of cruelty...Let not the oppressed return ashamed: let the poor and needy praise thy name. Arise, O God, plead thine own cause....*" Wherever there is darkness, there is cruelty but where light abounds, passion and praise are evident.

RADIO IN ABA

Rita Momah, my wife to be, was a second year medical student at the same University I attended (as a third year medical student) and was about to celebrate her birthday with a bang. It was going to be lavish, by University of Nigeria Enugu Campus (UNEC) standards, and I wanted to make a splash at the ceremony to affirm my (yet unmentioned) affection for her.

I, therefore, sought out a brand new stereo set to give her as a birthday gift. Having explored my local terrain of Enugu, and finding nothing worthy of her, I set out for Aba in nearby Abia State the morning of her birthday. The plan was to return the same day, and place the gift in her hands as a tribute to her birthday celebration and as proof of my love for her.

The three hour journey was uneventful to Aba. The purchase was quickly made, and I returned back with the late afternoon bus with the hopes and intentions of getting to Enugu before evening. I was supposed to attend some lectures the next morning, and attend the Birthday celebrations of Rita Momah that evening, but midway through the journey, and just as dusk was about to set, a bus in front of our mini-bus began to reverse hysterically with the conductor shouting *thieves, thieves, thieves!*

Our bus driver quickly took the cue and reversed sharply. There was obviously an ongoing robbery operation, and for the rest of that night no other vehicle went past that robbery point. Neither did the police show up!

As a result of this vehicular imposition, I slept in that mini-bus till 5am the next day alongside the other passengers. At the rising of the Sun, traffic restarted and on passing the site of the burglary that morning we saw bodies of dead human beings and clothes and utensils scattered on the ground. It was about 10am when I got into UNEC, and I headed - in my smug countenance and composure - straight to Rita Momah's accommodation (at Lady Ibiam hostel).

I handed over the gift to her, and she expressed her gratitude and opined that since she loved to listen to music it would aid her progress in the Music ministry greatly. What she did not realize, however, was that this was not any ordinary gift. It was a gift preceded by a life and death journey, and had been gravely dangerous to procure. This is why Jesus said *"greater love hath no man than this, that a man lay down his life for his friend"* (John 15:13).

Prayer: Thou Father of lights, shine upon my life, in Jesus name!

Never give in, and in nothing great or small, large or petty, never give in except to convictions of honor and God sense. Never yield to force; never yield to the apparently overwhelming might of the enemy

– Winston Churchill (1874-1965)

CHAPTER TWENTY-ONE

PERSISTENT LIGHT

"They know not, neither will they understand; they walk on in darkness (for) *all the foundations of the earth are out of course"* (Psalm 82:5).

Too many quit too early in their bid to birth light. They start with lights blazing, but after darkness resists and curtails their entry they fold up, turn back and quit rather than persist. **The only light that shines is the light that persists to the end.** It is the light that refuses to stop shining, no matter the odds against it, that shines for eternity!

In Job 28:3, the Bible says *"he setteth an end to darkness, and searcheth out all perfection:...."* The problem of darkness is not dependent on God, but on man's willingness to be a channel for God to shine through. God has given you and I the responsibility to be "... *the light of the world* (as) *a city that is set on a hill* (that) *cannot be hid,"* (Matthew 5:14). **Until the Church starts shining, the darkness in the world persists.**

In Matthew 5:16, Jesus said, *"let your light so shine before men, that they may see your good works, and glorify your Father which is in heaven."* **It is our persistently shining light that causes darkness to flee.** The words of our mouth and the life we live are shining lights to the world (Psalms 119:105 and Philippians 2:15). Through them, we can be heaven's tools to abrogate darkness if we stay the course.

In Isaiah 9:8, the Bible says *"...the Lord sent a word into Jacob, and it hath lighted upon Israel."* The worlds, and nay the church, are waiting for our light to obey the ordinances and precepts of the word of God. It is our responsibility not to hide that light but shine it bright. In Matthew 5:15, Jesus said, *"neither do men light a candle, and put it under a bushel, but on a candlestick; and it giveth light unto all that are in the house."* You are the answer to the darkness around the world today. Get up and shine!

LIGHT OF LIFE, OR CASTING SHADOWS?

God is persistent. He does not waver in His shine, and that persistency is what the Church must reflect. In James 1:17-18, Apostle James says *"every good gift and every perfect gift is from above, and cometh down from the **Father of lights**, with whom is **no variableness, neither shadow of turning**. Of his own will begat he us with the word of truth, that we should be a kind of first fruits of his creatures"* (James 1:17-18).

The Church must jettison the epileptic and erratic shining of light, and embrace the enduring light that never flickers or fades. This kind of light is the light God has called the Church to. For example, when He called Paul He told him *"I have set thee to be a **light** of the Gentiles, that thou shouldest be for **salvation unto the ends of the earth**"* (Acts 13:47). The light Paul carried was not to be intense in some parts of the earth only, but a light birthing salvation for the ends of the earth.

In the case of Jesus, He died so *"...He should be the first that should rise from the dead, and... shew light unto the people, and to the Gentiles"* (Acts 26:23). His light persisted to the Gentiles, and today the ends of the earth are lighted by that persistent light. The **light that disperses darkness is shone by those with persistence, not those who worship God on a weekly basis.** If the devil can stop light persistently shining in your life, he will consume your territory with darkness.

In James 4:7, God says *"submit yourselves therefore to God. Resist the devil, and he will flee."* The word *resist* means to strongly resist an opponent. **If there is no resistance, there is no fleeing of darkness,** and if there is no persistence, resistance is moribund. That is why God does not cast shadows, but rather shines light without equivocation. As the father of lights, He gives that same unwavering and persistent light to his children who are partakers of His divine nature (2 Peter 1:4) – and that includes you!

PERSISTENCE IN PRAYER

The prayer of the persistent will birth bright lights and breakthrough lifting. In Psalm 34:4-6, the Psalmist prayed saying *"I sought the Lord, and he heard me, and delivered me from all my fears. They looked unto him, and were **lightened**: and their faces were not ashamed. This poor man cried, and the Lord heard him, and saved him out of all his troubles."*

The rule of kingdom living is it does not take long if believers remain strong! In Ephesians 6:12-13, Apostle Paul said *"…we wrestle not against flesh and blood, but against principalities, against powers, against the rulers of the darkness of this world, against spiritual wickedness in high places, wherefore take unto you the whole **armor** of God that ye may be able to withstand in the evil day, and having done all to stand."*

Part of the armor needed to fight the evil forces of these last days is the armor of light. In Romans 13:11-12, Apostle Paul prays that *"…knowing the time, that now it is high time to awake out of sleep: for now is our salvation nearer than when we believed. The night is far spent, the day is at hand: let us therefore cast off the works of darkness, and let us put on **the armour of light**."*

Without persistent light in your armor, your prayer will be ineffectual. The prophet Elijajh's prayers were only as powerful as his light was persistent. In 1 Kings 18:44, he sent his servant to look to the sea for a sign and it *"…came to pass at the seventh time, that he said, Behold, there ariseth a little cloud out of the sea, like a man's hand. And he* said, *Go up, say unto Ahab, Prepare thy chariot, and get thee down that the rain stop thee not."*

No wonder Apostle James describes that experience, in 1 Kings 18:43-44, as "*...effectual fervent prayer of a righteous man (which) availeth much* (for)... *he prayed* **earnestly** *that it might not rain: and it rained not on the earth by the space of three years and six months. And he prayed again, and the heaven gave rain, and the earth brought forth her fruit*" (James 5:16-18).

This was no ordinary prayer; rather, it was passionate, persistent, and persuaded prayer that brought open heavens after three and a half years of drought. It took Elijah praying seven times, and his servant walking hundreds of miles between the sea shore and Mount Carmen, to see a fist like the size of a man's hand and bring his prophecy to pass (1 Kings 18:32-40). Stay persistent or shame persists!

EKWUEME...

The Igbo name *Ekwueme* means **he says, and he does as he said.** My late Dad used that name to describe me in July 2020, just a few weeks before he died. He and my mother were commending me for fulfilling my promises and being a man of my word. They said I backed up my words with action and as a result, I was an Ekwueme!

With my mother, in the background, he commended me for being committed, and stedfast when I made a promise. He reminisced on how, over the years, he had several people promise him heaven and earth but fail to deliver on their promises. He remembered how, on several occasions, I had rolled out a vision and against the odds went on to fulfill the vision in record time.

He said he was inspired by my persuasiveness, and determination to accomplish what ever I laid my hands to do. He, thereafter, encouraged and blessed me and asked me to continue in my steadfastness. He mentioned one or two challenges that I was facing and said with steadfastness they too would soon be resolved.

He died a few weeks later, but that name *Ekwueme* has never departed from my consciousness. I am more committed than ever before to demonstrate the faithfulness of God's word in deed and truth. As the apostle Paul said *"faithful is he that calleth you, who also will do it"* (1 Thessalonians 5:24).

Prayer: Lord deliver me from the impurity of double-mindedness, in Jesus name!

PART IV

Secrets to Shining

- Life of the Holy Spirit
- Listening
- Labor
- Love
- Looking
- Leadership
- Laughter

*A part-time Christian is
a full-time sinner!*

– Dr. Ferdinand Nweke
(Eternity Ministries, Abuja, Nigeria)

CHAPTER TWENTY-TWO

LIFE OF THE HOLY SPIRIT

"In him was **life***; and the* **life** *was the* **light** *of men. And the light shineth in darkness; and the darkness comprehended it not...And of his fulness have all we received, and* **grace** *for grace. For the law was given by Moses, but grace and truth came by Jesus Christ"* (John 1:4-5, 16-17).

God is the source of the true light that brings shining in life! Jesus said, in John 9:5, that *"as long as I am in the world, I am the light of the world."* He added, in John 12:46, that *"I am come a light into the world, that whosoever believeth on me should not abide in darkness."*

If God is your light, you cannot but shine in life! In Psalm 18:28-29, the Psalmist said God *"...wilt light* (his) *candle* (and) *the Lord my God will enlighten my darkness. For by thee I have run through a troop; and by my God have I leaped over a wall."*

These acts are indispensable and prototypical of life in the Spirit and why apostle Paul called life in the Spirit *"...liv(ing), mov(ing), and hav(ing) our being* (in Him);..." (Acts 17:28).

The five foolish virgins lost their position at the Marriage supper of the lamb because they did not take the oil they needed to light their lamps (see Matthew 25:10-13). They lived holy (typified by their virginity), but failed and were cast out of the marriage supper of the lamb because their lamps went out in darkness!

Without the Holy Spirit, failure is inevitable in these last days. It is those who "...*walk in the Spirit, (that)...shall not fulfil the lust of the flesh*" (Galatians 5:16) and those who implement "...*the law of the Spirit of life in Christ Jesus* (that are) *made...free from the law of sin and death*" (Romans 8:2).

OPTIMIZING THE OIL

The five foolish virgins were fiery saints of God but lacked oil in their lamps and wisdom for their jouney. They loved the Lord, and like the five wise virgins, "...*took their lamps, and went forth to meet the bridegroom*" (Matthew 25:1). But despite their hearts being holy, and having their lamps lighted, they lacked optimization of their oil. As a result they could not shine!

The word *oil* in Matthew 25:1-3 is the Greek word **Elaion,** and it means "*the indwelling (empowering) of the Holy Spirit.*" The word *optimize* means to *make the best or most effective use of something,* and even though the Church has more anointed, and Holy Ghost baptized believers, than ever before the dearth of optimized oil has left the Church dimmed and dysfunctional.

The latter day Church is guaranteed a more glorious destiny than the glory Moses exemplified in Exodus 34:29 when his face shone so much he had to wear a veil to cover his face. **There is an oil that makes the face to shine, and it is the life of the Holy Spirit.** In Psalm 104:15, the Bible says "...*wine that maketh glad the heart of man, and oil to make his face to shine, and bread which strengtheneth man's heart.*"

The shining Church is the glorious Church (Ephesians 5:25)! These ones are "...*able ministers of the new testament; not of the letter, but of the spirit: for the letter killeth, but the spirit giveth life. But if the ministration of death, written and engraven in stones, was glorious, so that the children of Israel could not stedfastly behold the face of Moses for the glory of his countenance; which glory was to be done away: How shall not the ministration of the spirit be rather glorious? For if the ministration*" *of condemnation be glory, much more doth the ministration of righteousness exceed in glory"* (2 Corinthians 3:6-9).

The latter day Church's secret to the exceeding glory is the presence of God within her by the person of the Holy Spirit. God fills believers with the Holy Spirit, according to 1 Cor 3:16, and to maintain the glory He adjures them to beware of the **anointing anathema.** In Songs of Solomon 2:15, the wise man said *"take us the foxes, the little foxes, that spoil the vines: for our vines have tender grapes."*

The word **tender,** as used in S.O.S 2:15, is the Hebrew word *Semadar* and it means to blossom. It takes His blessings to blossom, and partnership with him to walk in divine power.

THE FATHER OF LIGHTS

God is described as the *"…father of lights, with whom is no variableness, neither shadow of turning"* (James 1:11), because He (God) does not cast shadows but always produces shining! The panacea to darkness is always light, and there is no greater source than the father of lights.

In 1 Timothy 6:15-16, God is described as *"…the King of kings, and Lord of lords; Who only hath immortality, dwelling in the light which no man can approach unto; whom no man hath seen, nor can see: to whom be honour and power everlasting."*

It is the father of lights that determines your shining! If you are uninhabited by the God of light, your life will be darkness and void of impact. Who your lord is, will determine what light you shine on the earth. In Isaiah 9:8, the prophet said *"the Lord sent a word into Jacob, and it hath lighted upon Israel."*

A single eye produces a wholesome shining, according to Luke 11:34-36. The question, therefore, is **who are you looking at?** If you are focused on darkness, you can only produce darkness. But if you look on the father of lights, there will be uncontestable and undeniable shining!

Those who are guided by the Father of lights will avoid the repercussions of darkness. In Luke 6:39-40, Jesus spoke a parable asking "...*can the blind lead the blind? shall they not both fall into the ditch? The disciple is not above his master: but every one that is perfect shall be as his master.*"

THE ARMENIA TO AMERICA ABUNDANCE

In 1850, prophecies given by Efim Gerasemovitch Klubniken, an 11-year-old "Boy Prophet," had to do with a coming persecution of that area at the foot of Mount Ararat. The Lord showed him maps and writing of where they were to go and that area turned out to be America, with that prophecy was fulfilled, exactly as he described.

The *boy prophet's* prophecy was, however, not fulfilled until fifty-three years later. From his earliest childhood Efin had shown a gift for prayer, and was frequently going on long fasts, and praying around the clock. On the occasion of this prolonged fast, however, he persisted for seven days and nights, and during this time received a vision.

Though Efin could neither read nor write, he sat in the little stone cottage in Kara Kala, and after he saw before him a vision of charts and a message in a beautiful handwriting he asked for pen and paper and for seven days sitting at the rough plank-table where the family ate, he laboriously copied down the form and shape of letters and diagrams that passed before his eyes.

When he had finished, the manuscript was taken to people in the village who could read. It turned out that this illiterate child had written out in Russian characters a series of instructions and warnings. He stated that at some unspecified time in the future, every Christian in Kara Kala would be in terrible danger.

He foretold a time of unspeakable tragedy for the entire area, when hundreds of thousands of men, women, and children would be brutally murdered. The time would come, he warned, when everyone in the region must flee. They must go to a land across the sea. Although he had never seen a geography book, the Boy Prophet drew a map showing exactly where the fleeing Christians were to go.

To the amazement of the adults, the body of water depicted so accurately in the drawing was not the nearby Black Sea, or the

Caspian Sea, or even the farther-off Mediterranean, but the distant and unimaginable Atlantic Ocean! There was no doubt about it, nor about the identity of the land on the other side: the map plainly indicated the east coast of the United States of America. They were not to settle down there, but to continue traveling until they reached the west coast of the new land. There, the boy wrote, God would bless them and prosper them, and cause their seed to be a blessing to the nations.

In 1901, Efin announced that the time was near for the fulfillment of the words he had written down nearly fifty years before. He told the people of Kara Kala *we must flee to America. All who remain here will perish.* A few Kara Kala Pentecostal families packed up and left the holdings that had been their ancestral possessions, and though jeered by those who remained behind they left.

In 1914 a period of unimaginable horror arrived for Armenia. With remorseless efficiency the Turks killed over a million men, women and children, including every inhabitant of Kara Kala. Another half a million were massacred in their villages, in a pogrom that the world ignored. Meanwhile, the escaped Amrenians moved to Los Angeles – in fulfillment of the prophecy – and prospered.

Today, Armenian Americans are an integral part of the United State of America having become major players in the medical, entertainment, legal, military, and business circles. They are localized mostly in the California area, and have prospered there greatly. Though prophet Efim died in 1915, he saw a part fulfillment of God's prophecy for his people and emblazoned the ideals of a life lived in the fullness of the Spirit.

Prayer: Give me Light from the Father of lights, O God, in Jesus name!

*Where God leads, he supplies
the light to walk the path*

- BISHOP DAVID OYEDEPO
(PRESIDENT, LIVING FAITH
CHURCH WORLDWIDE)

CHAPTER TWENTY-THREE

LISTENING

"The entrance of thy words giveth light; it giveth understanding unto the simple" (Psalm 119:130).

A valuable secret to shining is listening to the word of God. If a person is bereft of an ear that hearkens diligently to the word of God, they will be without the benefit of the light that produces shining. The Word of God is the secret to a shining life and its absence the cause for an abandonment of the glory.

Where light appears, darkness disappears! In John 1:4-5, the Bible says *"in him* (the word of God) *was life; and the life was the **light** of men. And the **light** shineth in darkness; and the darkness comprehended it not."* It is not the false light, however, that promotes shining but the true light.

When a false gospel is preached, or believed, it casts a false shine on the individual. Those who live by the light of God's word, on the other hand, will shine to the ends of the earth. That is why Jesus called you and I, " *...the light of the world* (and) *a city that is set on an hill cannot be hid"* (Matthew 5:14).

It is also why, in Isaiah 60:1-3, the Lord says *"arise, shine; for thy light is come, and the glory of the Lord* is risen upon thee. For, behold, the darkness shall cover the earth, and gross darkness the people: but the *Lord* shall arise upon thee, and his glory shall be seen upon thee.

And the Gentiles shall come to thy light, and kings to the brightness of thy rising."

THE MYSTERY OF JOHN THE BAPTIST

Though John the Baptist did no miracle, as attested by John the beloved in John 10:41, he was acknowledged by Jesus as the one who "*...among them that are born of women, there hath not risen a greater than John the Baptist*" (Matthew 11:11). He attracted more people to the wilderness than any other prophet of his time, and was described by Jesus as a "*...a burning and a shining light: and ye were willing for a season to rejoice in his light*" (John 5:35).

John the Baptist shone brighter than any other prophet of his time, but the reason for his shining was he was first burning. The word for burning is the Greek word *Kaio,* and it means to be consumed or be lighted. It took the fired up word consuming John the Baptist to make his light shine, for as God asked, "*is not my word like as a fire?...*" (Jeremiah 23:29).

That word, however, had to be received and listened to by John the Baptist for his shining to manifest. In Matthew 11:18-19, Jesus endorsed the success of John the Baptist's ministry as due to wisdom. He said, "*...John came neither eating nor drinking, and they say, He hath a devil, The Son of man came eating and drinking, and they say, Behold a man gluttonous, and a winebibber, a friend of publicans and sinners. **But wisdom is justified of her children***" (Matthew 11:18-19).

It takes listening and obedience, however, to produce wisdom. In Proverbs 8:33-35, the wise man said "*hear instruction, and be wise, and refuse it not. Blessed is the man that **heareth me**, watching daily at my gates, waiting at the posts of my doors. For whoso findeth me findeth life, and shall obtain favour of the Lord.*"

Until a believer hears, watches, waits, and does the will of God they can't shine in life! That is why, in Daniel 12:3, the Bible says "*... they that be wise shall shine as the brightness of the firmament; and they that turn many to righteousness as the stars for ever and ever.*"

ENLIGHTENMENT FOR EXPANSION

The word used in Proverbs 3:3 for *understanding* is the word interpreted to *enlighten*. This word, *Sakal*, in the Hebrew means to have insight, discretion and understanding of a matter. When believers stop leaning on their wisdom, but instead seek His divine wisdom, it makes for a lighted journey in life.

In Proverbs 3:1-7, the wise man said *"My son, forget not my law; but let thine heart keep my commandments: For length of days, and long life, and peace, shall they add to thee. Let not mercy and truth forsake thee: bind them about thy neck; write them upon the table of thine heart: So shalt thou find favour and good understanding in the sight of God and man. Trust in the Lord* with all thine heart; and lean not unto thine own understanding. In all thy ways acknowledge him, and he shall direct thy paths. *Be not wise in thine own eyes: fear the Lord, and depart from evil."*

It takes light to live a life that is large! The Bible teaches that simpletons stay bereft of understanding. In Psalm 119:130, the Bible says *"the entrance of thy words giveth light; it giveth understanding unto the simple."* Those who are loyal to the call, no matter the cost, see the word of God grow continually. That word is called revelation and it stimulates a revolution that takes them out of the reach of their enemies.

BILLY JOE DAUGHERTY, SHERIDIAN CHRISTIAN CENTER AND VICTORY CHURCH

Billy Joe Daughtery moved from Magnolia, Arkansas to Tulsa, Okhlahoma and enrolled for a bachelor's degree (theology) at Oral Roberts University (ORU) in 1971. He graduated three years later from Oral Roberts University, Tulsa, Oklahoma in 1974. He and his wife, Sharon Daughtery, then attended classes at Christ for the Nations Institute in Dallas, Texas before returning to Tulsa to serve as youth ministers of Sheridan Christian Center in Tulsa, Oklahoma.

Daugherty became senior pastor there in 1976 when the pastor retired, and the Church grew from 300 to 2,000 under his leadership. He left the Church in 1980, after God told him He did not call him to be a pastor of the Sheredian Christian Center. He asked him to leave the Church to go and understudy Kenneth Copeland at Kenneth Copeland Ministries, in Newark Texas.

This instruction was doubly challenging to Billy Joe Daugherty, as he had been contrmporaries with Kenneth Copeland at ORU, and his ministry at Sheridian Christian center was flourishing. He, however, obeyed, and after two years of understudying Kenneth Copeland Ministries he returned to Tulsa, Oklahoma.

On his return to Tulsa, Okhlahoma God led him to start Victory Christian Church (VCC), at the Mabee Center of Oral Roberts University (ORU) and on their inaugural service they had over 4,000 people show up. Though he died in 2009, Billy Joe Daugherty's legacy lives on in the over 900 Victory Bible Intitutes his ministry started around the world, the Tulsa Dream center, and the 25,000 capacity VCC currently pastored by his son, Paul Daughtery.

Billy Joe Daughtery also served as an interim president of ORU, and transitioned the Tulsa-based Church from the Mabee center ORU to their own facility in 2007, after renting out the space for 25 years. He epitomizes the need to listen for God's direction before embarking on a project. He shone, in life and in death, because he was consumed by God's word and lived a life that was totally sold out to God.

He was once slapped by a visitor to the Church, while trying to greet the intruder. Instead of getting irate, and pressing charges against him Pastor Billy Joe Daugerthy dropped all charges against him, prayed for him, and requested he return to the Church when released.

Prayer: Give me a light, O Lord, that darkness cannot extinguish in Jesus name!

No food for a lazy man!

- LOCAL NIGERIAN PROVERB

CHAPTER TWENTY-FOUR

LABOR

*"The soul of the sluggard desireth, and hath nothing: but the soul of the diligent shall be made **fat**"* (Proverbs 13:4).

The power of labor is the key to reward. It (labor) is the horn that when exalted gives out the fresh oil that makes a man's face to shine. In Ezekiel 29:20-21, the Lord said *"I have given him the land of Egypt for his **labor** wherewith he served against it, because they wrought for me, saith the Lord God. In that day will I cause the horn of the house of Israel to bud forth, and I will give thee the opening of the mouth in the midst of them; and they shall know that I am the Lord."*

When **human effort is forfeited, divine anointing is frustrated**. Jesus could have raised Lazarus on day four, after he arrived Bethany, but he asked the people around him to roll away the stone first (see John 11:39-41). God gave the Israelites Manna but they had better be ready to go get it because God would not spoonfeed them with it (Exodus 16:4).

In like manner, Jesus called the disciples to the upper room for Pentecost in Luke 24:49. It was in their prayer and fasting for ten days, however, that they birthed the breakthrough baptism of the Holy Spirit and the Church was founded. The forfeiture of labor has robbed many of an otherwise glorious future. They lose their oil, and as a result can't glow!

In Proverbs 20:12-13, the wise man counsel led his generation that "*the hearing ear, and the seeing eye, the Lord* hath made even both of them (so) *love not sleep, lest thou come to poverty; open thine eyes, and thou shalt be satisfied with bread.*" Love of sleep is the enemy of the seeing eye or the hearing ear, and an albatross to a life lived with satisfaction.

CALLED TO BE PRODUCTIVE

Jesus was diligent to the end of His journey, and as a resut he saw what others never saw. The prophet Isaiah said, in Isaiah 53:10-12, that "*...it was the Lord's will to crush him and cause him to suffer, and though the Lord* makes his life an offering for sin, he will see his offspring and prolong his days, *and the will of the Lord* will prosper in his hand. After he has suffered, he will **see the light of life** and be satisfied; *by his knowledge my righteous servant will justify many...* (NIV)."

No man will remain at the bottom who employs the instrumentality of labor. The wise man, in Proverbs 13:4, said "*the soul of the sluggard desireth and hath nothing but the soul of the diligent shall be made fat.*" The interpretation of *fat*, in the Hebrew, is the word *Dashen* and it means to be *anointed, shine,* and to *take away the ashes* therein.

The Christian's heritage is one of productivity. In 2 Thessalonians 3:10-12, Paul teaches the Church that "*...if any would not work, neither should he eat for we hear that there are some which walk among you disorderly, working not at all, but are busybodies. Now them that are such we command and exhort by our Lord Jesus Christ, that with quietness they work, and eat their own bread.*"

This productivity is a signpost for promotion! In Proverbs 12:24, the wise man said "*the hand of the diligent shall bear rule but the slothful shall be under tribute.*" In Ecclesiastes 10:18, he adds "*by much slothfulness the building decayeth; and through idleness of the hands the house droppeth through.*"

LESSONS FROM LABOR!

Everyman God ever used was productive - from Jesus at carpentry, to Peter's fishing, or Paul's rigorous tent making. Diligence is an attitude required both for life and ministry. In Ephesians 4:28, the Bible says *"let us labor working with our hands the thing which is good that we may have to give to him that needeth."*

Jesus cried out for laborers, not loafers, in Luke 10:2. He told his disciples, *"...the harvest truly is great, but the labourers are few: pray ye therefore the Lord of the harvest, that he would send forth **labourers** into his harvest."* God has not called the Church to laze around, but rather to labor.

God is a laborer (1 Cor 3:9), and as partakers of His divine nature (2 Peter 1:4), the Church is called to labor. In 1 Corinthians 3:8-9, Apostle Paul said *"...every man shall receive his own reward according to his own labor. For **we are laborers together with God**: ye are God's husbandry, ye are God's building."*

The reward of labor is the anointing that makes the face to shine. When there is a dearth of labor, there is a lame Church that cannot change her generation. In Hebrews 6:11-12, the writer of Hebrews advised the Church to *"...desire that every one of you do shew the same diligence to the full assurance of hope unto the end (and) That ye **be not slothful**, but followers of them who through faith and patience inherit the promise."*

BISHOP PRESTON: FROM FOLLOWER TO FIELD COMMANDER

As I preached on a Sunday morning in November 2020, at my local Church - Miracle Temple Evangelistic Church (MTEC), Jackson MS - the prophetic word came to me saying *"a promotion is coming for Pastor Kenneth Preston."*

Though there were no vacancies for Bishop at that time, Pastor Kenneth Preston held unto that word. He was, at that time, serving as the administrative assistant for the second jurisdiction Bishopric, and was highly regarded in the jurisdiction.

A few days after the prophecy, the presiding bishop of the jurisdiction died and between December 2020 and May 2021, there was an election of a new bishop and Pastor Kenneth was elected.

He was consecrated in October 2021, and attributes his promotion to God's favor. His wife, lady Missisionary Preston, was of the opinion however that his promotion was adequate reward for his labor in the 2nd Mississippi jurisdiction in particular, and the Church of God in Christ (COGIC) ministry in general.

Prayer: The grace to labor above all others come upon me, in Jesus name!

Good people are like candles;
they burn themselves up
to give others light

- TURKISH PROVERB

CHAPTER TWENTY-FIVE

LOVE

*"So let all thine enemies perish, O Lord: but let them that **love** him be as the **sun** when he goeth forth in his might..."* (Judges 5:31).

Love is described as the fulfillment of the law. In Romans 13:8-10, Apostle Paul charges the Church to *"...love (one) another (and so)...fulfill the law (because)...thou shalt not commit adultery, thou shalt not kill, thou shalt not steal, thou shalt not bear false witness, thou shalt not covet...is briefly comprehended in this saying, namely, thou shalt love thy neighbour as thyself. Love worketh no ill to his neighbour: therefore love is the fulfilling of the law."*

Without love, the believer's shining is turned into a shadow! The Psalmist reflected on his enemies, and said *"let them be confounded and put to shame that seek after my soul: let them be turned back and brought to confusion that devise my hurt. Let them be as chaff before the wind: and let the angel of the Lord chase them. Let their way be **dark and slippery**: and let the angel of the Lord persecute them. For without cause have they hid for me their net in a pit, which without cause they have digged for my soul"* (Psalm 35:4-7).

Love is not optional in the tapestry of shining, but the cardinal rule for a life that burns with glory. In 1 John 1:5-7, Apostle John (the apostle of Love) states unequivocally that *"...God is light, and in him is no darkness at all. If we say that we have fellowship with him, and walk in darkness, we lie, and do not the truth: But if we walk in the light, as he is in the light, we have fellowship one with another, and the blood of Jesus Christ his Son cleanseth us from all sin."*

The word interpreted *light* in the above verse is the Greek word *Phos*, and it means to shine or to make manifest. These ones, who walk in the light of His resence by fellowship, are first and foremost lovers of God and the world around them.

That is why, in 1 John 2:8-11, apostle John says *"...darkness is past, and **the true light** now shineth. He that saith he is in the light, and hateth his brother, is in darkness even until now. He that loveth his brother abideth in the light, and there is none occasion of stumbling in him. But he that hateth his brother is in darkness, and walketh in darkness, and knoweth not whither he goeth, because that darkness hath blinded his eyes."*

You can't truly love and remain in the dark! The signature of a burning and shining star is the insignia of love. No wonder those who *"...deal their bread to the hungry, and...bring the poor that are cast out to their house, (and) when they see the naked...cover him (have) their light break forth as the morning, and...the glory of the Lord be thy reward"* (Isaiah 58:7-8).

WORSHIP: WHEN HEAVEN KISSES THE EARTH!

Rain represents His glorious presence. In Deuteronomy 28:12, the Bible says *"the Lord shall open unto thee his good treasure, the heaven to give the rain unto thy land in his season, and to bless all the work of thine hand: and thou shalt lend unto many nations, and thou shalt not borrow."*

When rain is absent, as a result of sadness and depression, the church becomes *"...clouds...**without water**, carried about of winds; trees whose fruit withereth, without fruit, twice dead, plucked up by the roots; raging waves of the sea, foaming out their own shame; wandering stars, to whom is reserved the **blackness of darkness** forever"* (Jude 1:12-13).

The solution to this drought of God's presence is worship! God is *"...thou (who) art holy, (and)...that inhabitest the praises of Israel"*

(Psalm 22:3). He charged Israel, in Zechariah 14:17, saying, "...*whoso will not come up of all the families of the earth unto Jerusalem to worship* the King, the *Lord* of hosts, even upon them shall be no *rain.*"

The kissing-ground between believers (the Bride) and Christ (the heavenly Bridegroom) is a heart full of worship! These are those God describes as shining as the noon day Sun in Judges 5:31. These ones "...*love Him* (and so will) *be as the sun when he goeth forth in his might....*"

Moses died angry, and resentful. He criticized the children of Israel for his failure to enter the promisd land (see Deuteronomy 3:26, 1:27 and Numbers 20:7-12), and at his death had to have "...*Michael the archangel contend with the devil...about* (his)...*body...*" (Jude 9) because his lack of love had breached the wall and given satan entrance against him.

Jacob, on the other hand, "...*when he was a dying, blessed both the sons of Joseph; and worshipped, leaning upon the top of his staff*" (Hebrews 11:21). Even though, like Moses, he had faced his fair share of disappointment and discouragement (Genesis 47:9) he died with worship not regret or resentment.

As a result, his legacy was a shining legacy! In Numbers 24:17-19, Balaam prophesies that "...*there shall come a **Star out of Jacob**, and a Sceptre shall rise out of Israel, and shall smite the corners of Moab, and destroy all the children of Sheth. (And) out of Jacob shall come he that shall have dominion, and shall destroy him that remaineth of the city.*"

DARK GLASS EQUALS DIMMED GLORY

I Corinthians 13 is considered the holy grail of Love in the Bible. It is the consummation of God's concepts and thoughts on love, and ends with a focus on what would transpire in a home or Church where love is transcendeth and exalted. In 1 Corinthians 13:11-12, Apostle Paul said "*when I was a child, I spake as a child, I understood as a child, I thought as a child: but when I became a man, I put away childish things. For now we see through a **glass, darkly**; but then **face to face**: now I know in part; but then shall I know even as also I am known.*"

The highest level of love is the face to face encounter or relationship, and as long as there are dark glasses present, the fullness of God's glory cannot be manifest. In Proverbs 27:18-19, we see an example of the strength of face to face relationships. It says "*whoso keepeth the fig tree shall eat the fruit thereof: so he that waiteth on his master shall be honoured. As in water face answereth to face, so the heart of man to man.*"

The transparent and sincere love relationship births honor, not shame! It is the reason glory follows some and eludes others. For example, in Psalm 112:4, the Psalmist said "*unto the upright there ariseth light in the darkness: he is gracious, and full of **compassion**, and righteous.*"

Without love, darkness becomes the status quo, and glory a far flung hope. It takes a heart full of love to shine bright on the stratosphere of life. When there is love, God will be "*...an everlasting light, and thy God thy glory. Thy sun shall no more go down; neither shall thy moon withdraw itself: for the Lord* shall be thine everlasting light, and the days of thy mourning shall be ended" (Isaiah 60:15-21).

The signature of shining is love, not hatred or bitterness. That is why Apostle Paul told the Church in Philippi to "*do all things without murmurings and disputings that ye may be blameless and harmless, the sons of God, without rebuke, in the midst of a crooked and perverse nation, among whom ye **shine** as lights in the world*" (Philippians 2:14-15).

He adds, in 1 Thessalonians 5:4-8, that "*...ye, brethren, are not in darkness, that that day should overtake you as a thief* (but) *...are all the children of **light**, and the children of the day: we are not of the night, nor of darkness. Therefore let us not sleep, as do others; but let us watch and be sober. For they that sleep sleep in the night; and they that be drunken are drunken in the night. But let us, who are of the day, be sober, putting on the breastplate of faith and **love**; and for an helmet, the hope of salvation.*"

Where there is hatred and vilification, darkness is evident. In Psalm 69:20-26, the Psalmist said "*...let their eyes be **darkened**, that they see not; and make their loins continually to shake. Pour out thine indignation upon them, and let thy **wrathful anger** take hold of them. Let their habitation be desolate; and let none dwell in their tents. For they* *persecute him whom thou hast smitten; and they talk to the **grief** of those whom thou hast wounded."*

DAVID WILKERSON: GOD'S LOVE AGENT!

David Wilkerson (1931-2011) was a youth pastor in rural Pennsylvania when God called him to minister in inner city New York. He had seen an artist's impression of six kids, who belonged to a gang called the dragons, and were being sentenced to prison for the murder of a fifteen year old poliomyelitis patient.

Their faces expressed despondency, hopelessness, and dismay and soon after that David felt the Lord telling him to leave the comfort of his pastorate in rural Pennsylvania to set up a new ministry base in Brooklyn, New York. That was in 1958, and more than fifty years later *Teen Challenge*, which David formed on arriving Brooklyn New York City, is a global household name.

It has the highest rate of success for recovering addicts staying sober and drug-free (97%), and has touched lives around the globe. The teen challenge organization has a presence in over 1,000 locations, offices in over 77 countries of the world, with more than 173 residential programs and 241 centers in the USA. In the movie, *the Cross and the switchblade*, David famously confronts a drug Czar, who threathened to kill him, saying *if you cut me in a thousand pieces, each piece will cry out I love you.*

David Wilkerson, in 1971, re-located to Texas and started another organization called world challenge designed to bring the ministry of the word of God to the world. This arm of the ministry printed world-wide tracts and teachings that were shipped all around the world, and organized teen-themed crusades designed to reach the lost with the saving gospel of the Lord Jesus Christ.

In 1986, while walking down Time Square, after a street rally to reach the lost of New York City, God directed David to start a Church in downtown New York City. They bought out the famous Mark Hellinger cinema hall, after initially using rented facilities, and the Times Square Church was born. It encompassed thousands of

New Yorkers' from over a hundred different nations and from this ministry base missions, ministers' conferences and humanitarian aid were given.

After more than fifty years of marriage and ministry, the curtains were drawn on this General of the faith's life as he travelled on the roads of Texas. He was killed in a head-on collision and died instantly. His wife, though injured as well in the car crash, died nine months later from complications arising from cancer and not the car crash.

David Wilkerson's legacy, however, continues today in the thousands of men and women whose lives have been forever changed through the ministries he founded. As stated in a tribute by Nicky Cruz, at his death *David Wilkerson was like somebody who was not only my spiritual father, but much more than that is gone.*

Prayer: Let the love of God be shed abroad from my heart by the Holy Spirit, in Jesus name!

If you look at God you attract Godderisms, but if you look to men you attract mannerisms!

- Tobe Momah M.D.

CHAPTER TWENTY-SIX

LOOKING

"They looked unto him, and were lightened: and their faces were not ashamed" (Psalm 34:5).

If the Church is going to be a light in a dark world, they cannot be escapable or mistaken for someone or something else. The words *cannot be hid,* as used in Matthew 5:14 to describe *a city that is set on an hill,* is from the Greek word *krupto* that is interpreted *impossible to escape notice.* There is something wrong with a church that is the light of the world, but not reflecting the brightness of his rising! If the Church is truly the light of the world, then why isn't she a shining light for Jesus?

In psalm 123:2, a visual personification describing how the believer should look at the master is instituted. It says, *"...as the eyes of servants look unto the hand of their masters, and as the eyes of a maiden unto the hand of her mistress; so our eyes wait upon the Lord our God, until that he have mercy upon us."* The look of a servant will break the barriers to shining! It is a look of submission, salutation, and subjection to God's will.

The Bible talks about the stronghold of Zion, which was in Jerusalem. Before its conquest, however, a unique reason David was regaled by God as *"...a man after His own heart..."* (Acts 13:22) was revealed. In 2 Samuel 5:8, David told his soldiers that *"whosoever getteth up to the gutter, and smiteth the Jebusites, and the lame and the blind that are hated of David's soul, he shall be chief and captain. Wherefore they said, The blind and the lame shall not come into the house. said on that day, who so ever get up to the gutter and smite had the Jabber size that people who lived in Jerusalem and the lame and the blind that I hate."*

David hated blind ignorance! If you want to taste the shine of heaven, and the riches of God like David did, you have got to hate ignorance and desire knowledge. Could it be that the tolerance of blindness and the lame has curtailed the Church of Jesus Christ from being chief? Are you blinded from the revelation of Jesus, and as a result your face is not lightened? In Psalm 34:5, the Bible says *"they looked unto him, and were lightened: and their faces were not ashamed."*

KEEP YOUR OWN VINEYARD!

Who you look to determines who looks at you! The wise man said, in Songs of Solomon (S.O.S) 1:5-6, that *"I am black, but comely, O ye daughters of Jerusalem, as the tents of Kedar, as the curtains of Solomon. Look not upon me, because I am black, because the sun hath looked upon me: my mother's children were angry with me; they made me the keeper of the vineyards; but mine own vineyard have I not kept."*

Black, as stated in S.O.S, is the Hebrew word *shachor* that signifies, not a skin complexion, but a lack of shining. It was his distractibility that precipitated his darkness, and his lack of focus that dimmed his flourishing. He states that his siblings were angry with him because he was so busy looking after every other person's ministry, calling, or destiny that he left his own vineyard unoccupied.

In Proverbs 29:18, the Bible says *"where there is no vision, the people perish: but he that keepeth the law, happy is he."* The word *perish*, used in Proverbs 29:18, means vacant, empty, or unoccupied. Until you look at God's vision for your life, you can't fulfill your lot in life. **No one can take you where your eyes don't first see**. Are you looking in the right direction? Is your eye focused on the purpose of God for your life? I believe there are a lot of blessings the church is missing because she is distracted and has her vision looking in the wrong direction.

Your revelation is tied to your righteousness! When Moses and the people of Israel were unable to drink the bitter waters of Marah, Moses "...*cried unto the Lord; and the Lord shewed him a tree, which when he had cast into the waters, the waters were made sweet: there he made for them a statute and an ordinance, and there he proved them and said, If thou wilt diligently hearken to the voice of the Lord* thy God, and wilt do that which is right in his sight, and wilt give ear to his commandments, and keep all his statutes, I will put none of these diseases upon thee, which I have brought upon the Egyptians: for I am the *Lord* that healeth thee" (Exodus 15:25-26).

The place of their hurt became the theater of their healing because the man Moses looked unto God's sightings of a tree, and not the pain around him. That is why, in the chronicles of his life, he is described as an apostle who "...*by faith...forsook Egypt, not fearing the wrath of the king (and) endured, as **seeing** him who is invisible*" (Hebrews 11:27).

The Prophet Moses was leading 6 million individuals through the wilderness, and told Hobab, his brother in law, "...*we are journeying unto the place of which the Lord* said, I will give it you: come thou with us, and we will do thee good: for the *Lord* hath spoken good concerning Israel....Leave us not, I pray thee; forasmuch as thou knowest how we are to encamp in the wilderness, and thou mayest be to us instead of ***eyes** and it shall be, if thou go with us, yea, it shall be, that what goodness the Lord* shall do unto us, the same will we do unto thee" (Numbers 10:29-32).

The outcome of a wilderness journey without eyes is wasting! Moses, though a towering intellectual, who had built the cities of Rameses, and had advanced degrees in history, international economy, politics and Architecture from the finest citadels of learning in Egypt, took time to seek out eyes for his journey. He knew that a commission without a vision will end in termination. He was a man who didn't know the demographics and the topography of the wilderness, and was not afraid to ask for help when he needed it. No wonder he shone bright in Israel (2 Corinthians 3:7-11).

VISION VIOLATORS; BLESSING BANKRUPTERS!

The devil attacks vision more than anything else. If the devil can distract you, he can destroy you. In 2 Corinthians 4:3-6, the Bible says that "...*if our gospel be hid, it is hid to them that are lost: In whom the god of this world hath blinded the minds of them which believe not, lest the light of the glorious gospel of Christ, who is the image of God, should shine unto them. For we preach not ourselves, but Christ Jesus the Lord; and ourselves your servants for Jesus' sake. For God, who commanded the light to shine out of darkness, hath shined in our hearts, to give the light of the knowledge of the glory of God in the face of Jesus Christ.*"

When the god of this world (satan) blinds the eyes of men, that they might not behold the glorious gospel, it is because he knows looking into the perfect law of liberty is the only way they can shine their light to a dark and dying world. If he (satan) can blind you, shining is impossible. That is why elder James said, in James 1:25, that "...*whoso looketh into the perfect law of liberty, and continueth therein, he being not a forgetful hearer, but a doer of the work, this man shall be blessed in his deed.*"

No one can take you where your mind cannot see! Every building was once a vision, a picture, or a concept in the mind of the architect. Whatever you see today was someone's vision yesterday. Stop whining about what you should be warring about, and stop been distracted by what you should be destroying! That is why Paul prayed for the Church in Ephesus...*that the God of our Lord Jesus Christ, the Father of glory,...give unto you the spirit of wisdom and revelation in the knowledge of him* (and that) *the eyes of* (their)... *understanding being enlightened...may know what is the hope of his calling, and what the riches of the glory of his inheritance in the saints, and what is the exceeding greatness of his power to us-ward who believe, according to the working of his mighty power*" (Ephesians 1:17-19).

If you and I get the eyes of our understanding enlightened, the riches of the glory of his inheritance in the saints towards us will make us shine. Paul in essence tells the Ephesian Church that I know you have eyes, but asks if their eyes were enlightened? Many of us have eyes, but we have eyes that are not seeing the spiritual! In 2 Corinthians 4:18, Paul said "*we look not at the things which are seen, but at the things which are not seen: for the things which are seen are temporal; but the things which are not seen are eternal.*"

RAPID REPAIR BY THE REDEEMER!

The surgeon had just told Rev. Ashbrook, the then District Superintendent of the Louisiana District of the Assemblies of God that he had less than six months to live because he had an inoperable lung mass. He then added that, with the best of treatment, they would prolong his life for at most six months to a year. In that one moment, the revered gentleman and his wife faced down the surgeon and told him that in the absence of a cure from medicine or surgery, they would rather depend on God for his healing.

That diagnosis was in the 1960's! Rev. Ashbrook lived another forty years pastoring megachurches from Hong Kong to Louisiana without missing a step. Even though his faith was severely challenged on several occasions, he never quit. His son John remembers him, a times, as been sickly and weak while preaching, but nevertheless kept preaching till he ended his sermon.

One day, while he was preaching from Romans 8:11, he discovered a pivotal scripture that changed his health forever. God showed him that the Holy Spirit in him could do what was needed – quicken his mortal body! That scripture says, "*…if the Spirit of him that raised up Jesus from the dead dwell in you, he that raised up Christ from the dead shall also quicken your mortal bodies by his Spirit that dwelleth in you.*"

He lifted up his arms in surrender and began to claim that promise for his physical body. After the service, his body felt revived by the quickening power of the Holy Spirit, and he went on finish his term successfully as the Louisiana State Assemblies of God District Superintendent. After he retired, he served as the senior pastor of an International Assemblies of God Church in Hong Kong (where he rpeached five services every Sunday), and even covered a missionary who was on furlough for a year in Mongolia.

At the time of his passing at nearly eighty years of age, he had proven the Word of God in Romans 8:11. He had inspired so many with his testimony and life, and among several Assembly of God ministers (including Jesse Duplantis), he had served as a mentor and motivator. He walked where others feared to thread, and accomplished more than legions of ordinary men do in their lifetimes.

Prayer: Transform my life O Lord, by showing me your face, in Jesus name!

Walking in the light means for many of us walking according to our standard for another person. The deadliest Pharisaism today is not hypocrisy, but unconscious reality

– Oswald Chambers
(Author/Chaplain/
Missionary 1874 – 1917)

CHAPTER TWENTY-SEVEN

LEADERSHIP

"The Lord sent a word into Jacob, and it hath lighted upon Israel" (Isaiah 9:8)

In the book of Matthew 15:13-14, Jesus counsel led against the blind leading the blind. He said, *"...every plant, which my heavenly Father hath not planted, shall be rooted up. Let them alone: they be blind leaders of the blind. And if the blind lead the blind, both shall fall into the ditch."*

The dearth of godly leadership is why so many believers end up in the ditches of life. There are so many blind leaders who are leading, and it is only where there *"...is the fountain of life* (that) *in thy light shall we see light"* (Psalm 36:9). Where the fountain is dry, light is absent and catastrophe is inevitable.

Apostle Paul, speaking in Romans 2:19-20, described the instructed-out-of the-Word believer as *"...a guide of the blind, a light of them which are in darkness, an instructor of the foolish, a teacher of babes, which hast the form of knowledge and of the truth in the law."*

The Lord sent a word into Jacob, and it lighted upon the nation of Israel (Isaiah 9:8), because it is who you accompany that determines what you accommodate. Anytime you want to move up in life, you must have some one to look up to. If you have nobody to look up to, you will remain stranded on the journey of life!

Every Paul needs an Ananias to give him light (Acts 9:17), and every Baruch a Jeremiah to guide and instruct him through dark circumstances (Jeremiah 45:5). Leadership is not a popularity contest, but it is stating God's word and implementing it, no matter whose ox is gored. It means bringing everyone along to God's destination and destiny for their lives by leading them there.

Leadership is also not lording it over the followers (1 Peter 5:3), but leading them as peers. In Micah 3:5-7, prophet Micah says *"thus saith the Lord concerning the prophets that make my people err, that bite with their teeth, and cry, Peace; and he that putteth not into their mouths, they even prepare war against him. Therefore* **night** *shall be unto you, that ye shall* **not have a vision***; and it shall be* **dark** *unto you, that ye shall not divine; and the sun shall go down over the prophets, and the* **day shall be dark** *over them. Then shall the seers be ashamed, and the diviners confounded: yea, they shall all cover their lips; for there is no answer of God."* When leaders lord, instead of lead, their light goes out and their life grinds to a halt.

DITCHES OR HILLS?

You cannot go from the gutter most to the uttermost if you follow blind leaders. The gutters of life are full of blind leaders leading their followers into the ditches of life, according to Luke 6:39. These wrongly led followers need to change their leadership if they want to make their stars shine. In Ecclesiastes 10:15, the Bible said *"the labor of the foolish wearieth every one of them, because he knoweth not how to go to the city."*

The position a child of God is supposed to occupy is on the hilltop, not the ditch! Jesus said, in Matthew 5:14-15, that *"ye are the light of the world. A city that is set on an hill cannot be hid* (and) *neither do men light a candle, and put it under a bushel, but on a candlestick; and it giveth light unto all that are in the house."*

The five wise and five foolish virgins, in Matthew 25, epitomize the lives of believers who end up in hills or ditches respectively. All ten virgins departed from their homes with lights burning, and hearts ready for the marriage supper of the land. After some perceived delay, they slept off only to wake up when the bridegroom arrived.

On his arrival, the foolish virgins turned to the wise for oil asking "…*give us of your oil; for our lamps are gone out*" (Matthew 25:8). The wise, however, answered saying, "*Not so; lest there be not enough for us and you: but go ye rather to them that sell, and buy for yourselves*" (Matthew 25:9).

Unfortunately by the time the five foolish virgins returned, they had been ditched to the gutters (Matthew 25:10), and cast out of the marriage supper of the lamb. While the five wise virgins gained entrance to the Marriage supper of the lamb, the foolish were shut out. The proof of wisdom is the presence of an oil that directs and leads. In Ecclesiastes 8:1, the wise man asks, "*who is as the wise man? and who knoweth the interpretation of a thing? (For) a man's wisdom maketh his face to **shine**, and the boldness of his face shall be changed.*"

LIBERTY, LIGHT, AND LEADERSHIP

The leadership you follow will determine the light and the liberty you manifest. In 2 Corinthians 3:16-18, "*nevertheless when it shall turn to the **Lord**, the vail shall be taken away. Now the Lord is that Spirit: and where the Spirit of the Lord is, there is **liberty**. But we all, with open face beholding as in a glass the glory of the Lord, are changed into the same image from glory to glory, even as by the Spirit of the Lord.*"

As long as the Holy Spirit is the architect of your journey, you will behold the glory of God that makes shining incontrovertible. When shadows are eliminated, and the Father of Lights beams forth, your first fruits from the Word of God will manifest. In James 1:16-18, Elder James says "*do not err, my beloved brethren. Every good gift and every perfect gift is from above, and cometh down from the **Father of lights**, with whom is no variableness, neither **shadow of turning**. Of his own will begat he us with the word of truth, that we should be a kind of first fruits of his creatures.*"

The moon has no light of its own, and it is simply positioned next to the sun to reflect light from it. It (the moon) is too positioned to escape the shining from the sun. **Who you follow determines what kind of light you shine!** It takes a consummate and Christ-like leader to keep your light shining bright. If the person leading you is "not lighted," your initial light will eventually go out.

In Job 29:24-25, Job said "...*the **light of my countenance** they cast not down* (and) *I chose out their way, and sat chief, and dwelt as a king in the army, as one that comforteth the mourners.*" Those who sit chief, therefore, are motivational leaders who inspire others by their light.

The trajectory a follower goes is dependent on who he or she follows. If that leader is lighted, they too will be lighted but if the leader abides in darkness so will they abide in darkness. That is why the wise man, in Proverbs 28:12, says "*when righteous men do rejoice, there is great glory: but when the wicked rise, a man is hidden.*"

REINHARD BONNKE AND RICHARD NGIDI

There was a great man of God, who worked with Reinhard Bonnke, named Richard Ngidi. He was a Zulu preacher from South Africa, and this man was gifted in miracles, signs and wonders. During those days, Bonnke would preach and step down from the platform for Richard Ngidi to do what he knows best - which was pray for the sick.

He was really the kingpin of the early healing ministry in Southern Africa, and was a concrete support to Reinhard Bonnke as Bonnke's ministry was growing rapidly. He spearheaded many Christ For All Nations (CFAN) crusade including their first Gabarone, Botswana crusade. At a particular crusade, however, Pastor Ngidi did not show up.

He had been overheard telling an associate of Reinhard Bonnke's that he was the man doing the whole work and yet Reinhard Bonnke was taking the credit. He then added that "*the day I leave Bonnke that day will mark the end of him and his ministry.*" He began to think of himself as the maker of Reinhard Bonnke, and did not show up purposefully to embarrass Reinhard Bonnke.

Bonnkke waited, waited and waited for him yet he didn't show up. Frustrated and disappointed, Reinhard mounted the platform fully depending on the Holy Spirit. As a result, God used him mightily that day in miracles and that marked the beginning of his ministerial success.

Instead of that day being the end of Bonnke, it became his beginning and unfortunately the end of Ngidi. Times passed, and while CFAN exploded with millions attending its miracle crusades, Ngidi's trajectory in ministry declined. He was later seen at one of Reinhard Bonnke's crusades, and seeing multitudes like never before, he said "*I missed it, I missed it...*" and left the venue.

That was the last time the world saw Richard Ngidi. He died shortly after that in 1985 from a diabetic coma. Today everybody knows Reinhard Bonnke but no one knows Richard Ngidi. What Richard did not realize early enough is that it is God's work, and it is bigger than anyone. You are not that important, or as Reinhard Bonnke was fond of saying *do not be moved by men's criticism or praise, and you will not be made by either.*

Prayer: Make me a lighted believer, O Lord, in Jesus name!

Light

(*Aunty Annie's* Executive team Motto)

L = Lead by Example

I = Invest in Employees

G = Give Freely

H = Honor God

T = Treat all business contacts with respect

CHAPTER TWENTY-EIGHT

LAUGHTER

*"If I **laughed** on them, they believed it not; and the **light** of my countenance they cast not down"* (Job 29:24).

Shining is standing out so bright that some will assume that you are God's favorite! **It is the spirit of cheer that guarantees the spirit of conquest**. In Proverbs 17:22, the Bible says, *"a merry heart doeth good like a medicine: but a broken spirit drieth the bones."* Every time you want to take a step toward shining, you must first take another step towards laughter first.

Believers have eternal rest and can afford to laugh, notwithstanding their surrounding circumstances, because they know they have the last laugh always. In Job 5:22-24, Eliphaz said, *"at destruction and famine, thou shalt **laugh**...For thou shalt be in league with the stones of the field: and the beasts of the field shall be at peace with thee. And thou shalt know that thy tabernacle shall be in peace...."*

There is strength in laughter! It is not only a heartfelt sign of confidence in God but a veritable weapon of war. In Psalm 2:4-5, the Psalmist says, *"He that sitteth in the heavens shall laugh; the Lord shall have them in derision...and vex them in His sore displeasure."*

The prophet Isaiah tells us the anointed of the Lord *"...shall not fail nor be discouraged, till he have set judgment in the earth: and the isles shall wait for his law...*(as the) *Lord* have called thee in righteousness, and will hold thine hand, and will keep thee, and give thee for a covenant of the people, for a *light of the Gentiles; To open the blind eyes, to bring out the prisoners from the prison, and them that sit in darkness out of the prison house"* (Isaiah 42:4-7).

The shining Christian is a shouting believer! In Isaiah 42:11-13, the Bible says *"sing unto the Lord a new song, and his praise from the end of the earth, ye that go down to the sea, and all that is therein; the isles, and the inhabitants thereof. Let the wilderness and the cities thereof lift up their voice, the villages that Kedar doth inhabit: let the inhabitants of the rock sing, let them shout from the top of the mountains. Let them give glory unto the Lord, and declare his praise in the islands. The Lord shall go forth as a mighty man, he shall stir up jealousy like a man of war...."*

Whenever God rises up as a mighty man, it is because someone gave glory, or sang praise unto the Lord with shouting. In 1 Thessalonians 5:15-18, the Bible says *"rejoice evermore. Pray without ceasing. In everything give thanks: for this is the will of God in Christ Jesus concerning you."* It is in such an atmosphere of unmitigated praise that the fullness of the Holy Spirit shines forth. It is, no wonder, therefore that 1 Thessalonians 5:19 requests the believer to *"quench not the Spirit."*

HAVE YOU LIVED, BUT NEVER LAUGHED?

The Shunnamite woman was a paradox of contradictions. She was wealthy, influential, great, well-connected, surrounded by her family and seemingly content (2 Kings 4:8-17) but there was something she wanted. When the prophet of God told her she would have a child in a year's time, notwithstanding her husband's biological inadequacies, she replied *"...nay, my lord, thou man of God, do not lie unto thine handmaid"* (2 Kings 4:16).

She had lived, but never laughed and in about a year's time her laughter was fulfilled as she held her son in her arms (2 Kings 4:17). This Shunammite woman had never experienced the God of more than enough! If you want to shine in life, you must come out of the dark room and show the world laughter, joy and rejoicing!

Fear is the dark room where the negatives of life are produced, and there must be no room for fear if you want the light of the gospel to shine from your life. In Psalm 27:1-3, David said *"the Lord is my light and my salvation; whom shall I fear? the Lord is the strength of my life; of whom shall I be afraid? When the wicked, even mine enemies and my foes, came upon me to eat up my flesh, they stumbled and fell. Though an host should encamp against me, my heart shall not fear: though war should rise against me, in this will I be confident."*

You cannot soar in life, and be sour all the time. On the contrary, if you have want a continual feast, then you must have a merry heart (Proverbs 15:15). In the Psalms, the Psalmist describes a strong man who, about to get married, *"…rejoiceth as a strong man to run a race* (for) *his going forth is from the end of the heaven, and his circuit unto the ends of it and there is nothing hid from the heat thereof"* (Psalm 19:5-6).

Where there is laughter, there will always be light and when there is rejoicing there will always be radiance! God called you to change the earth with your light, but it will not be possible without laughter. In Psalm 104:15, the Psalmist said, *"…wine that maketh glad the heart of man, and oil to make his face to shine, and bread which strengtheneth man's heart."* Whenever there is gladness of heart, there will always be the oil of shining.

After God saved Mordecai and Israel, and destroyed Haman and his genealogy, the Bible says *"…the city of Shushan rejoiced and was glad (and) the Jews had light, and gladness, and joy, and honour. And in every province, and in every city, whithersoever the king's commandment and his decree came, the Jews had joy and gladness, a feast and a good day…"* (Esther 8:15-17).

So many believers spend their time beating themselves up, instead of laughing through their storms. In Isaiah 12:3-4, the prophet Isaiah said *"…with joy shall ye draw water out of the wells of salvation and in that day shall ye say, Praise the Lord, call upon his name, declare his doings among the people, make mention that his name is exalted."*

THE REPROACH OF RACHEL VS THE JOY OF JOB

Rachel was the second wife of Jacob. She had been a woman filled with tantrums (as evidenced by her use of an aphrodisiac called mandrake in Genesis 30:14), melancholic attitudes (as buttressed by her cry to Jacob saying *give me children or I die* - Genesis 30:1) and by the name she gave her second child (*Benoni* which means son of my sorrow). The Bible is explicit with her mood disorders, and as a result she died in ignominy buried by the side of the road (Genesis 35:19).

Job, on the other hand, became the wealthiest man in the east because he was a man whose "*...glory was fresh...and...bow renewed in* (his) *hand. (And so) unto* (him) *men gave ear, and waited, and kept silence...and after* (his) *words they spake not again; and* (his) *speech dropped upon them....They waited for* (him) *as for the rain; and they opened their mouth wide as for the latter rain* (and) *if* (he) ***laughed*** *on them, they believed it not; and the **light** of* (his) *countenance they cast not down. I chose out their way, and sat chief, and dwelt as a king in the army, as one that comforteth the mourners*" (Job 29:20-25).

This man, who was the richest man in the east, refused to give himself over to brow beatings, backbiting, and bitterness when he faced challenges. He remained joyful and full of laughter instead, and the light of his countenance brought forth glory and riches to him and his family. Even when his wife came to him and said, "*...curse God and die*" (Job 2:9), he refused and instead asked her "*...shall we receive good at the hand of God, and shall we not receive evil?*" (Job 2:10).

Job never stopped thanking and praising God notwithstanding his circumstances. He said, "*...though he slay me, yet will I trust in him: but I will maintain mine own ways before him. He also shall be my salvation:...*" (Job 13:15-16). Rachel, on the contrary, continued her lifelong attitude of mournfulness and consequently developed a notoriety for idolatry (Genesis 31:19b) that eventually terminated her life journey prematurely (Genesis 35:19).

VAN GOGH: A LIFE ECLIPSED AT DAWN BY MDD

Van Gogh (1853 – 1890) commissioned over two hundred paintings, which are today worth billions of dollars in the last two years of his life. He is considered, in art circles, a genius who used bright colors to highlight his paintings like few before or after him have done. He, however, started his career trying to be an evangelist. His father, a Dutch reformed minister, considered Van Gogh the successor to his ministry, as the first born son in the family. After training stints in Holland, France and Belgium that ended in abysmal failure, Van Gogh's father contemplated putting him in a mental health institution. The reasons for this were not far-fetched. Van Gogh, compared to his contemporaries, dressed differently and spoke austerely with little conviction. He was an introvert, and spent most of his time alone with few social interactions.

His one outlet, however, was his brother Theo. Van Gogh confided in him about his love for the arts, after helping his uncle retail some art work in Lewisham, England. He told him, "*I will rather be an evangelist with my art and use my paintings as God's voice*" than go into ministry. With encouragement from Theo, and support from family, Van Gogh enrolled in art schools in Paris, France at the age of Twenty-eight. Impressionists all around Europe gave Van Gogh's art encouraging words, especially seeing he had real-world views of his paintings. For example, he painted a picture of a slum in Belgium he had lived in as an itinerant preacher. Over the next ten years, Van Gogh painted outstanding artwork, but was only able to sell one of them for one thousand four hundred dollars to the Duchess Anna Boch. He pushed his potential helpers away with his melancholic moods, and spent months in mental health institutions undergoing treatment. He, eventually, strayed from the faith, indulging in alcohol and harlots and repeatedly suffered from sexually transmitted diseases including Syphilis and Gonorrhea. His life, that generated worthwhile art, was unfortunately wasted by depression as his health failed.

In 1890, Van Gogh died after a prolonged illness aged thirty-seven years of age. He had no dependants and was estranged at the time of his death from his brother Theo and other immediate family members. He left behind artwork that keeps alive the Van Gogh name, but Major Depressive Disorder (MDD) and Generalized anxiety Disorder (GAD) prematurely sounded his death knell, and thus ended the career of one of the most promising artists ever produced! It is a paradox that the paintings that brought laughter to so many,were painted by a man so beleaguered by anhedonia and melancholy.

Prayer: Turn again our captivity, O Lord, as the streams in the south in Jesus name!

PART V

The Light that Limits

- Flickering Light
- Filibuster Light
- Frustrating Light
- Futuristic Light
- Fainting Light
- Flowless Light
- Frightened Light

Splendor without spirituality is stupidity!

- TOBE MOMAH M.D.

CHAPTER TWENTY-NINE

FLICKERING LIGHT

"...even things without life giving sound, whether pipe or harp, except they give a distinction in the sounds, how shall it be known what is piped or harped? For if the trumpet give an uncertain sound, who shall prepare himself to the battle?" (1 Corinthians 14:7-8).

Nothing diminishes the brightness from a light source like a flickering light. The word, *flicker,* is defined as moving irregularly or unsteadily, and whenever there is instability excellence is extinguished. In Genesis 49:3-4, Jacob told his first born son, *"Reuben, thou art my firstborn, my might, and the beginning of my strength, the excellency of dignity, and the excellency of power: Unstable as water, thou shalt not excel...."*

The outcome of a flickering lifestyle is failure! A light that flickers cannot dispel the darkness, and except the Church shines her light with consistency and character the darkness in her environment cannot be dispelled. In Malachi 4:2, the Prophet Malachi said *"...unto you that fear my name shall the Sun of righteousness arise with healing in his wings; and ye shall go forth, and grow up as calves of the stall."*

The power of the Sun is in its consistency. It shines from one end of the earth to the other, and is likened to *"...a bridegroom coming out of his chamber, and rejoiceth as a strong man to run a race (whose)...*

going forth is from the end of the heaven, and his circuit unto the ends of it: and there is nothing hid from the heat thereof" (Psalm 19:5-6).

The strongman's rejoicing and running reflect the Sun's shining. Like the Sun, he must be **clear, confident, and have a champion's mentality** to shine bright. There is no room for instability and wavering in the life of the believer who wants to dispel darkness by their light. That is why, in James 1:6-8, Elder James states that "*...he that wavereth is like a wave of the sea driven with the wind and tossed. For let not that man think that he shall receive any thing of the Lord. A double minded man is unstable in all his ways.*"

DON'T PLAY THE VICTIM!

One of the results of playing the *victim* card is a flickering light lifestyle. Instead of addressing the root issues, such as loss of confidence or character flaws, some individuals would rather play the victim card and seek out pity. The son of the prophet, who asked two fellows to smite him, illustrates this principle.

In 1 Kings 20:37-40, this son of the prophet said to the second fellow, "*...smite me, I pray thee. And the man smote him, so that in smiting he wounded him. So the prophet departed, and waited for the king by the way, and disguised himself with ashes upon his face. And as the king passed by, he cried unto the king: and he said, Thy servant went out into the midst of the battle; and, behold, a man turned aside, and brought a man unto me, and said, Keep this man: if by any means he be missing, then shall thy life be for his life, or else thou shalt pay a talent of silver. And as thy servant was **busy here and there**, he was gone....*"

The distracted and inconsistent son of the prophet, in the above verse, illustrates the flickering light individual. He or she is "*...busy here and there...*" (1 Kings 20:40) and as a result of their broken focus lost the little they already had. There are people who are wounded, bruised and covered in ashes like this son of the prophet (1 Kings 20:35-42), because of a lack of tenacity and purpose.

The last days believer must have "*...loins...girded about, and... lights* burning (so they may be)...*like unto men that wait for their lord,* *when he will return from the wedding; that when he cometh and knocketh, they may open unto him immediately"* (Luke 12:35-36). The word *girded* is the Greek word *perizonnumi* and it means to be dressed in readiness or to fasten one's belt.

The truly combustible and lighted life is the one whose mind is set and willing to undergo whatever task the master has for him or her. Their eyes are fixed and their focus is unbroken. They are those the Lord *"...wilt keep him in perfect peace,* (because their)*...mind is stayed on* (Him)*...as he trusteth in thee"* (Isaiah 26:3). The proof of trust is focus, and the cause of perfidy is flickering vision.

THE POWER OF A SINGLE EYE

The single eye produces a wholesome shining, but the duplticious eye limits light's emanation! If someone is solely focused on darkness, they can only produce darkness. But if you look on the father of lights, there will be uncontestable and undeniable shining. In James 1:17, the Bible says that *"every good gift and every perfect gift is from above, and cometh down from the Father of lights, with whom is no variableness, neither shadow of turning."*

In Luke 11:34-36, Jesus said, *"the light of the body is the eye: therefore when thine eye is single, thy whole body also is full of light; but when thine eye is evil, thy body also is full of darkness. Take heed therefore that the light which is in thee be not darkness. If thy whole body therefore be full of light, having no part dark, the whole shall be full of light, as when the bright shining of a candle doth give thee light."*

Who you look at, will determine what light you shine on the earth! If it is the father of lights, everything around you will be full of light but if it is *"...the rulers of the darkness of this world..."* (Ephesians 6:12), all you will have will be darkness and a life void of impact. **God's word always comes back with excess baggage** (Isaiah 55:10-11)! Start looking unto him alone, for *"they* (that) *look unto him,* (are)*...lightened: and their faces...not ashamed"* (Psalm 34:5).

The unstoppable life is a life built on the Word of God. The wise man said, in Proverbs 31:30-31, that *"there is no wisdom nor understanding nor counsel against the Lord. The horse is prepared against the day of battle: but safety is of the Lord."* If the vision is clear, then people can run with it (Habbakuk 2:2). If it is flickering, however, there will be a *staccato* approach to the race that curtails speed. No wonder the wise man said, in Ecclesiastes 7:11, that *"wisdom is good with an inheritance and by it there is **profit** to them that **see the sun**."*

BATTLES FOR BREAKTHROUGH AND BALANCE!

Pastor Shane Warren repeatedly shares his father's powerful story of breakthrough and then, through a loss of balance, unmitigated loss. At a point in their life, the Warren family were living in a Tennessee hotel room as Shane's dad and Mom had no source of income. Shane and his brother were the butt of classmates' jokes, as the school bus picked and dropped them up from their city hotel routinely.

On one occasion, however, the Warren family were invited to a Church service nearby. At the meeting, Shane's parents' gave their lives to Jesus. Soon after, a prophet from Beaumont, Texas came visiting their local Assembly of God Church. This prophet walked up to Shane's father, and told him he had a hundred dollars in his pocket which was his last one hundred dollars. He told him *"I know that is your last hundred dollars but God said to ask you to sow that money into this ministry and He will bless you abundantly."*

He added that Shane's Dad would rise to become a multimillionaire but if he forgot God, his end would be worse than his beginning. Shane's father sowed that one hundred dollars, as the prophet commanded, and within one month Shane got a job as a car salesman, and prospered. The owner of the car showroom wanted to sell it, and chose Shane's Dad to sell it to. Within a few years, Shane's dad had transformed that dealership and bought another 20 to 30 dealerships till he became the biggest car dealer in the state of Tennessee.

Pastor Shane says he remembers the family travelling on vacations abroad, and his Dad would have uncountable wads of one hundred dollar bills in his briefcase. They were living tastefully, but exactly what the prophet said happened. Shane's dad forgot God, and his end was worse than his beginning. He stopped going to church, and forgot the warning the prophet had given him.

He died broke, broken hearted and a few years after his death, his wife died. The family had ridden the tidal waves of poverty and prosperity and it had consumed their parents. As a result, Pastor Shane adopted a balanced attitude towards money. He sees it as a tool to do the work of the Lord with, but not a master that controls one's life and motives. As a result he has seen unprecedented success as a minister, business owner, and parent.

Prayer: Give me an unbreakable spiritual focus, in Jesus name!

Inertia causes Implosion,
but Spontaneity brings
Sharp Sightedness

- TOBE MOMAH M.D.

CHAPTER THIRTY

FILIBUSTER LIGHT

*"But all things that are reproved are made manifest by the **light**: for whatsoever doth make manifest is **light**. Wherefore he saith, awake thou that sleepest, and arise from the dead, and Christ shall give thee **light**. See then that ye walk circumspectly, not as fools, but as wise"* (Ephesians 5:13-15).

The word *filibuster* means to delay, put off until later, or cause to be late. It is a foolish kind of light, that stays on the shelf and continues to be an onlooker instead of participating in the timings of God. In Ephesians 5:16, the Apostle Paul advises the last day Church to *"redeem the time, because the days are evil. Wherefore be ye not unwise, but understanding what the will of the Lord is."*

A woman who has a filibuster light will wait, when she should push, at the time of her child's delivery. The child inevitably becomes a victim of his or her mother's indecisiveness, and that one act of filibustering can have life long deleterious effects on the health of the child.

In Hosea 13:13-14, the Bible says *"the sorrows of a travailing woman shall come upon him: he is an **unwise** son; for he should not stay long in the place of the breaking forth of children. I will ransom them from the power of the grave; I will redeem them from death: O death, I will be* *thy plagues; O grave, I will be thy destruction: repentance shall be hid from mine eyes."*

It takes wisdom to be delivered from death! In Ecclesiastes 7:16-17, the wise man counsel led the Church to *"be not righteous over much; neither make thyself over wise: why shouldest thou destroy thyself? Be not over much wicked, **neither be thou foolish: why shouldest thou die before thy time?"***

THE PATH LESS TRAVELLED

Wisdom is the path less travelled in the world today. The wise man said, in Ecclesiastes 7:24-25, *"all this have I proved by wisdom: I said, I will be wise; but it was far from me. That which is far off, and exceeding deep, who can find it out? I applied mine heart to know, and to search, and to seek out wisdom, and the reason of things, and to know the wickedness of folly, even of foolishness and madness:"*

The Proverbs 31 woman *"...openeth her mouth with wisdom..."* (Proverbs 31:26), but she was a rarity. In Proverbs 31:10, the wise man asked *"who can find a virtuous woman? for her price is far above rubies."* The path of wisdom is a path less travelled, but the reason is because more follow the foolish and filibuster light instead of the constant light from the word of God (Psalm 119:130).

As the end of the age approaches, wisdom's necessity and its increased requirement will be validated more and more. It (wisdom and knowledge) are described, in Isaiah 33:6, as *"...the stability of thy times, and strength of salvation* (with) *the fear of the Lord* ...his treasure." One of the characteristics of the last days is the spirit of Elijah. In Malachi 4:5-6, he said *"...I will send you Elijah the prophet before the coming of the great and dreadful day of the Lord: And he shall turn the heart of the fathers to the children, and the heart of the children to their fathers, lest I come and smite the earth with a curse."*

Elijah, however, took the path less travelled! He was on the offensive, unlike the generality of the prophets of his day who were on the defensive and hiding in caves (1 Kings 21:20 and 18:4). For example, when he met Obadiah, the prophet was told by the King's servant that "*…as soon as I am gone from thee, that the Spirit of the Lord* shall carry thee whither I know not; and so when I come and tell Ahab, and he cannot find thee, he shall slay me: but I thy servant fear the *Lord* from my youth" (1 Kings 21:20).

Beware of being too predictable! Don't be frigid, but fluid! Avoid a filibuster light, and stop a foolish life. Elijah was spontaneous, and not stubborn to the Holy Spirit. In John 3:8, Jesus said *"the wind bloweth where it listeth, and thou hearest the sound thereof, but canst not tell whence it cometh, and whither it goeth: so is every one that is born of the Spirit."*

GOD'S WORD IS CURRENT, NOT CONVENTIONAL!

In Matthew 4:4, Jesus said *"Man shall not live by bread alone, but by every word that proceedeth out of the mouth of God."* The word *proceedeth* is the Greek word *ekporeuomai,* and it means to go forth continually. His word is current, and not dependent on the convention of the day or the community the word was preached in.

The light of God's word is not a filibuster or flustering word. Rather, it is fastidious and firm. In Hebrews 4:12, it is described as "… *quick,…powerful, and sharper than any twoedged sword, piercing even to the dividing asunder of soul and spirit, and of the joints and marrow, and is a discerner of the thoughts and intents of the heart."*

In Psalm 74:20, the Psalmist asks the believer to *"have respect unto the covenant: for the dark places of the earth are full of the habitations of cruelty."* The covenant of God is current, unchangeable, and inalienable and is the secret to ridding the earth of the dark places of cruelty. He said, in Psalm 89:34, *"my covenant will I not break, nor alter the thing that is gone out of my lips."*

A Church steeped in Mystery is a Church guaranteed militancy for mastery. The mysterious Church is what makes the devil unable to stop her. Just like it is impossible to keep the wind, water, or oil under seal, it is impossble to put the Holy Spirit in a box.

The Word of God's light is positionally based! If the light is wrongly positioned, no matter how great the quality might be, it won't manifest its potential benefits. In Philippians 2:15-16, the Church is urged to "...*be blameless and harmless, the sons of God, without rebuke, in the midst of a crooked and perverse nation, among whom ye shine as lights in the world; **Holding forth the word of life;** that I may rejoice in the day of Christ, that I have not run in vain, neither laboured in vain.*"

KENNETH HAGIN'S MOVEMENT FROM TEXAS TO OKLAHOMA

Kenneth Hagin (1917 – 2003) was an itinerant preacher with the Assemblies of God, Texas district, who after pastoring more than 12 Churches in the area, heard God ask him to move to Oklahoma to start a teaching and evangelistic ministry. He got married to Oretha Rooker in 1938 and together they had two children, Kenneth Hagin Jnr and Patricia Harrison.

In 1966, he moved to Tulsa, Oklahoma at almost 50 years of age, and took up space in an office owned by Evangelist T.L Osorne. At nearly 60 years of age, he started Rhema Bible Training Center, Tulsa, Oklahoma and over the next 25 years trained more than 25,000 Bible school students and published more than 247 books.

Today, there are more than 65 million Kenneth Hagin books in circulation, alongside international Bible training centers in fourteen different countries. The alumni have planted over 1,500 congregations worldwide, and there are still ministry programs and outreaches conducted on scheduled television, radio and print media with Kenneth Hagin's thumbprint evident on them.

Even though his evangelistic and teaching ministry spanned just the last 35 years of his ministry, he lived a full life. He was questioned repeatedly by fellow clergy when he moved from Texas (a burgeoning metropolis) to the back woods of Tulsa, Oklahoma in the 1960's, but today he has been vindicated.

His life is considered inseparable from the Word of faith movement, that brought untold wealth, revelation and influence to the Charismatic sphere of Christianity. His reach was across denominations, and at his death was acknowledged by *proteges* from around the world as the touchbearer of the Word of Faith who brought the message of faith to a generation of believers.

Prayer: Make me what you made to be, O Lord, in Jesus name!

When there is hesitancy in the pulpit,
there will be confusion in the pew

\- Dr. Jesse Duplantis
(Evangelist, Jesse Duplantis
Ministries, Destreham, La)

CHAPTER THIRTY-ONE

FRUSTRATED LIGHT

*"And this is the condemnation, that **light** is come into the world, and men loved darkness rather than light, because their deeds were evil. For every one that doeth **evil hateth the light**, neither **cometh to the light**, lest his deeds should be reproved. But he that doeth truth cometh to the light, that his deeds may be made manifest, that they are wrought in God"* (John 3:19-21).

To frustrate something is to stop a plan or attempted action from progressing, succeeding, or being fulfilled. It means leaving unused, and setting it aside as idle instead of flipping the switch. They are those apostle Paul said, *"...frustrate the grace of God..."* (Galatians 2:21) because they are not crucified with Christ and so do not live by the faith of the Son of God (Galatians 2:20).

These ones hide the light, instead of shining their light. They *"...light a candle,* (but)*...put it under a bushel,* (instead of) *on a candlestick..."* (Matthew 5:15). God's original intention for His Church was for her to be *"...the light of the world* (and) *a city that is set on an hill* (that) *cannot be hid"* (Matthew 5:14).

They were designated as cities, not a town or village, because inherent greatness lies within her. It is the light bearing Church that will *"...shine before men, that they may see your good works, and glorify your Father which is in heaven*" (Matthew 5:16). The individual who covers their light, on the other hand, will have the "*...face of the covering cast over all people, and the vail that is spread over all nations*" (Isaiah 25:7) over their lives.

The worst enemy of light is self! In Isaiah 8:19-22, the Lord asked "*...should not a people seek unto their God? for the living to the dead? To the law and to the testimony* (and) *if they speak not according to this word, it is because there is no **light** in them...And they shall look unto the earth; and behold trouble and darkness, dimness of anguish; and they shall be driven to darkness.*"

The life that seeks the way of the wicked and its wickedness, will not see His light because they are already frustrating His grace. It is what the believer lets that will be let! In 2 Thessalonians 2:7-8, the Aposte Paul states that "*...the mystery of iniquity doth already work: only he who now letteth will let, until he be taken out of the way. And then shall that Wicked be revealed, whom the Lord shall consume with the spirit of his mouth, and shall destroy with the **brightness** of his coming:*"

RECOGNIZING AND RECEIVING HIS RADIANT LIGHT

When Paul was converted on the road to Damascus, by the person of Jesus, "*they that were with him saw the light, but they heard not the voice of him that spake to him*" (Acts 22:9). Today God is asking us to go beyond just seeing to recognizing and recieving the person behind the light. In John 1:12, Apostle John states that "*as many as received him, to them gave he power to become the sons of God, even to them that believe on his name.*"

It is not enough just to know about Jesus - we must also Know him experientially, intimately and reverently. The veracity of the light is in its effect on our life as Christians and not just for us to fall down and get up unchanged. The reason for light is for it "*to shine in darkness and* (for) *the darkness not to comprehend it*" (John 1:5).

Light cannot be stopped from shining, no matter the level of darkness! The real enemy to recognizing and receiving the light, however, is the devil. In 2 Corinthians 4:4, Apostle Paul says that "*the god of this world hath blinded the minds of them which believe not lest the light of the glorious gospel of Christ, who is the image of God, should shine unto them."*

Satan does this because of the limitless potentials inherent in recognizing and receiving the light. Ephesians 1:18 tells us that if our *"eyes of understanding are enlightened* (then) *we may know the hope of his calling and the riches of the glory of his inheritance in the saints and what is the exceeding greatness of his power to us-ward who believe."* If we don`t recognize and recieve His light, however, life becomes a routine rigmarole, and a mundane manifestation that is lived without expectation or zest due to the non-recognition and non receptivity of divine light.

THE GOD OF THE MASTER BREAKTHROUGH!

The God who makes sudden breakthrough possible was visible in the Battle between Israel and the Philistines in 2 Samuel 5:20-21. It says, *"...David came to Baalperazim, and David smote them there, and said, The Lord hath broken forth upon mine enemies before me, as the breach of waters. Therefore he called the name of that place Baalperazim. And there they left their images, and David and his men burned them."*

God wants to be our Baal-Perazim or possessor of the breaches upon our enemies. The word *Baal-Perazim* is a Hebrew word that means God of the master breakthrough. It means *Lord,* or *owner, of breaches,* or *breakings forth.* "Baal" may refer to *Jehovah* and *perāzim* means the *fissures* or gullies on the mountain-side i.e. like the breach made by waters.

The scene of the victory was most likely a hill deeply scarred with water-courses. The force with which God broke through the army of the Philistines is compared with that of a torrent breaking its way through all obstacles. The situations they think you can't escape from, God will give you escape from them. The situation they thought you will never be able to avoid, God will make you overcome them. You must, however, yield totally unto the Lord and then you can overcome. It will not be because of your ability, but like David against the Philistines, it will come from the Lord!

There is one breakthrough idea, one breakthrough book, one breakthrough recipe, one breakthrough paper or one breakthrough song that will shift your life for ever. It took only one idea for William Colgate to move from pauper to prosperous. It took one song to bring Fannie Crosby who composed Blessed Assurance to fame, and it took just one sermon called *blessed from where you bleed* for T.D Jakes to come from a back of the woods preacher to a household name.

In Reinhard Bonnke's ministry, it was one miracle that *launched his ship*. He had invited a well-known South African healing Evangelist, named John Bosman, and after he excused himself on the grounds God told him to return to Pretoria, Reinhard Bonnke took the bull by the horns and preached to the teeming crowd. Before he started preaching, however, God spoke to him and said *"my word in your mouth is as powerful as My word in My mouth."*

After preaching the ABCs of the gospel, he remembers seeing a visage - that later came to characterize the presence of the Holy Spirit in his ministry – and afterwards a woman running from the back of the audience screaming *I can see, I can see*. He then laid hands on a four year old boy who was born crippled, and he miraculously got up from his hands running. Many others were healed, saved and delivered and after that Christ for All Nation's ministry of Miracles, signs and wonders was born.

ALLENBY AND THE DELIVERANCE OF JERUSALEM

General Edmund Allenby and his British troops were getting into position to apprehend Jerusalem. Allenby was known as a Christian and follower of the Bible, and is reported that the night before the invasion, he prayed that he might take the city without destroying the holy places. He had wired London for instructions and had received a scripture verse as a reply; *"As birds flying, so will the LORD of hosts defend Jerusalem; defending also he will deliver it; and passing over he will preserve it"* (Isaiah 31:5).

He was so excited about this verse that he read it aloud before all his troops that were positioned in the foothills of Jerusalem. Allenby commandeered every available aircraft for a fly-over. On the morning of December 10, what seemed like hundreds of planes skirted low over the Temple mount.

When the planes went up a cloud covering hid them so that they were not seen, only their sound was heard. Fliers were dropped that said, 'surrender immediately, you don't have a prayer.' and were signed by Allenby. What the General did not know was that the Turks believed in an old prophesy that they would never lose the Holy City until "a man of Allah came to deliver it" and the River Nile flows in Palestine.

According to reports, the signature of Allenby on the paper dropped from the sky was interpreted by them to mean the word 'Allah' in Arabic meaning 'God' and 'beh' in Arabic that means 'son'. The Turks were looking at a demand to surrender signed by Allah-beh, the son of God. Also, at that time British Military engineers had piped fresh water from River Nile to Palestine, and thus Palestine was flooded.

In response, the Turks hoisted a white flag and surrendered the city without firing a single shot. This was an incredible fulfillment of Biblical prophesy which put Israel under British mandate. This mandate, called the Balfour Declaration, called for a Jewish homeland and set the foundation for modern Israel. Jerusalem had been under Muslim control for centuries.

After the Turks surrender, General Allenby mounted off of his white horse as he entered Jerusalem through the Jaffa Gate because he knew from the bible that only the Messiah will enter the city on a white horse. The lesson from General Allenby is the power of following divine wisdom, no matter how unconventional if one wants not to frustrate the grace of God.

Prayer: Lord deliver me from everything not planted by God in my life, in Jesus name!

If Jesus is Ahead,
He can Handle what is Behind!

- TOBE MOMAH M.D.

CHAPTER THIRTY-TWO

FUTURISTIC LIGHT

*"Say not thou, what is the cause that the former days were better than these? for thou dost not enquire wisely concerning this. Wisdom is good with an inheritance: and by it there is profit to them that **see the sun**"* (Eccl 7:10-11).

The kingdom of God does not come by observation, but by revelation. What you see today determines what you manifest tomorrow! Too many stay in observation mode, and miss their manifestation as a result. In Luke 17:20-21, the Bible says *"...the kingdom of God cometh not with observation. Neither shall they say, Lo here! or, lo there! for, behold, the kingdom of God is within you."*

God gives the vision, and that is the race set before you. All you have got to do is run that race and as you do what God's called you to do, and don't get bogged down in the details in between, God will make a way for you. In Hebrews 12:1-2, He said *"...seeing we also are compassed about with so great a cloud of witnesses, let us lay aside every weight, and the sin which doth so easily beset us, and let us run with patience the race that is set before us, looking unto Jesus the author and finisher of our faith;...."*

What paralyses many from running their race is futuristic quest for understanding. They want to know every detail before they commence their journey, but that is unbiblical. In Mark 4:26-29, Jesus told his disciples "...*so is the kingdom of God, as if a man should cast seed into the ground; And should sleep, and rise night and day, and the seed should spring and grow up, he knoweth not how. For the earth bringeth forth fruit of herself; first the blade, then the ear, after that the full corn in the ear. But when the fruit is brought forth, immediately he putteth in the sickle, because the harvest is come.*"

Many don't go to bed, in the first place, because they want to know how the seed grows, comes up and becomes a plant. You don't need to know all the details; you just need to know the next step. In Matthew 6:34, Jesus told his disciples to "t*ake therefore no thought for the morrow: for the morrow shall take thought for the things of itself. Sufficient unto the day is the evil thereof.*" This attitude, however, was the product of the single-eyed life spoken of by Jesus in Matthew 6:22. It says, "*the light of the body is the eye: if therefore thine eye be single, thy whole body shall be full of light.*"

Discover your Light; Deliver your Life

Too many have broad visions, but they get bogged down in the minute details along the way. You don't, however, need to know the details to obey God. When God called Saul in Acts 9:15-16, he told Ananias "...*he is a chosen vessel unto me, to bear my name before the Gentiles, and kings, and the children of Israel: For I will shew him how great things he must suffer for my name's sake.*"

Paul, who was formerly Saul, later witnessed of his suffering saying "*God, who commanded the **light** to shine out of darkness, hath **shined** in our hearts, to give the **light** of the knowledge of the glory of God in the face of Jesus Christ but we have this treasure in earthen vessels, that the excellency of the power may be of God, and not of us (and though)... troubled on every side,...not distressed,...perplexed, but not in despair, ... persecuted, but not forsaken, cast down, but not destroyed; always bearing* *about in the body the dying of the Lord Jesus, that the life also of Jesus might be made manifest in our body"* (2 Cor 4:6-10).

If Paul had been told about the future *"...afflictions,... necessities,...distresses, ...stripes, ...imprisonments, ...tumults, ...labors, ...watchings, ...fastings"* (2 Corinthians 6:4-5), he may never have stepped out in faith to preach the gospel. He was given enough light for the next step, and as he took it his path got brighter and brighter.

When Jesus told Peter to come and walk on the water in Matthew 14:28, he could have argued about his lack of understanding of the principles of floatation but he did not. He eventually walked on water (Matthew 14:29), and left the skeptics, doubters and overly inquisitive in the boat. Faith requires standing on what you can't see, and holding what you can't touch (Hebrews 11:1)!

THE VISION WILL SPEAK

The prophet Habakkuk said, in Hab 2:2-3, *"write the vision, and make it plain upon tables, that he may run that readeth it. For the vision is yet for an appointed time, but at the end it shall speak, and not lie: though it tarry, wait for it; because it will surely come, it will not tarry."*

Some forsake their future brightness because they want to know the futuristic light ahead of time. The vision will speak, because Jesus *"...hath done all things well"* (Mark 7:37). The more you look for things that don't concern you, the more likely you will derail from the plan of God for your life.

In Ecclesiastes 7:10, the wise man said unnecessary introspection about the whys, what, and how are not a wise use of one's time! That is why Jesus, when asked about the man born blind in John 9, did not bother about the cause or source of the man's blindness but instead declared that *"as long as I am in the world, I am the light of the world"* (John 9:5). Those who don't beleaguer themselves with questions about providence and progeny shine as lights in the world for they *"...must work the works of him that sent me, while it is day: (for) the night cometh, when no man can work"* (John 9:4).

The Holy Spirit is able to lead you in the right direction, if you trust in the light He gives today and not looking for some futuristic light. For example, after Delilah betrayed Samson into the hands of the Philistines, he got blinded by them (see Judges 16:21) and had a young child lead him to two pillars that upheld the building. In his darkness, he turned to a young lad – who can be considered a representation of the Holy Spirit – and by following him step by step, slew more Philistines in his death than all his twenty years as judge of Israel live (see Judges 16:30). Those who dedicate themselves to God's ways and wisdom, instead of decoding the past and analyzing the future, will see and reflect the sun in its brightness (Eccl 7:10-11).

Born for a Time Such as This!

In 1971, Rev. Burke was pastoring an Assembly of God Church in Oklahoma, USA when God spoke to him about going on a mission trip to Nigeria. He had never been outside the USA, and he decided to share his vision with the ministry leaders. Aside the fact that Nigeria was just coming out of a Civil war, that had decimated the country economically and numerically, the leadership felt it was too risky and refused to sanction Rev. Burke's trip.

His wife remembers her husband bucking the leadership, and self-funding his trip to Nigeria without due authorization from the Assembly of God leaders. She recalls him flying out of the USA through New York, with just enough to get him to Nigeria and back. She was a young mother and school teacher, and for six weeks she waited to hear from him but to no avail.

She did not have any contact numbers or addresses in Nigeria, and instead decided to send a letter with some financial support to his last known abode in New York. She states that the telegram arrived New York just in time for him to get it, and facilitate Rev. Burke's trip back to Oklahoma.

Apparently, he had had a very eventful trip with outbreaks of revival meetings in Lagos keeping him in Nigeria longer than he had initially proposed. He developed life-long ministry acquaintances, and returned several more times to Nigeria as a guest minister to several Churches. He saw "...*the fields* (as)...*white already to harvest*" (John 4:35) and himself born for a time like that.

Prayer: May my urgency to preach the gospel overtake my understanding, in Jesus name!

I will rather die trusting
God, than live in unbelief

\- SMITH WIGGLESWORTH
(1859 – 1947)

CHAPTER THIRTY-THREE

FAINTING LIGHT

*"Let their eyes be **darkened**, that they see not; and make their loins continually to shake"* (Psalm 69:23).

The light that faints is a limiting light. It impairs vision, and limits speed. In Psalm 38:10, the Psalmist describes these fainting lights even further. He said *"my heart panteth, my strength faileth me* (and) *as for the light of mine eyes, it also is gone from me."* It is not the will of God for a believers lights to faint, but rather for it to increase from stregth to strength.

The wise man, in Proverbs 4:18, describes the pattern for the believer's light. He said, *"...the path of the just is as the shining light, that shineth more and more unto the perfect day. The way of the wicked is as darkness: they know not at what they stumble"* (Proverbs 4:18-19). Lack of faith or weakness in trust of God is the root cause of the fainting lights so pervlent in today's Church.

Apostle Paul advises the Church, in Thessalonica, that you*"... are not in darkness, that that day should overtake you as a thief. Ye are all the **children of light**, and the children of the day: we are not of the night, nor of darkness. Therefore let us not sleep, as do others; but let us watch and be sober. For they that sleep sleep in the night; and they that be drunken are drunken in the night. But let us, who are of the day, be sober, putting on* *the breastplate of **faith** and **love**; and for an helmet, the hope of salvation"* (1 Thessalonians 5:4-8). .

Where ever Faith and love are present light is available, but where they are absent there is faintness! In Psalm 69:23, the Psalmist describes an unstable believer whose loins or mind were repeatedly shaken or manipulated. It says, *"let their eyes be darkened, that they see not; and make their loins continually to shake."*

END OF ELI, AND SAMUEL AT SHILOH

While the whole nation of Israel *"...from Dan even to Beersheba knew that Samuel was established to be a prophet of the Lord* (as) *the Lord appeared again in Shiloh* (and)...*revealed himself to Samuel in Shiloh by the word of the Lord"* (1 Samuel 3:19-21), the eyes of the High Priest, Eli, were dimming.

In 1 Samuel 3:1-3, the Bible says *"...the child Samuel ministered unto the Lord before Eli. And the word of the Lord was precious in those days* (for) *there was no open vision. And it came to pass at that time, when Eli was laid down in his place, and his **eyes began to wax dim**, that he could not see; And ere the lamp of God went out in the temple of the Lord...."*

While the vision was getting sharper for Samuel, in Shiloh, it was diminishing at the same location for Eli. The reason was not location, age, or time in ministry but Eli's faintness of heart. In 1 Samuel 2:29, the prophet asked Eli why *"...kick ye at my sacrifice and at mine offering, which I have commanded in my habitation; and honourest thy sons above me, to make yourselves fat with the chiefest of all the offerings of Israel my people?"*

The eventual outcome was the sudden death of Eli, his two sons, and a daughter in law following a loss in a battle with the Philistines (1 Samuel 4:1-10). He (Eli) lost strength because he stopped listening to God (1 Samuel 2:29), and tried to placate his incestuous sons instead of pruning them from their offices.

In Psalm 80:17-19, the Psalmist prayed saying *"let thy hand be upon the man of thy right hand, upon the son of man whom thou madest* *strong for thyself. So will not we go back from thee: quicken us, and we will call upon thy name. Turn us again, O Lord God of hosts, cause thy face to **shine**; and we shall be saved."* Where God's hand is strong, His face shines but where His face is covered, clarity and courage are nullified.

THE DAYSTAR THAT DESTROYS DARKNESS!

The kind of light the Christian is expected to shine forth is akin to the Daystar. It is the kind of light that heralds a new day, and represents a bright dawn. In 2 Peter 1:17-19, apostle Peter says *"we have also a more sure word of prophecy; whereunto ye do well that ye take heed, as unto a light that shineth in a dark place, until the day dawn, and the day star arise in your hearts."*

The root cause to the Daystar's brightness was confidence in the more sure word of prophecy. Instead of fainting lights, the Daystar is a light-bringing, morning star-like representation of a bright dawn. In Psalm 84:11-12, the Psalmist declared that *"...the Lord God is a sun and shield: the Lord will give grace and glory: no good thing will he withhold from them that walk uprightly. O Lord of hosts, blessed is the man that trusteth in thee."*

Where ever there is trust in God, or strength in God, there will be a shining forth from like the Sun. In Luke 1:78-79, another evidence of the power of the daystar to destroy darkness is re-emphasized. It says, *"through the tender mercy of our God; whereby the dayspring from on high hath visited us, to give light to them that sit in darkness and in the shadow of death, to guide our feet into the way of peace."*

The word, *Dayspring*, is interpreted from the original Greek word *anatello*, and it means *a rising of light*. Strength is the stabilizer for insight and without it darkness is relentless. In John 12:35-36, the Bible says *"...a little while is the light with you. Walk while ye have the light, lest darkness come upon you: for he that walketh in darkness knoweth not whither he goeth. While ye have light, believe in the light, that ye may be the children of light."*

In Isaiah *50:10-11*, the prophet Isaiah gives a strategy for shining, and demolition of darkness. He said, *"who is among you that feareth the Lord, that obeyeth the voice of his servant, that walketh in darkness, and hath no light? let him trust in the name of the Lord, and stay upon his God."*

There is a tool darkness cannot resist and that is trust, faith or strength in God. Until the hand of God is upon you, with the strengthening of the Holy Spirit, light is foolhardy and prayer is brittle. Revival in prayer is hinged on light but it starts with strengthening. Until you are rooted, your glory can't be released. In Isaiah 27:6, the prophet Isaiah said *"He shall cause them that come of Jacob to take root: Israel shall blossom and bud, and fill the face of the world with fruit."*

UMA UKPAI: THE MIRACLES THAT HEALED HIS CRIPPLED CHILDREN

Dr. Uma Ukpai is a foremost evangelist in Nigeria, who has been pivotal to the spread of the gospel in that country. A USA-trained Bible scholar, he returned home in 1974 and launched the Uma Ukpai Evangelistic Association (UUEA). The Association has a weekly program themed Thank God it is Wednesday, that brings thousands to their headquarters in Uyo, Nigeria.

He has preached all over the world, as well as mentored several ministers of the gospel. His million-man crusades have witnessed signs and wonders, and he has facilitated the development of the Uma Ukpai Polytechnic, Uma Ukpai University, and Schools of business and theology in Ohafia and Uyo, Nigeria respectively.

In the beginning, though, he was faced with certain obstacles. He tells the story repeatedly of how his first son was born crippled, and while at a hospital waiting the birth of his second child, a nurse chided him. She said, *"Is that your son still crippled? If God can heal, why does He not start from your own house?"* That statement provoked a holy hatred and an anointed anger that birthed a righteous rebellion in Uma Ukpai against the sickness in his son's life.

He told the nurse, *"because of your basket mouth, that boy will walk today!"* He went home and raised song after song to the Lord. Then God answered him mightily. His son miraculously got out of bed and started walking, dancing, and praising God with his father. He also told his father that while he was slain in the spirit, angels were operating on him and he can now walk, jump and leap without assistance or pain. On arrival at the hospital, Uma showed the nurse and his now post-partum wife their son as he walked unaided.

On another occasion, his oldest daughter was born crippled. He challenged God to do what He had done with his son. God told him He would heal her during the Miracle Convention Crusade at the end of the year. At the outset of the miracle crusade, he called his daughter forth and declared God's word over her. She fell down and slept for a few hours. When she woke up, she had been totally healed.

Today, Dr. Uma Ukpai counts more than a hundred individuals from USA to Africa who have been healed from paralysis under his ministry. He always attributes it to God's goodness. He challenges believers to stand on God's word no matter how vilified or derogatory the world gets concerning our faith in Jesus Christ.

Prayer: Dark veils covering my glory, catch fire in Jesus name!

Those who Flow Glow!

- TOBE MOMAH M.D.

CHAPTER THIRTY-FOUR

FLOWLESS LIGHT

*"And the Gentiles shall come to thy light, and kings to the brightness of thy rising....Then thou shalt see, and **flow** together, and thine heart shall fear, and be enlarged; because the abundance of the sea shall be converted unto thee, the forces of the Gentiles shall come unto thee"* (Isaiah 60:3-5).

The static Church is a stagnant Church. A wise man once said that if you fish out of a bath tub every week, you will only catch the same fish. The only way to change the static is to spread your wings and fly on the everlasting arms of the Father. In Deuteronomy 33:26-28, Moses said *"there is none like unto the God of Jeshurun, who rideth upon the heaven in thy help, and in his excellency on the sky. The eternal God is thy refuge, and underneath are the everlasting arms: and he shall thrust out the enemy from before thee; and shall say, Destroy them. Israel then shall dwell in safety alone:....."*

The prophet Jeremiah challenged the Moabites to stop *"being at ease from youth and* (not) *settle on their lees* (lest)*...He* (God) *send unto him* (Moab) *wanderers that shall cause him to wander and empty his vessels"* (Jeremiah 48:10-11). The worst wanderers and the emptiest entertainers are those who refuse to adapt to change. *Getting off the lees* is an archaic Bible phrase meaning to shake off the dregs they have settled into and keep moving by the power of the Holy Spirit.

In Romans 8:14-15, Paul says, "*as many as are led by the Spirit of God, they are the sons of God for ye have not received the spirit of bondage again to fear but have received the Spirit of adoption whereby we cry Abba Father.*" Those who walk in bondage to fear have not allowed the dynamism of the Holy Spirit in their lives but have continued in business as usual. **Routine is not righteousness and habit is not holiness.** It is not right because you have always done it that way but because God says so!

THE LIGHT INSIDE THE BUSHEL

The last days' learning curve is a steep learning curve for some in the Church. There will be those in the Church who are "*ever learning and never able to come to the knowledge of the truth*" (2 Timothy 3:7) because they are "*...reprobate concerning the faith*" (2 Timothy 3:8).

These ones do not shine because their foundation in faith is skewed. Until you stand on the mountain top, in faith, your light is non directional and of no benefit to the nation. In Matthew 5:14-16, Jesus said "*ye are the light of the world* (and) *a city that is set on an hill* (that) *cannot be hid. Neither do men light a candle and put it under a bushel but on a candlestick* (to) *give light unto all that are in the house*"

In Psalm 147:19-20, the Psalmist adds that "*He showed His word unto Jacob* (and) *His statutes and his judgments unto Israel* (for)...*they have not known them.*" He shows His word to the believer, not to hide it (or put it under a bushel), but to declare it to the unknowing congregation. *There must be a flow from His Spirit for there to be His glow in your life!*

The Hebrew word for *flow*, as used in Isaiah 60:5, is the Hebrew word *Nahar* which means to *sparkle*, be *cheerful*, or be *lightened*. It says, "*then thou shalt see, and flow together, and thine heart shall fear, and be enlarged; because the abundance of the sea shall be converted unto thee, the forces of the Gentiles shall come unto thee.*"

Too many start and stop, and as a result, miss out on His light in their lives. **The false light of flow less ness has stifled the sparkle in many Christian's lives.** It is like a pinhole camera, whose radiation is determined or dependent on the consistent flow of light through its apertures. In Rev 3:15-16, God warns the Church in Laodecia saying *"I know thy works, that thou art neither cold nor hot: I would thou wert cold or hot. So then because thou art lukewarm, and neither cold nor hot, I will spue thee out of my mouth."*

GRACE FOR GRACE

Every believer receives the same amount of grace Jesus operated on the earth with. In John 1:14-17, John the Baptist said *"...He of whom I spake,...that cometh after me is preferred before me for he was before me. And of His fullness have all we received, and grace for grace. For the law was given by Moses, but grace and truth came by Jesus...."*

The consistency in receiving will determine the grace available to the individual. While God has made available *"...all His fullness..."* (John 1:16) to the believer, many shutter what they receive from the Father based on their theology. For example, some believe in salvation but can't accept prosperity from God. Some receive forgiveness from God, but forfeit healing because of their religious mindset.

When Jesus was here on earth, he told the Pharisees and scribes, that they *"make the word of God of none effect through...tradition..."* (Mark 7:13). God wants His fullness released, with the equivalent grace upon one's life, but it takes a people who are receptive to manifest His grace. Without a receiving of His fullness, otherwise termed a flow, there will be no manifestation of His grace in that person's life.

God has called the Church to ever increased shining light, and not a staccato kind of shining light. In Proverbs 4:18, the Bible says *"...the path of the just is as the shining light, that shineth more and more unto the perfect day."* The Lord is not a respecter of persons (see Acts 10:34; Romans 2:11; Ephesians 6:9 and 1 Peter 1:17), but *"...in every nation he that feareth him, and worketh righteousness, is accepted with him"* (Acts 10:35).

THE MISTAKE OF MALAWIANS

Pastor Shane Warren is an avid traveler. On one of his numerous flights to Malawi, he happened to sit next to a Food and Agricultural Organization (FAO) officer. He asked the officer why there was so much famine in Malawi. The FAO officer's reply startled Pastor Shane, and formed one of his sermons to his congregation on his return.

The FAO officer told Pastor Shane that the problem was that the *Malawians ate their seeds!* He stated that the FAO supplies more than enough seedlings to Malawi to come out of famine, but rather than plant their seedlings and wait for the harvest, they ate their seedlings.

In Genesis 8:22, the Bible says, *"while the earth remaineth, seedtime and harvest, and cold and heat, and summer and winter, and day and night shall not cease."* There is something called time between seed and harvest, and when there is lack of consistency in sowing, there will be an absence of divine surplus.

Prayer: Powers assigned to stop my light from shining, die in the name of Jesus.

Fear tolerated is Faith contaminated!

- KENNETH COPELAND
EVANGELIST/TEACHER TEXAS, USA

CHAPTER THIRTY-FIVE

FRIGHTENED LIGHT

"The people that walked in darkness have seen a great **light:** *they that dwell in the land of the shadow of death, upon them hath the light* **shined"** (Isaiah 9:2).

When there is fear in the land, dimness and danger pervades the land. In Isaiah 59:7-10, the Lord said *"their feet run to evil, and they make haste to shed innocent blood: their thoughts are thoughts of iniquity; wasting and destruction are in their paths. The way of peace they know not; and there is no judgment in their goings: they have made them crooked paths: whosoever goeth therein shall not know peace. Therefore is judgment far from us, neither doth justice overtake us: we* **wait for light,** *but behold obscurity; for brightness, but we* **walk in darkness.** *We grope for the wall like the blind, and we grope as if we had no eyes: we stumble at noon day as in the night; we are in desolate places as dead me."*

It does not matter how long you wait for light, if there is fear pervading your existence that light will only turn to darkness. In 1 John 4:17-18, Apostle John said *"herein is our love made perfect, that we may have boldness in the day of judgment: because as he is, so are we in this world. There is no fear in love; but perfect love casteth out fear: because fear hath torment. He that feareth is not made perfect in love."*

The word used for *torment* in *fear hath torment* in 1 John 4:18 is the Greek word *Kolasis,* and it means to curtail, limit, restrain, or make someone a dwarf. The root cause why many will not have boldness on the day of judgement, when they stand before his inapproachable light (1 Timothy 6:16), is because their light has been dimmed and dwarfed by fear.

Rather than approach God amidst a frightened light, on the day of judgement, God expects those "...*that feareth the Lord, (and) that obeyeth the voice of his servant, that walketh in darkness, and hath no light* (to)...*trust in the name of the Lord, and stay upon his God*...(and) **walk in the light of your fire,** *and in the sparks that ye have kindled*" (Isaiah 50:10-11).

Those believers who fear God, insead of man, and trust and stay upon Him will God turn their darkness into light and give them a light to walk in! In Isaiah 8:17-22, the children of Israel were been asked to turn their allegiance from God to belial out of fear. In utter disregard to that ideology, the prophet said "...*I will wait upon the Lord, that hideth his face from the house of Jacob, and I will* **look** *for him. Behold, I and the children whom the Lord* hath given me are for signs and for wonders in Israel from the *Lord* of hosts, which dwelleth in mount Zion. *And when they shall say unto you, Seek unto them that have familiar spirits, and unto wizards that peep, and that mutter: should not a people seek unto their God? for the living to the dead? To the law and to the testimony: if they speak not according to this word, it is because there is* **no light** *in them.... And they shall look unto the earth; and behold trouble and darkness, dimness of anguish; and they shall be driven to darkness*" (Isaiah 8:17-22).

JOB: FROM FRIGHT TO LIGHT

The one mistake in Job's life and ministry was fear. A great man, who invested in God, his community and his family, he built a financial empire that was unprecedented. Job, however, lost it all due to fright! He told all that cared to listen *"For the thing which I greatly feared is come upon me, and that which I was afraid of is come unto me"* (Job 4:23).

He stayed paranoid, and remained plundered but in Job 42:5-6 he said *"I have heard of thee by the hearing of the ear: but now mine eye seeth thee. therefore I abhor myself, and repent in dust and ashes."* The fright blinded his light, and until he overcame his fear of the unknown God he could not turn his captivity. As soon as Job saw light, however, his life turned right!

In Job 42:10-13, the Bible said *"...the Lord turned the captivity of Job, when he prayed for his friends: also the Lord gave Job twice as much as he had before. Then came there unto him all his brethren, and all his sisters, and all they that had been of his acquaintance before, and did eat bread with him in his house: and they bemoaned him, and comforted him over all the evil that the Lord had brought upon him: every man also gave him a piece of money, and every one an earring of gold. So the Lord blessed the latter end of Job more than his beginning: for he had fourteen thousand sheep, and six thousand camels, and a thousand yoke of oxen, and a thousand she asses. He had also seven sons and three daughters."*

When light comes, your destiny helpers emerge! You know you are loved and accepted, not rejected and hated, according to the word and favor of God that smiles upon you. The aftermath of Job's turmoil was greater glory. In James 5:11, the apostle James said *"we count them happy which endure. Ye have heard of the patience of Job, and have seen the end of the Lord; that the Lord is very pitiful, and of tender mercy."*

FEAR NOT; ONLY BELIEVE!

In Luke 8, Jesus was heading to the home of Jairus (a ruler of the Jewish Synagogue) when he was intercepted by the woman with the issue of blood in Luke 8:43-48. In the pandemonium that ensued, someone walked up to the centurion and told him *"...thy daughter is dead; trouble not the Master"* (Luke 8:49).

Rather than resign himself to fate, and accept the status quo, Jesus told Jairus *"...Fear not: believe only, and she shall be made whole...."* (Luke 8:50). Jesus knew that the only panacea to the principalities troubling Jairus daughter was for her father to believe. But until He stopped fear, he could not believe as his light would be impeded.

This analogy is re-iterated in Jesus commandment to Martha. In John 11:40, Jesus said to her *"…if thou wouldest believe, thou shouldest see the glory of God?"* It takes believing for light to shine upon an individual, but first fear must be abrogated not aggravated!

Eventually, Jesus reached Jairus's home, and though jeered, mocked and ridiculed by those in his home (Luke 8:53), *"…He put them all out, and took her by the hand, and called, saying, Maid, arise. And her spirit came again, and she arose straightway: and he commanded to give her meat. And her parents were astonished:…"* (Luke 9:54-56).

No man epitomizes failure from frightened light like King Saul. Chosen as King by Samuel, under God's direction (1 Samuel 10:20-25), he was offered a path out of endemic ignominy (1 Samuel 9:21) but failed because of the fear of man. In 1 Samuel 15:24-28, he lost the Kingship of Israel because of fear saying to prophet Samuel, who had accosted him for sparing King Agag, that he did it because *"he feared the people and obeyed their voice"* (1 Samuel 15:24).

The Bible says in Proverbs 29:25 that, *"the fear of man brings a snare…."* Because King Saul feared the people he became ensnared in battles he should not have fought and wars he should never have started. In Psalm 27:1, the Psalmist declares *"the Lord is my light and my salvation; whom shall I fear? the Lord is the strength of my life; of whom shall I be afraid?"* Until you rid yourself of the fear of man, you cannot attain and percieve the true light from God.

FINDING A JOB IN NEW YORK

In 2005, I arrived New York City after working as a missionary doctor in Gimbie, Ethiopia. I had volunteered at the Adventist health hospital in Western Wellagoa, Ethiopia for six months, and wanted to start my post-graduate residency training in the USA. I was, however, given no chance at employment in the American health care system by my peers and family. I had no clinical experience in America, had average scores on my entrance exams and was – in their view - just not connected enough.

I was called over adventurous, stubborn and proud by friends and family and asked to return to London, United Kingdom and get my career off the ground again. I had, however, heard God's voice in September 2003 telling me to re-locate to New York City. He had said, *re-locate to New York City, and set up the base of your ministry there.* He had sent me to New York City, and while traveling to and fro different volunteer positions at the Long Island Jewish hospital, New Hyde Park, Cornell New York Presbyterian Hospital Manhattan, and Afam Comprehensive clinic, Brooklyn God kept re-assuring me that He, who sent me to New York, would complete it by finding me a job.

I was living with my Aunt and Uncle in Long Island, New York, while my wife was in Ethiopia initially, and then later with my parents in Nigeria. I was not earning any income, and was reprimanded on several fronts by family and friends for abandoning my family. Within a few months of arriving New York, however, I was offered a surgical residency position and my access to becoming an attending/consultant in the American medical system began.

I had opportunities to have my perspective skewed by the *frightened light* others were throwing at me, but the constant re-iteration by God of His purpose for me gave me proper perspective. I followed God to Ethiopia, and He showed up for me in New York! Apparently, the Chancellor of Loma Linda Univesity, Dr. Richard Hart, who had signed my recommendation letter for residency application had trained the surgeon who offered me a position at the Brooklyn hospital center named Stephen Carryl. He was a student at Loma Linda, and had risen to become the Chair of General Surgery at the Brooklyn hospital I had applied to.

I had been introduced to him, by his altruistic secretary, and after I left he told her to call me back for a meeting at about 6pm. I worked into his office that evening, and he made an offer of a position as a non designated preliminary General surgery resident to me. He told me, *go home and get your wife and I will see you on July 1st, 2005.* I went back to Nigeria, applied for my wife and I's work permit at the American embassy in Lagos and within days my wife and I were in the United States and living in our apartment in Brooklyn with both of us working and earning a decent income. One step of faith initiated by God, in London, made what today's sucess story possible!

Prayer: Shadow of death assigned against my star expire, in the name of Jesus!

PART VI

Leveraging the Light

- Jesus
- Just
- Joy
- Justice
- Just Because God Said So
- Jury
- Jolt

Until you are rooted,
you can't be released!

- Tobe Momah M.D.

CHAPTER THIRTY-SIX

JESUS

"Then spake Jesus again unto them, saying, I am the light of the world: he that followeth me shall not walk in darkness, but shall have the light of life" (John 8:12).

To leverage is the ability to influence a system, or an environment, in a way that multiplies the outcome of one's effort without a corresponding increase in the consumption of resources. In other words, leveraging is the advantageous condition of having a relatively small amount of cost yield a relatively high level of returns.

Jesus is the Church's Number one leverage. Without Him, we can do nothing (John 15:5), and through Him, we can do all things (Philippians 4:13). He is *"...the light of the world* (who gives them) *that follow* (Him)*...the light of life"* (John 8:12), and *"...of his fulness have all we received,...grace for grace"* (John 1:16).

In the world we live in, with daily increasing darkness in spite of the Church's light, the children of God must lean on *"...the light of the world..."* (John 8:12) and not themselves to dispel the darkness. As long as believers carry His light, which is assertive and initiating, no devil can stop or stagnate them.

That is why He (Jesus) is called *"...the true Light, which lighteth every man that cometh into the world"* (John 1:9) and when that *"... light shineth in darkness;...the darkness comprehended it not"* (John 1:5).

There is a kind of light that when you live by it, your journey is not all toil and gruesome turmoil.

Rather, your journey through life is lighter and without struggle. That is the reason, in Simon's testimony of Him, in Luke 2:31-32 he said "...*thou* (God) *hast prepared before the face of all people; A light to lighten the Gentiles, and the glory of thy people Israel.*"

YOU CAN'T SEE TILL YOU GET INTO SILOAM!

In John 9:1-5, Jesus encountered the man at the pool of Siloam. The apostle John states that "...*as Jesus passed by, he saw a man which was blind from his birth. And his disciples asked him, saying, Master, who did sin, this man, or his parents, that he was born blind? Jesus answered, Neither hath this man sinned, nor his parents: but that the works of God should be made manifest in him. I must work the works of him that sent me, while it is day: the night cometh, when no man can work. As long as I am in the world, I am the light of the world.*"

The word *seeing* as used in John 9:7b, where Jesus said to him *Go, wash in the pool of Siloam, (which is by interpretation, Sent.) He went his way therefore, and washed, and came **seeing*** is interpreted from the original Greek as *something physical with spiritual results.* The power of His word brings you liberty (John 8:31-35), and that liberty births unprecedented light for your next level. **Embrace liberty, and experience light!**

Rather than liturgy, Jesus was a giver of life. Instead of theological debates and sociological discourses, Jesus was consumed with "... *do*(ing) *the will of him that sent me, and to finish his work*" (John 4:34). Consumed with the desire to bring sight to this perennially blind individual, Jesus "...*spat on the ground, and made clay of the spittle, and...anointed the eyes of the blind man with the clay, and said unto him, Go, wash in the pool of Siloam (which is by interpretation, Sent)* ...", (John 9:6-7).

The word Siloam is from the Original Greek word *apostelenos* and it means to be *set at liberty*! Jesus was telling this individual who was born blind that until you are set at liberty, you can't really see.

Every thing else would be a camouflage, or temporary relief but when you taste true liberty for yourself, you will experience insight, revelation and light that no devil can take away.

The pool Siloam had a precarious set of stairs that travelled hundreds of miles down a 250 feet pool, and for a blind male these could be nervy to navigate. Liberty is, however, worth obtaining as long as it comes from Jesus instruction. The blind man, eventually, "...*went his way therefore, and washed, and came seeing*" (John 9:7).

The Bible says, in 2 Corinthians 3:17-18, that "...*the Lord is that Spirit: and where the Spirit of the Lord is, there is liberty. But we all, with open face beholding as in a glass the glory of the Lord, are changed into the same image from glory to glory, even as by the Spirit of the Lord.*" The Spirit of liberty gives a change in the degree of light available!

THE POWER IN THE BLOOD OF JESUS

Don't take the blood of Jesus for granted. It is not some old wives tale or fable but the most potent force on the earth today. People blurt out *the blood of Jesus* or *I plead the blood* at the slightest infringement of their solitude. But it is not a label or a lip balm to assuage some frayed nerves, but a potent destroyer of devils.

Acording to Hebrews 2:14-15, "*forasmuch then as the children are partakers of flesh and blood, he also himself likewise took part of the same; that through death he might destroy him that had the power of death, that is, the devil; and deliver them who through fear of death were all their lifetime subject to bondage.*"

The blood of Jesus destroys devils! It is a deliberate tool in God's armamentarium and one He would like the Church to deploy more. In 1 John 3:8, the Bible says "*For this purpose the Son of God was manifested, that he might destroy the works of the devil*"and in Rev 12:11, adds that "...*they overcame him by the blood of the Lamb, and by the word of their testimony; and they loved not their lives unto the death.*"

It is a supernatural tonic that opens eyes, quickens bodies, and stimulates understanding. In Hebrews 10:19-22, the Bible says "*having therefore, brethren, boldness to enter into the holiest by the blood of*

Jesus, by a new and living way, which he hath consecrated for us, through the veil, that is to say, his flesh; And having an high priest over the house of God; Let us draw near with a true heart in full assurance of faith...."

Where ever the blood and body of Jesus is available, a new and living way will be made accessible! The death of Jesus created access for those in the holy place and outer court to enter the Holy of holies (see Matthew 27:51). It (the blood of Jesus) gives revelation so that you can see more than you had seen before. You don't get the leveraging light until you partake in the blood of Jesus. After Jesus resurrection, He appeared to two disciples on the road Emmaus and after exhaustively outlining scriptures and illustrating the Word of God, He "*...took bread, and blessed it, and brake, and gave to them. And their eyes were opened, and they knew him;...*" (Luke 24:30-31).

It took the breaking of bread for them to know him. Light is far from those who ignore the blood of Jesus. According to Apostle Paul, "*...Christ...suffer*(ed),*...that he should be the first that should rise from the dead, and **should shew light** unto the people, and to the Gentiles*" (Acts 26:23). It **is in His suffering that we see our shining** for "*... if we walk in the light, as he is in the light, we have fellowship one with another, and the blood of Jesus Christ his Son cleanseth us from all sin*" (1 John 1:7).

GODWIN EWU AND THE GOD OF EXCEEDING GRACE!

Godwin Ewu is today An associate professor of Community Medicine at the University of Abuja Medical school. A frontline fighter in the battle against COVID-19 in Nigeria, he was also the erstwhile Head of TB/DOTS clinic of University of Abuja Teaching Hospital, Gwagwalada. He, in tandem with the current pandemic, has sucessfully faced similar earth shaking trials headlong and succeeded.

In 1994, he was dismissed from the University of Nigeria College of Medicine with little hope of ever re-starting his studies. He had been an ardent Christian, and participated actively in the Christian Union Campus fellowship and the Christian Medical and Dental association (CMDA) which was then called NCCMDS.

Unfortunately, he was unsuccessful at the 2nd MB exam, and like several others in his third year medical school class was asked to withdraw. He, rather than give up his dream, decided to apply to the University of Jos in North central Nigeria. He was accepted, and rose through the ranks to become President of the local and national chapter of CMDA Nigeria.

He finished in record tme, and started a fellowship in Community medicine buoyed by his interest in Community Medicine. He finished, again in record time, and was accepted as a faculty at the department of Community Medicine University of Abuja Teaching Hospital, Gwagwalada, Nigeria.

Today, while his colleagues are beleaguered by a change in tides and alternative career paths, Godwin has carved a nitch for himself as the man to beat in combating COVID-19 in Abuja. His success rates at the Gwagwalada isolation center has earned him pluses, with paundits amazed at how he picked himself up from such a life shattering moment.

He attributes it all to Jesus, however, and states that he is who he is because of the Grace of God. He currently serves as the national Missions director for the Nigerian CMDA, and is an active part of his local Church.He is happily married, and blessed with adorable children. Truly, the *"the lines are fallen unto* (him) *in pleasant places;* (and so he)...*has a goodly heritage"* (Psalm 16:6).

Prayer: Hidden darkness, jump out of my life, in Jesus name!

If you don't have Character,
you will become a Character!

\- D.K Olukoya
Mountain of Fire and
Miracles mInistries

CHAPTER THIRTY-SEVEN

JUST

*"The path of the **just** is as the **shining light**, that shineth more and more unto the perfect day"* (Proverbs 4:18).

Many want the ever increasing light, elucidated by the wise man in Proverbs 4:18, but fail in the area of character. The word translated *just* in Proverbs 4:18 is from the Hebrew word *tsaddiq* and it means to be righteous, innocent, and blameless.

Those who must leverage their light, and manifest an Assertive Initiative lifestyle, are those who have a character building testimony. These ones are not fiddling believers, but fierce devotees who live life precariously and love God jealously. These ones live by faith, tenacious in their trust of God.

In Hebrews 10: 35-39, the Bible says *"cast not away therefore your confidence, which hath great recompence of reward. For ye have need of patience, that, after ye have done the will of God, ye might receive the promise. For yet a little while, and he that shall come will come, and will not tarry. Now the **just shall live by faith**: but if any man draw back, my soul shall have no pleasure in him. But we are not of them who draw back unto perdition; but of them that believe to the saving of the soul."*

Those who operate with an ever increasing light lifestyle live by faith! These truism is repeated four times in scripture (Galatians 3:11, Hebrews 10:38, Habbakuk 2:4, Romans 1:17), and serves to re-iterate the fact that shining is the privilege of those living by faith. These *just* are those who, no matter how dark the situation, their light never stops shining.

The just are not justified by good works or people's praises, but by the blood of Jesus. They are those "...*whom* (God) *did foreknow, (and)...did predestinate to be conformed to the image of his Son, that he might be the firstborn among many brethren. Moreover whom he did predestinate, them he also called: and whom he called, them he also justified: and whom he justified, them he also glorified*" (Romans 8:29-30). **The end of a justified life is always a glorified life!**

Not Drawing Back!

One of the greatest challenges to a life of Ever Increasing Shining and ever radiating light is the soul that draws back! In Hebrews 10:38-39, the Bible says "...*the just shall live by faith: but if any man draw back, my soul shall have no pleasure in him. But we are not of them who draw back unto perdition; but of them that believe to the saving of the soul.*"

This kind of faith that saves the soul, however, is not man made or human engineered, but a supernatural kind of faith. According to Habakkuk 2:4, the prophet Habakkuk said "*behold, his soul which is lifted up is not upright in him: but the just shall live by his faith.*"

The word *his faith* utilized in Habakkuk 2:4b is not the faith of the individual, but in the original Hebrew it is the **faith of God**. It is that kind of faith that keeps your shining ever increasing. In Galatians 2:20, Apostle Paul testifies that the secret to his ever increasing light was the faith of the son of God.

He said,"...*the life which I now live in the flesh I live by the faith of the Son of God, who loved me, and gave himself for me*" (Galatians 2:20), and in Romans 3:22 further elucidates this fact further by saying "...*the righteousness of God which is by faith of Jesus Christ unto all and upon all them that believe:...*"

The supernatural faith of God must always be the goal of the Church. The faith of God must be what the Church lives for, exhibits, and pursues after. If she draws back, however, God says it is a set up for perdition or loss that can be physical, spiritual or eternal. When the Church stops pressing (Philippians 3:14), she enters perdition, and when she stops stretching, she stops shining!

Until there is a quest for excellence, the evidence of light in a person's life will be missing. In Ecclesiastes 2:13-14, the wise man said "*...I saw that wisdom excelleth folly, as far as **light excelleth darkness**. The wise man's eyes are in his head; but the fool walketh in darkness....*"

THE PARADIGM OF LIGHT

A wicked thought that is permeating the 21st century is the notion that darkness can stop the stars from shining forth. In Job 22:12-14, Eliphaz said "*is not God in the height of heaven? and behold the **height of the stars**, how high they are! And thou sayest, How doth God know? can he judge through **the dark cloud**? Thick clouds are a covering to Him, that he seeth not; and he walketh in the circuit of heaven.*"

The custodians of Job's day believed they were safe, because their acts were oblivious to God. They expected a dark cloud to shut out God, unaware that those who are righteous have a darkness-penetrating light that leaves every pursuit penetrable and any accomplishment attainable. They are, therefore, undeterred till they accomplish their goal.

This false perception that God was exempt from human affairs existed in the days of David also. He knew better because he was "*...a man after God's heart...*" (Acts 13:22). He said, "*...the darkness hideth not from thee (God); but the night shineth as the day: the darkness and the light are both alike to thee for thou hast possessed my reins: thou hast covered me in my mother's womb* (Psalm 139:12).

Those who God possesses will portray the paradigm of true light. They are not "*...false apostles, (and) deceitful workers, (who) transform themselves into the apostles of Christ...for Satan himself is transformed into an angel of light*" (2 Corinthians 11:13-15) but bonafide believers who have staked their claim and made commitments to stay connected eternally.

Gloria Braimoh: From Shuttered to Shining!

Barrister Gloria Braimoh is a cosmopolitan gospel singer, with best selling songs such as *Open heavens*, *Miracle worker* and several other chart topping singles. She was in the University of Nigeria when she gave her life to Jesus and that opened vistas of ministry opportunities for her.

She, however, came from a Roman Catholic background and her father was particularly not impressed by her new found faith. She was deprived of basic necessities, as a result of her commitment to Christ, and had to depend on friends and the campus fellowship to finish law school.

After her graduation, she worked for a few years at a telecommunications firm and got married to a local pastor in her Church. She was later to find out, however, that he was not heterosexual and was unwilling to consummate their relationship. She eventually got divorced from him and for nearly twenty years lived as a single singer.

In 2021, after many successful albums and stage performances, she was shuttered by some music promoters for reasons best known to them. She was not able to minister on platforms she had been used to ministering for years, and along the way she had to change her Church as well.

Throughout her ordeals, however, she persisted in her faith in Christ. She did not draw back, but kept releasing song after song. Eventually, she reconciled with her Eighty year old father, released a joint duet with him, and got married to her (Italian-based) husband after a life of singleness of more than twenty years.

Truly, Gloria's story is that of God turning one's captivity for His glory. She was the one "...*the Lord* turned again (her) *captivity*... (and they) *were like them that dream. Then was* (her) *mouth filled with laughter, and* (her) *tongue with singing: then said they among the heathen, The Lord* hath done great things for them (for) *the Lord* hath done great things for us; whereof we are glad" (Psalm 126:1-3).

Prayer: May my light never stop shining, in Jesus name!

*Nothing stops Darkness faster
than a Champion Mindset!*

- Tobe Momah M.D.

CHAPTER THIRTY-EIGHT

JOY

*"God came from Teman, and the Holy One from mount Paran. Selah. His glory covered the heavens, and the earth was **full of his praise and his brightness** was as the light; he had horns coming out of his hand: and there was the hiding of his power"* (Habakkuk 3:3-4).

Leverage is the ability to influence a system, or an environment in a way that multiplies the outcomes of one's efforts. It is the advantageous condition of having a relatively small amount of cost yield a relatively high level of returns. Joy is an amplifier of light for future generations.

In Proverbs 15:30, the wise man said *"the light of the eyes rejoiceth the heart: and a good report maketh the bones fat."* There is a direct correlation between joy and light, and how much joy is allowed into one's life will determine how much light they leave for future generations.

The Lord, speaking in Psalm 132:16-17, said *"I will also clothe her priests with salvation: and **her saints shall shout aloud for joy**. There will I make the horn of David to bud: I have ordained **a lamp** for mine anointed."* **Where the joy is sounded, the light must shine forth!**

He adds, in Isaiah 35:6-10, that the *"...the eyes of the blind shall be opened, and the ears of the deaf shall be unstopped. Then shall the lame man leap as an hart, and the tongue of the dumb sing: for in the wilderness shall waters break out, and streams in the desert. And the parched ground shall become a pool, and the thirsty land springs of water:... And the ransomed of the Lord shall return, and come to Zion with songs and everlasting joy upon their heads: they shall obtain joy and gladness, and sorrow and sighing shall flee away."*

When there is a desire for light, there must also be a readiness for singing and rejoicing. These sort end in everlasting joy that perpetuates light for future generations. In Isaiah 58:9-12, the Lord says *"...if thou take away from the midst of thee the yoke, the putting forth of the finger, and speaking vanity; And if thou draw out thy soul to the hungry, and satisfy the afflicted soul; then shall thy light rise in obscurity, and thy darkness be as the noon day....And thou shalt raise up the foundations of many generations; and thou shalt be called, The repairer of the breach, The restorer of paths to dwell in."*

Joy is a catalyst for light. Without it, darkness is perpetuated for generations. The recovery of joy is the beginning of the discovery of light. In Esther 8:15-16, after the blood-sucking attack from Haman had been annulled and Mordecai promoted to Haman's former position, the *"...city of Shushan rejoiced and was glad. (And) the Jews had light, and gladness, and joy, and honor."*

Their light arose from the place of Joy, and their shining from a lifestyle of rejoicing. The Psalmist acknowledged this, and prayed in Psalm 35:4-7, to *"...let them be confounded and put to shame that seek after my soul: let them be turned back and brought to confusion that devise my hurt. Let them be as chaff before the wind: and let the angel of the Lord chase them. Let their way be **dark** and slippery: and let the angel of the Lord persecute them. For without cause have they hid for me their net in a pit, which without cause they have digged for my soul."*

Two Patriachs, Two Prayers, and Two Places!

Moses was well positioned to bring light to his generation, as the deliverer of Israel. Instead, his anger streak made him miss the promised land (Numbers 20:7-12), and nearly got him killed (see Exodus 4:24-26).

His anger erupted on multiple occasions, and even in death, when the enemies of his soul came for his body "...*Michael the archangel,...contend(ed) with the devil...*(and) *disputed about the body of Moses,* (but) *durst not bring against him a railing accusation, but said, The Lord rebuke thee*" (Jude 9).

He went to his grave in regret, and kept saying to the Israelites "...*the Lord was wroth with me for your sakes, and would not hear me: and the Lord said unto me, Let it suffice thee; speak no more unto me of this matter. Get thee up into the top of Pisgah, and lift up thine eyes westward, and northward, and southward, and eastward, and behold it with thine eyes: for thou shalt not go over this Jordan*" (Deut 3:26-27).

Jacob, on the other hand, died blessing his progenitors. He had had a tough life, as he confessed to Pharaoh in Genesis 47:9, but "*by faith...when he was a dying, blessed both the sons of Joseph; and worshipped, leaning upon the top of his staff*" (Hebrews 11:21). He had endured the loss of his parents, betrayal from his maternal uncle, hatred from his brother, and the rape of his only daughter. Not to be deterred, however, he persisted in worship and "...*he charged them, and said unto them, I am to be gathered unto my people: bury me with my fathers in the cave that is in the field of Ephron the Hittite, in the cave that is in the field of Machpelah, which is before Mamre, in the land of Canaan, which Abraham bought with the field of Ephron the Hittite for a possession of a burying place*" (Genesis 49:29-30).

Jacob refused to let sorrow of heart stop his entrance into the place of his solution. His worship opened the doors for him to be buried in the promised land, while Moses's anger shut the door to the promised land against them. The promise of God to Jacob, which arose from the blessings of God upon Abraham, that "...*I will make thy seed to multiply as the stars of heaven,...*" (Genesis 26:4) came to pass because Jacob chose worship instead of worry, and praise instead of pity. Joy is a lever for light, and a feeder for fruitfulness. In Isaiah 29:17-18, the Lord God said "...*in that day shall the deaf hear the words of the book, and the eyes of the blind shall see out of obscurity, and out of darkness. The meek also shall increase their joy in the Lord, and the poor among men shall rejoice in the Holy One of Israel.*"

JACOB'S WELL

The well Jesus met the Samaritan woman in John 4, is famously called Jacob's well. It has, however, been historically traced back to the Abrahamic wells (Genesis 26:15) that Isaac fought to retain. After a protracted conflict, that saw Isaac gain and lose *Esek* and *Sitnah* to the Philistines (see Genesis 26:19-22), God blessed Jacob with the wells of Rehoboth and Beersheba (Genesis 26:22-33). It was at this dark well, that had been beleaguered by conflict (*Esek*), and hostility (*Sitnah*), that Jesus brought the woman of Samaria the waters of life. He told her, "*whosoever drinketh of the water that I shall give him shall never thirst; but the water that I shall give him shall be in him a well of water springing up into everlasting life*" (Hebrews 11:13).

The healing virtues of this well were, however, enshrined in the life of peace and praise that Isaac had repeatedly demonstrated in the face of provocation from King Ahimelech and his army commander, Phicol. He told them, after digging his third well called Rehoboth (Genesis 26:22), and building an altar of worship to the Lord (Genesis 26:24), that "…*wherefore come ye to me, seeing ye hate me, and have sent me away from you?*" (Genesis 26:27).

In reply, "…*they said, We saw certainly that the Lord was with thee: and we said, Let there be now an oath betwixt us, even betwixt us and thee, and let us make a covenant with thee; That thou wilt do us no hurt, as we have not touched thee, and as we have done unto thee nothing but good, and have sent thee away in peace: thou art now the blessed of the Lord. And he made them a feast, and they did eat and drink. And they rose up betimes in the morning, and sware one to another: and Isaac sent them away, and they departed from him in peace*" (Genesis 26:28-31).

The blessings from Jacob's well were generational in impact, but they stemmed from a lifestyle of peace and praise by his father Isaac. The ability to forgive multiplies an outpouring of God's supernatural light to coming generations.

In 1 John 1:4-7, the Bible says "…*these things write we unto you, that your joy may be full. This then is the message which we have heard of him, and declare unto you, that God is light, and in him is no darkness at all. If we say that we have fellowship with him, and walk in darkness, we lie, and do not the truth: But if we walk in the light, as he is in the light, we have fellowship one with another, and the blood of Jesus Christ his Son cleanseth us from all sin."*

There are a select group of individuals who will inhabit God's mountain and be joyful in prayer. These ones are not moribund in God's presence, but aggressive in prayer, and yet still enjoy themselves in the presence of the Lord! They lay down their lives for kingdom service, and are oiled by a covenant relationship with God that is hinged on service and worship. They are "*...them* (God) *will bring to* (His) *holy mountain, and make joyful in* (His) *house of prayer: their burnt offerings and their sacrifices shall be accepted upon* (His) *altar; for mine house shall be called an house of prayer for all people"* (Isaiah 56:7).

MILLIONAIRES WITH MDD!

A group of celebrated American millionaires met at a hotel in Chicago in the 1920's. They were venerated and envied by millions of their peers and citizens; but less than thirty years later, the majority of them had died by suicide. The emptiness of everything they owned and the futility of the fantasy life they lived drove them to suicide.

First of all was Leo Fraser. He became the first President of the Bank for International Settlements in 1935, and served as professor of public law at Columbia University. In 1945, while President of First National Bank of New York, he shot himself in the head at his summer home in North Granville, NY. He was fifty-five. In his suicide note, he said, "I have been depressed mentally and suffered from melancholia that gets steadily worse."

Another of the millionaires at the meeting was Jesse Livermore, also known as the Great Bear, the Wall Street Wonder, and the Cotton King. He was one of the most flamboyant and successful market speculators in the history of Wall Street. During his three-decade career as the King of the Speculators, he reportedly made and lost four separate multi-million-dollar fortunes. He was also one of the prominent speculators later blamed for having precipitated the

Great Crash of 1929, during which he claimed to have made over $100 million. Livermore committed suicide at New York's Sherry-Netherland Hotel a week after Thanksgiving in 1940.

Last but not the least, was Ivar Kreuger. A Swedish businessman, he founded and ran Kreuger & Toll into a multi-billion-dollar match conglomerate. Kreuger, like other financial crooks of his era, was essentially running a huge pyramid scheme through a complex structure of hundreds of subsidiary shell companies, hiding his manipulation by cooking the company books and insisting that financial statements not be audited.

Kreuger & Toll securities were among the most widely held in the United States, and when the company went under in 1932, investors lost millions in the largest bankruptcy of its time. The scandal led to the passage of laws requiring mandatory audits of all companies with listed securities. Kreuger shot himself to death on 12 March 1932.

The elderly, white male are in the highest socio-economic class in the USA, but have the highest suicide risk. Money can't buy happiness, and neither can possessions. Jesus said, *"Take heed, and beware of covetousness: for a man's life consisteth not in the abundance of the things which he possesseth"* (Luke 12:15).

Prayer: Baptize me with the Spirit of righteousness, Peace, and Joy in the Holy Ghost, in Jesus name.

No devil can Steal what God has Sealed with the Holy Spirit!

- MATTHEW ASHIMOLOWO
(SENIOR PASTOR KINGSWAY INTERNATIONAL CHRISTIAN CENTER, LONDON UK)

CHAPTER THIRTY-NINE

JUSTICE

"Justice and *judgment* are the habitation of thy throne: mercy and truth shall go before thy face. Blessed is the people that know the joyful sound: they shall walk, O Lord, in the **light** of thy countenance"* (Psalm 89:14-15).

When light is present, there is no need for a middle man between God and man. The power of light rebukes openly (Ephesians 5:13), and shines light with ferocity on anything around it. It does not concede to intimidation, but immediately directs judgment for the most high God and Judge of all the earth. The greatness of our God is in the brightness of His shining, but for that light to shine His body (the Church) must take off the veil, and shine the light by letting judgement reign in her midst.

In Psalm 27:1-3, the Psalmist declared that *"the Lord* is my light and my salvation; whom shall I fear? the *Lord* is the strength of my life; of whom shall I be afraid? When the wicked, even mine enemies and my foes, came upon me to eat up my flesh, they stumbled and fell. Though an host should encamp against me, my heart shall not fear: though war should rise against me, in this will I be confident."

Too many believers allow injustice because they do not carry His light! When the Lord is your light, you pray prayers like David who said *"deliver me not over unto the will of mine enemies: for false witnesses are risen up against me, and such as breathe out cruelty. I had fainted, unless I had believed to see the goodness of the Lord* in the land of the living" (Psalm 27:12-13).

It is easy to quit when you lack the light leveraged by justice. The day of judgement is fast approaching, and with it consequences for sin. One of the catastophes of sin is darkness. In Isaiah 60:1-3, the Prophet Isaiah adjures the Church to *"Arise, shine; for thy light is come, and the glory of the Lord* is risen upon thee. *For, behold, the darkness shall cover the earth, and gross darkness the people: but the Lord* shall *arise upon thee, and his glory shall be seen upon thee. And the Gentiles shall come to thy light, and kings to the brightness of thy rising."*

The light that justice emanates is illustrated by the pillar of cloud that guided Israel when they left Egypt. In Exodus 14:19-20, the Bible says *"...the angel of God, which went before the camp of Israel, removed and went behind them; and the pillar of the cloud went from before their face, and stood behind them: And it came between the camp of the Egyptians and the camp of Israel; and it was a cloud and **darkness** to them, but it gave **light** by night to these: so that the one came not near the other all the night."*

The Israelites were beneficiaries of the light of God's double edgedness. The same pillar of cloud that gave light to Israel, brought darkness to Egypt. As a result, Egypt was halted in their tracks as they tried to pursue the Israelites. Every where darkness reigns, there is pity, paralysis, and powerlessness, but where light resides there is progress, power, and prosperity.

When God chooses to fight injustice, like He did against the Egyptians, He places the pillar of cloud and fire between them (Exodus 14:19). Rather than making excuses for injustice, enforce it by taking a stand on the side of Justice. In Amos 5:15, the prophet Amos said *"hate the evil, and love the good, and establish judgment in the gate: it may be that the Lord God of hosts will be gracious unto the remnant of Joseph."*

THE ENEMY CALLED INJUSTICE

The man or woman raised by injustice because of their influence in the judicial system will have that same source of power de-articulated and thus become powerless. In Job 31:21-22, Job said *"if I have lifted up my hand against the fatherless, when I saw my help in the gate, then let mine arm fall from my shoulder blade, and mine arm be broken from the bone."*

God hates injustice! In Amos 5:24, the prophet prayed *"... let judgment run down as waters, and righteousness as a mighty stream."* In Psalm 89:14-15, the Psalmist added that *"**justice** and **judgment** are the habitation of thy throne: mercy and truth shall go before thy face and blessed is the people that know the joyful sound: they shall walk, O Lord, in the **light** of thy countenance."*

This correlation between injustice and lack of insight is corroborated further by Isaiah saying *"their feet run to evil, and they make haste to shed innocent blood: their thoughts are thoughts of iniquity; wasting and destruction are in their paths. The way of peace they know not; and there is **no judgment** in their goings:...Therefore is judgment far from us, neither doth justice overtake us: we **wait for light**, but behold obscurity; for brightness, but we **walk in darkness**. We grope for the wall like the blind, and we grope as if we had no eyes: we stumble at noon day as in the night; we are in desolate places as dead men"* (Isaiah 59:7-10).

If you get anything because of undue influence, especially against the powerless, it leads down the path of deep darkness. It (injustice) turns your life backward, and de-articulates your future.

GOD OF VENGEANCE

There are a generation of believers who have not known the God of vengeance and so are sadly bereft of light. In Isaiah 47:1-3, God told Babylon *"...I will take vengeance, and I will not meet thee as a man. As for our redeemer, the Lord* of hosts is his name, the Holy One of Israel. Sit thou silent, and get thee into darkness, O daughter of the Chaldeans: for thou shalt no more be called, The lady of kingdoms."

Only those who accept the God of Vengeance can God shine upon and deliver their enemies to darkness. In Psalm 18:27-29, the Psalmist cried "...*thou wilt save the afflicted people; but wilt bring down high looks. For thou wilt light my candle: the Lord my God* will enlighten my darkness. *For by thee I have run through a troop; and by my God have I leaped over a wall.*"

When a person hates the good and loves the evil, they do injustice and their lives continually go back and forth as a result. This mal-behavior further makes them oblivious of God or the revelation of His word. In Micah 3:4, prophet Micah says, "*then shall they cry unto the Lord, but he will not hear them: he will even hide his face from them at that time, as they have behaved themselves ill in their doings.*"

The heavens are closed unto the unjust, so that they lack vision or dreams. In Micah 3:6-7 prophet Micah says, "*therefore night shall be unto you, that ye shall not have a vision; and it shall be dark unto you, that ye shall not divine; and the sun shall go down over the prophets, and the day shall be dark over them. Then shall the seers be ashamed, and the diviners confounded: yea, they shall all cover their lips; for there is no answer of God.*"

The distance one is willing to pay for justice, therefore, determines the entry point God gives such a one into His presence! **When there is fairness, God's fullness is quickly manifest.** In Micah 3:8, the prophet says "*...I am full of power by the spirit of the Lord, and of judgment, and of might, to declare unto Jacob his transgression, and to Israel his sin.*" Those who speak truth to power without wavering, and keep the faith notwithstanding the odds, are rewarded with His fullness and power.

In Psalm 94:1-2, the Psalmist cried "*O LORD, God of vengeance, O God of vengeance, shine forth! Rise up, O judge of the earth; repay to the proud what they deserve!*" The manifestation of vengeance is a shining activity. When God manifests His vengeance on your behalf, shining is inevitable. Impunity, on the other hand, is the enemy of your shining in Life! What you tolerate is why you are not celebrated. The God of vengeance will shine brightest when vengeance is executed, and not when impunity is tolerated.

No wonder the Psalmist advocated for a quick vengeance by God in Psalm 82:1-5. He said, "*God standeth in the congregation of the mighty; he judgeth among the gods. How long will ye judge unjustly, and accept the persons of the wicked?....Defend the poor and fatherless: do justice to the afflicted and needy.Deliver the poor and needy: rid them out of the hand of the wicked. They know not, neither will they understand; they **walk on in darkness**: all the foundations of the earth are out of course.*"

Any foundation that is shrouded in injustice and ignorance is laden with darkness, and shining is impossible. The secret to victory in life is Light! That light is leveraged by justice, so that "*as soon as they hear of me, they shall obey me: the strangers shall submit themselves unto me and the strangers shall fade away, and be afraid out of their close places...*(for) *It is God that avengeth me, and subdueth the people under me*" (Psalm 18:44-47).

NOT MOVING WITH "THE MOVERS"

In my third year of medical school, I and several other Christian medical students from the University of Nigeria Enugu Campus set out from Enugu to Port-Harcourt in a rented bus owned by "the Movers" to attend anational conference convened by the Christain Medical and Dental Association (CMDA). The carnival-like athmosphere in the bus was, however, soon cut short by gun shots, and bangings on our bus to open up.

Rather than open up, however, the students responded in praise and prayer! The bus, which up to that point had been epileptic and problematic, took off and we got away from what seemed like an armed robbery scene. By the time we got to our destination, it was already morning of the next day as what was supposed to be a two hour trip had dragged on for more than twelve hours.

On arrival, we learnt that those robbers had robbed, raped and ravaged several travelers before us and we were fortunate to have escaped unhurt. The God of vengeance showed up for more than seventy vulnerable college students that night, and amidst an atmosphere of praise and prayer, defended them with a heavenly host that made them impregnable to satanic plots and devices.

Prayer: God of vengeance, fight for me and give me light in Jesus name.

The danger of darkness is prosecution, instead of persecution!

- Tobe Momah M.D.

CHAPTER FORTY

JUST BECAUSE I SAID SO

"In the beginning God created the heaven and the earth. And the earth was without form, and void; and darkness was upon the face of the deep. And the Spirit of God moved upon the face of the waters. And God said, Let there be light: and there was light" (Genesis 1:1-3).

God spoke to a world that was worthless, wallowing in despair, and wasting and His word brought order to chaos, and distinction to what was once devastated by sin. The reason is **just because He said so!** His word *let there be light* caused there to be "...*light* (which He saw) *was good and God divided the light from the darkness*" (Genesis 1:3-4).

You have the same power to speak and create your world! In Ecclesiastes 8:4, the wise man said *"where the word of a king is, there is power: and who may say unto him, what doest thou?"* That king with power in his or her words is the Church because God "...*hath made us kings and priests unto God and his Father;...*" (Revelation 1:6).

When a believer ignores his or her heritage of dominion and royalty (1 Peter 2:9), they walk on in a darkness that cascades eventually into death and destruction. In Psalm 82:5-7, God says *"they know not, neither will they understand; they walk on in darkness: all the foundations of the earth are out of course. I have said, **Ye are gods;***

and all of you are children of the most High. But ye shall die like men, and fall like one of the princes."

The lack of understanding about been a partaker of his divine nature (2 Peter 1:4), is why many continue to walk in darkness when they can instead speak light to their circumstances! The generations following are waiting for the gods in the Church to arise so they can leverage their light for future generations. Enough of the moaning, complaining and pity partying. Speak light to your darkness, and watch it transform.

THUNDERS AND LIGHTNINGS!

Lightnings and thunder will emerge from the same thunderstorm at differing speeds. While lightning travels at 185,000 meters per second, sound travels at 343 meters per second. An observer will, therefore, hear the sound from a thunderstorm more than five seconds after seeing a lightning flash from that same thunderstorm. **There can be no lightning, however, without an initial thunder** just like there can be no light without the thunder of our words.

In Psalm 77:17-18, the Psalmist said *"...the skies sent out a sound: thine arrows also went abroad. The voice of thy thunder was in the heaven: the lightnings lightened the world: the earth trembled and shook."* Even though in the natural, it looks like light emerges without provocation before thunder, it is actually the voice of thunder that heralds the lightning.

Until the Church begins to thunder like God does, the leveraging light effect she embodies will be masked. The Bible says, in John 12:28-29, that *"...came there a voice from heaven, saying, I have both glorified it, and will glorify it again* (and) *the people therefore, that stood by, and heard it, said that it thundered:..."*

The God of heaven thundered in agreement with His Son, and in 2 Peter 1:17, Luke 9:29-35 and Matthew 17:5 he thundered again to affirm His son. On the latter occasion, Jesus was translated *"...as he prayed* (with) *the fashion of his countenance...altered, and his* raiment…white and glistering" (Luke 9.29) and had a "…a bright cloud overshadowed them…" (Matthew 17:5).

When the Church starts thundering, like God does, the blazing brightness and the glistening glory that encompassed Jesus while on the mountain will encompass her (the Church). **The light is not supposed to be a luxury, but the birthright of every praying, believing and understanding Christian** which he or she can then pass on to future generations – like Jesus did on the mount of transfiguration to Peter, James, and John (Matthew 17:5-9, and Luke 9:29-35).

THERE IS POWER IN THE SPOKEN WORD

Where ever and whenever there is obedience to God's word, there is a bursting forth of sight and light. In Jeremiah 1:11-12, God asked the prophet Jeremiah "…what seest thou? And I said, I see a rod of an almond tree. Then said the Lord unto me, Thou hast well seen: for I will hasten my word to perform it."

The trigger for the sight, however, was the word of God spoken to Jeremiah in Jeremiah 1:4-9. Without the spoken word, the seeing vision is curtailed! It was what God spoke that He saw (Genesis 1:1-3), and not the other way around.

Paul, recognized this critical nexus, and declared in 2 Corinthians 4:13-17 that "we having the same spirit of faith, according as it is written, I believed, and therefore have I spoken; we also believe, and therefore speak; Knowing that he which raised up the Lord Jesus shall raise up us also by Christ Jesus, and shall present us with you. For all things are for your sakes, that the abundant grace might through the thanksgiving of many redound to the glory of God. For which cause we faint not; but though our outward man perish, yet the inward man is renewed day by day. For our light affliction, which is but for a moment, worketh for us a far more exceeding and eternal weight of glory; While we look not at the things which are seen, but at the things which are not seen: for the things which are seen are temporal; but the things which are not seen are eternal."

What started as faith filled speaking metamorphosed into eternal envisioning, because one faith filled word can change everything. Jesus told his disciples "*...whosoever shall say unto this mountain, Be thou removed, and be thou cast into the sea; and shall not doubt in his heart, but shall believe that those things which he saith shall come to pass; he shall have whatsoever he saith*" (Mark 11:23).

A closed mouth is a closed destiny! When the believer's mouth is opened, with his or her heart in belief, light shines forth. In Habakkuk 3:3-4, the Bible tells us "*God came from Teman, and the Holy One from mount Paran. Selah. His glory covered the heavens, and the earth was full of his praise. And his brightness was as the light; he had horns coming out of his hand: and there was the hiding of his power.*" Words of praise herald the brightness of His light and power!

Any word God speaks "*...shall not return...void, but it shall accomplish that which* (He) *please, and it shall prosper in the thing whereto* (He) *sent it*" (Isaiah 55:11). It is whatever pleases God that shines forth. He said, in Psalm 135:6-7, that "*whatsoever the Lord pleased, that did he in heaven, and in earth, in the seas, and all deep places by caus(ing) the vapors to ascend from the ends of the earth, (and)... mak(ing) lightnings for the rain....*"

Too Much Unfinished Business!

Dr. Creflo Dollar is the pastor of Mega Churches in Atlanta, Georgia and New York city, New York. He is happily married to Taffi Dollar, and together oversee a network of over a hundred Churches affiliated with their World Changers Church. He has preached all over the world, is a highly sought after speaker, and a writer of several best selling books.

On one occasion, he had finished preaching in California, and was heading back to the aiport when the car he was in began to soumersault. He came out without a scratch, against the expectation of onlookers, and remembers hearing a voince saying "too much unfinished business" as the car summersaulted.

He has since that incident in 2009, expanded his ministry to destitutes, prostitutes, and includes judicial and socio political advocacy. He attributes his near death experience with this wake up to preach the gospel urgently and without compromise. He sees that occasion, as God's mandate to him to win as many souls before returning to heaven.

Prayer: Everything God has said about my life, manifest in Jesus name!

No Jury, No Glory!

- Tobe Momah M.D.

CHAPTER FORTY-ONE

JURY

*"...rise, and stand upon thy feet: for I have appeared unto thee for this purpose, to make thee a minister and a **witness** both of these things which thou hast seen, and of those things in the which I will appear unto thee; Delivering thee from the people, and from the Gentiles, unto whom now I send thee, to open their eyes, and to turn them from darkness to **light**, and from the power of Satan unto God, that they may receive forgiveness of sins, and inheritance among them which are sanctified by faith that is in me"* (Acts 26:16-18).

When we say *jury* many think of a group of individuals who will determine the guilt or innocence of the person in the witness box. God, on the other hand, is looking at the jury in terms of a group of individuals who a witness must make an impression on to gain their acceptance. You and I are that witness, and the world is our jury.

The primary role of the Christian witness is not to be intimidated by the jury, but to be *"...the light of the world* (as) *a city that is set on an hill cannot be hid. Neither do men light a candle, and put it under a bushel, but on a candlestick; and it giveth light unto all that are in the house"* (Matthew 5:14-15).

It is either you are casting light or driving darkness on your world! The Bible says, "...*none of us liveth to himself, and no man dieth to himself. For whether we live, we live unto the Lord; and whether we die, we die unto the Lord: whether we live therefore, or die, we are the Lord's. For to this end Christ both died, and rose, and revived, that he might be Lord both of the dead and living*" (Romans 14:7-9).

WHY ARE YOU IN THE WITNESS BOX?

In Psalm 49:16-20, the Bible says "*be not thou afraid when one is made rich, when the glory of his house is increased; For when he dieth he shall carry nothing away: his glory shall not descend after him. Though while he lived he blessed his soul: and men will praise thee, when thou doest well to thyself. He shall go to the generation of his fathers; they shall never see **light**. Man that is in honour, and understandeth not, is like the beasts that perish.*"

Some opulent and wealthy individuals don't leave a legacy for the future, and the primary reason is because they don't know why "...(he or she) *is in honor, and understandeth not,* (and so are)...*like the beasts that perish*" (Psalm 49:20). The reason you are in the witness stand is to give a reflection of Christ, as you may be the only Bible some people ever read. Apostle Paul describes the Church in Corinth as "... *our epistle written in our hearts, known and read of all men: Forasmuch as ye are manifestly declared to be the epistle of Christ ministered by us, written not with ink, but with the Spirit of the living God; not in tables of stone, but in fleshy tables of the heart*" (2 Corinthians 3:2-3).

The same paradigm that swallowed one individual, can lift up the other because one understood his honor while the other did not. A man or woman who does not understand why he or she is in the witness box, will make a shipwreck of their destiny. When there is a lack of understanding, the light for the next generation is extinguished. When you are standing before the jury, understand it is for a season and it has a reason.

Samson lost his eye sight after he became entangled with Philistine women (including Delilah). He was set in honor as a

Judge in Israel, but because he was living a purposeless life he was soon blinded by the Philistines. It says in Judges 16:21 that "...*the Philistines took him, and put out his eyes, and brought him down to Gaza, and bound him with fetters of brass; and he did grind in the prison house.*"

In his blindness, however, he asked the lad who led him around to "*suffer me that I may feel the pillars whereupon the house standeth, that I may lean upon them*" (Judges 16:26). He pushed on the pillars that held the auditorium the Philistines had gathered to mock him and as a result "...*the house fell upon the lords, and upon all the people that were therein. So the dead which he slew at his death were more than they which he slew in his life*" (Judges 16:30).

He (Samson) did more with his eyes blinded, than with them open! Until he began to see as God saw, he never accomplished his long term divine goals. Don't live life so purpose less you leave no light for the following generations to follow! That is why Apostle Paul told Agrippa, that Jesus appeared unto him and told him to "... (be*) a witness both of these things which thou hast seen, and of those things in the which I will appear unto thee; Delivering thee from the people, and from the Gentiles, unto whom now I send thee, to open their eyes, and to turn them* **from darkness to light**, *and from the power of Satan unto God, that they may receive forgiveness of sins, and inheritance among them which are sanctified by faith that is in me*" (Acts 26:16-18).

ISAAC: FROM BLINDNESS TO BRILLIANCE

The Bible says, in Gen 27:1-2, that "...*when Isaac was old, and his eyes were dim, so that he could not see, he called Esau his eldest son, and said unto him, My son: and he said unto him, Behold, here am I. And he said, Behold now, I am old, I know not the day of my death:*"

He wanted to bless Esau after the flesh (Genesis 25:28) because he was blind to their purpose, and as a result he was about to perish. After Jacob had deceived Esau, however, and obtained the inheritance from their father Isaac, Esau said "...*in his heart, the days of mourning for my father are at hand; then will I slay my brother Jacob*" (Gen 27:41).

The minute Isaac understood God's spiritual permutations about his sons' destinies, his health was transformed. Instead of dying at One hundred years of age (see Genesis 26:34), as his son Esau expected, he lived to the ripe old age of one hundred and eighty years and then died (see Genesis 35:28). His health trajectory was amended when his life purpose was altered! After he blessed Jacob, instead of Esau, he knew by divine revelation, that "...*one people shall be stronger than the other people and the elder shall serve the younger*" (Genesis 25:23).

The day all this changed, however, was after he blessed Jacob. The Bible says, in Hebrews 11:20, that "*by faith, Isaac blessed Jacob and Esau concerning things to come.*" The walk of faith births legacy and leaves light for the following generations. Until an individual leaves a life of faith, that is solely focused on pleasing God and no else, he won't be able to bring a witness to the jury that will impact them and affirm his convictions.

Jesus chastised the Israelites of his day, when he said to them "*I receive not honor from men but I know you, that ye have not the love of God in you. I am come in my Father's name, and ye receive me not: if another shall come in his own name, him ye will receive. How can ye believe, which receive honour one of another, and seek not the honour that cometh from God only?*" (John 5:41-44). It takes a Godly witness to shine the light the world sees (Matthew 5:14-16).

DR. PIERRE'S PEERLESS PROBLEMS

Dr. Pierre was the poster child of the American dream. A Haitian immigrant, he had moved to the United States in the 1980's as a teenager, and quickly rose to the top of the academic ladder as a specialist in Orthopedic Surgery. He was articulate, handsome, charismatic, and skillful in the operating room.

He was, also, happily married with seven children. After a career that spanned three boroughs in New York and several hospitals, Dr Pierre was implicated by the Department of Justice (DOJ) in a financial racket that involved charging medicare millions of dollars for procedures that were not performed.

For once, his veritable and famed charm looked like it would be unable to get him out of a difficult position. He had for years used that charm on medical students, residents, nurses, drug reps, and administrative personnel without fail but now it looked as if the DOJ would not be charmed. He went to court and lost, and on his way to serve a seven year sentence he asked the judge one last favor.

He wanted to stop at the graveside of his parents, and ask for their forgiveness. Accompanied by his lawyer, Dr Pierre kneeled at his parent's graveside and pulled out a pistol and shot himself. He was determined not to spend seven years in jail and had ended his life instead. He had given a false witness to the world, and could not live with the repercussions of his actions.

Today, his wife and seven children are still picking up the pieces from a life that was everything on paper but real. Beleaguered by demons of greed, fame, and appetite Dr Pierre had substituted his reality for a façade. His brilliance was not enough to shield him from brutishness, neither was his learning enough to make him a true light for the next generation.

Prayer: Masquarading power attacking my star die, in the name of Jesus.

Once your eyes get used to Darkness,
it is jolting to see light!

- TOBE MOMAH M.D.

CHAPTER FOURTY-TWO

JOLT

"...*if the Spirit of him that raised up Jesus from the dead dwell in you, he that raised up Christ from the dead shall also quicken your mortal bodies by his Spirit that dwelleth in you*" (Romans 8:11).

The jolt of the Holy Spirit is the difference between the letter that kills and the spirit that giveth life. It is the abrupt shaking or push from the Holy Spirit, and is exemplified in Romans 8:11. It says "...*if the Spirit of him that raised up Jesus from the dead dwell in you, he that raised up Christ from the dead shall also quicken your mortal bodies by his Spirit that dwelleth in you.*" That quickening is the jolt of the Spirit, and is otherwise defined as the **Jesus Ordered Light** that **Transforms**.

When the mother of the founder of the China Inland missions, Taylor James Hudson, was *jolted* by the Holy Spirit to pray for her son in the 1840's, she obeyed. The result of that jolt is a four generational lineage that has served in China as missionaries for five generations. She stopped what she was doing, in the city of London, to pray for her then atheistic son and that *jolt* has reverberated for ages.

The Psalmist prayed to the Lord to, "*make (His)...face...shine upon thy servant; and teach me thy statutes*" (Psalm 119:135). The revelation birthing light is a jolt, and it comes with a lightening effect to others. In Psalm 119:130, he said *"the entrance of thy words giveth light* (and) *giveth understanding unto the simple."*

The patriarch Abraham saw God's *jolting* actions upon his wife, Sarah (Romans 4:17-20), and he relayed that same light to his Son when God asked him to crucify his son Isaac. In Romans 4:19-20, it says Abraham *"...being not weak in faith,...considered not his own body now dead, when he was about an hundred years old, neither yet the deadness of Sarah's womb* (by) *staggering not at the promise of God through unbelief...."*

He was, therefore, easily persuaded when God told him to sacrifice Isaac, because he believed *"...God was able to raise him up, even from the dead; from whence also he received him in a figure"* (Hebrews 11:19).

ARISE AND SHINE

The word, *arise*, as used in *"Arise, shine..."* (Isaiah 60:1) is the Hebrew word *Qum*, and it means to *take a stand or stir up*. The aftermath of taking a stand is the light that baptizes generations following. That is why, in response to taking a stand and been stirred up, the Bible says *"...thy light is come, and the glory of the Lord is risen upon thee. For, behold, the darkness shall cover the earth, and gross darkness the people: but the Lord shall arise upon thee, and his glory shall be seen upon thee. And the Gentiles shall come to thy light, and kings to the brightness of thy rising"* (Isaiah 60:1-3).

Taking a stand is akin to the jolt of the Holy Spirit, and propagates life changing light and glory! Until you make a decisive jolt-like decision, your light will remain dim and your brightness covered by the dark. In Ephesians 5:12-14, Paul said *"it is a shame even to speak of those things which are done of them in secret. But all things that are reproved are made manifest by the light: for whatsoever doth make manifest is light. Wherefore he saith, Awake thou that sleepest, and arise from the dead, and Christ shall give thee light."*

The word *reprove*, as used in Ephesians 5:13, is the Greek word *Elegxo* and it means to convince with solid, compelling evidence with the intention to expose, connect, or prove wrong. Light clarifies, but it is amplified by a jolt in the spirit. The word used for manifest, in Ephesians 5:13, is the Greek word *Phaneroo*, and it means to make visible or clear. Clarity is a sure platform for verification of the light, and when revealed, evil "...*deeds* (are)... *reproved. But he that doeth truth cometh to the light, that his deeds may be made manifest, that they are wrought in God*" (John 3:20-21).

Let There Be Light!

When God said, "...*let there be light...*" (Genesis 1:3), the "...*earth was without form, and void; and darkness was upon the face of the deep...*" (Genesis 1:2). That word from God jolted the earth out of the darkness and disorder the earth was in. Out of this came forth, "...*light and God saw the light, that it was good: and God divided the light from the darkness*" (Genesis 1:3-4).

The light that came on that day, however, was not the physical light of the sun, moon, and stars - which were created on day 4 (see Genesis 1:14-19). Rather, it was the assertiveness of God's word that changed the darkness, and heralded a new dawn for creation. The word used for light, in Genesis 1:3, is the Hebrew word *Owr* and it means to be clear, bright, day, concrete, or lightning.

When God spoke the word *let there be light* to a dark and dying world, he spoke it with clarity, concreteness, and color! The power of that word jolted the powers of "...*darkness* (that were)...*upon the face of the deep* (so that)...*the Spirit of God moved upon the face of the waters*" (Genesis 1:3). It is the assertively initiated and spoken word that quickens the Spirit of God to birth the change that lasts generations.

No wonder, in Hebrews 11:3, the Bible says "*through faith we understand that the worlds were framed by the word of God, so that things which are seen were not made of things which do appear.*" The Word of God stirred the Spirit of God's jolt which causes an irrepressible light effect on the earth. Truly, "*it is the spirit that quickeneth; the flesh profiteth nothing....*" (John 6:63).

BETTY BAXTER: GOD'S HAND MAIDEN FOR MIRACLES!

Betty Baxter (1927 -) was brought up in a Christian home in Minneapolis, Minnesota. Ever since she was a child, she had known nothing but pain. She suffered from severe scoliosis, which had crippled her to the point of incapacitation. After giving her life to Jesus, she understood that the will of God was to heal, not hurt; to deliver, not destroy. Without bitterness, grudging, or envy, she waited devotedly for God's healing stream.

One day, she went int a coma and while in the coma, Jesus appeared to her and told her he would heal her on the first day of autumn by 3pm. She asked her mother to buy her a blue dress and white shoes for the occasion. Her mother told her God had given her the same date and time for her healing. Their expectation was pumped, and they waited earnestly. Her mother attempted to invite her pastor but he declined, stating he had another appointment in Indiana on that day.

Her husband thought she was deranged, and the medical doctors taking care of Betty opined that she was hallucinating and maybe the medications had affected her mentally. As the day drew closer, Betty's mother planned an elaborate ceremony and invited Christian Church members (from her Nazarene Church) and neigbors. Together, they prayed, and extolled God for His mighty works as the d-day and time on the clock approached.

On the day Jesus healed her, light shone and a great wind blew into the house and Betty stood up straight. For the first time, she stood taller than her three-year-old brother and there was no scar or surgical incision. In less than a second, she was straightened by the power of God. Betty's parents, siblings and neighbors witnessed the miracle and the local metropolitan newspaper reported the story.

Betty went on to become a healing evangelist alongside Oral Roberts, and sharing her testimony at his crusades. She functioned in the office of an evangelist, and retired in 2003 from active preaching after a visit to California. Betty Baxter's story has brought thousands, if not millions, to the cross of Jesus Christ and reawakened the power of devotion in capturing Jesus' attention.

Prayer: Touch me with your power and presence, O God, in Jesus name.

PART VII

Commanders of Combustion

- Candle of the Holy Spirit
- Communion
- Cry
- Conversations
- *Carpe Diem*
- Circumspect
- Christ

Set yourself on Fire and the World will come and Watch you Burn!

\- GLORIA COPELAND
(TEACHER/AUTHOR
FORTH WORTH, TEXAS)

CHAPTER FORTY-THREE

CANDLE OF
THE HOLY SPIRIT

*"For thou wilt **light my candle**: the Lord my God will **enlighten my darkness**. For by thee I have run through a troop; and by my God have I leaped over a wall. As for God, his way is perfect: the word of the Lord* is tried: he is a buckler to *all those that trust in him"* (Psalm 18:28-30).

One of the key attributes of God's last day army is the fire of the Holy Ghost. In Joel 2:1-3, the prophet Joel said, "...*the day of the Lord cometh, for it is nigh at hand; A day of darkness and of gloominess, a day of clouds and of thick darkness, as the morning spread upon the mountains: a great people and a strong; there hath not been ever the like, neither shall be any more after it, even to the years of many generations. A fire devoureth before them; and behind them a flame burneth: the land is as the garden of Eden before them, and behind them a desolate wilderness; yea, and nothing shall escape them."*

These fiery ones are commanders of combustion in these last days. They provoke flames of fire and devour their enemies through the candle of the fire of the Holy Spirit. In Malachi 4:5-6, God said "*behold, I will send you Elijah the prophet before the coming of the great and dreadful day of the Lord and he shall turn the heart of the fathers to the children, and the heart of the children to their fathers, lest I come and smite the earth with a curse."*

Elijah is tantamount to a man carrying the combustible candle of the Lord. Following his encounter on Mount Carmel with the prophets of Baal (1 Kings 18:24-38), the last day Church is a fiery Church, and they don't just converse about combustion but are commanders of combustion. One of the characteristics of light is that, like combustion, it is commanded (2 Corinthians 4:6) not suggested!

When the man with the measuring line went to measure Jerusalem, "...*another angel went out to meet him, and said unto him, Run, speak to this young man, saying, Jerusalem shall be inhabited as towns without walls for the multitude of men and cattle therein for I, saith the Lord, will be unto her* **a wall of fire** *round about, and will be the glory in the midst of her"* (Zechariah 2:3-5). Without this wall of fire around the Church, her glory is moribound and stifled.

The secret to the glorious Church, that Jesus is coming back for (Ephesians 5:25), is the fire of the Holy Ghost. That is why Jesus said *"I am come to send fire on the earth; and what will I, if it be already kindled? But I have a baptism to be baptized with; and how am I straitened till it be accomplished"* (Luke 12:49-50). He (Jesus) is the Baptizer with the Holy Ghost and fire (Matthew 3:12), and the reason *"...His candle shined upon my head, and why by his light I walked through darkness"* (Job 29:3).

Razed to Be Raised!

Gezer was a town of unfulfilled expectations. It was abandoned, misused, abused and had unmet potential. Its name, from the original Hebrew, means portion and signifies how many believers leave their allocated portions wasted and unexploited. In Joshua 16:9-10, "...*the separate cities for the children of Ephraim were among the inheritance of the children of Manasseh, all the cities with their villages. And they drave not out the Canaanites that dwelt in* **Gezer***: but the Canaanites dwell among the Ephraimites unto this day, and serve under tribute."*

Eventually the king of Egypt came with a mission; he razed the city of Gezer down and Solomon raised it up as a City with purpose and plan from its rubbles. In 1 Kings 9:15-17, the Bible says *"...this is the reason of the levy which king Solomon raised; for to build the house of the Lord, and his own house, and Millo, and the wall of Jerusalem, and Hazor, and Megiddo, and* **Gezer***. For Pharaoh king of Egypt had gone up, and taken Gezer, and burnt it with fire, and slain the Canaanites that dwelt in the city, and given it for a present unto his daughter, Solomon's wife. And Solomon built* **Gezer***,...."*

God has a plan for you but you must first be razed by the fire of the Holy Ghost before you can be a blessing to them. The tragedy of our time is not unanswered prayers or unoffered prayers, but unoffered lives! The fire of the Holy Spirit is the barometer the last days judgement will be based on (see 1 Corinthians 3:13-15 and Matthew 25:`1-12), and until the Church regains her flames of fire (Hebrews 1:7; Psalm 104:4) status, her glory will be forfieted!

After razing Gezer, and raising a celebrated city out of her relics, it (Gezer) was eventually turned into a city of refuge or safety for men and women from all corners. In Joshua 21:20-21, the *"...families of the children of Kohath, the Levites which remained of the children of Kohath, even they had the cities of their lot out of the tribe of Ephraim. For they gave them Shechem with her suburbs in mount Ephraim, to be a* **city of refuge** *for the slayer; and* **Gezer** *with her suburbs,"*

Today, the remnants of Gezer are still available for tourists and travelers in Israel. It is considered a major thoroughfare, and was strategically situated at the junction of the international coastal highway, and the highway connecting it with Jerusalem through the valley of Ajalon. More than seven thousand years later, the rebuilt city of Gezer still stands, and this is the lot of those who God razes and raises up! In 1 Corinthians 3:13-15, the Bible says *"...the fire shall try every man's work of what sort it is. If any man's work abide which he hath built thereupon, he shall receive a reward. If any man's work shall be burned, he shall suffer loss: but he himself shall be saved; yet so as by fire."*

ARE YOU KINDLED OR KAPUT?

The Holy Spirit, according to John 7:37-39, is that river of living water that refreshes the believer and without Him, everything eventually evaporates, becomes extinct and goes *kaput*. The rivers of life are where the reviving's of God are present. Ezekiel talks about these flowing rivers in Ezekiel 47:9. He says, "...*it shall come to pass, that everything that liveth, which moveth, whithersoever the rivers shall come, shall live: and there shall be a very great multitude of fish, because these waters shall come thither: for they shall be healed; and everything shall live whither the river cometh.*"

There are no limits to the fire of the Holy Ghost! If it is kindled, it will be unstoppable, no matter how rocky the opposition. In Jeremiah 21:13-14, God said "...*I am against thee, O inhabitant of the valley, and rock of the plain, saith the LORD; which say, who shall come down against us? or who shall enter into our habitations? But I will punish you according to the fruit of your doings, saith the LORD: and I will kindle a fire in the forest thereof, and it shall devour all things round about it.*"

The mission of Jesus on earth was to kindle fire on the earth (Luke 12:49-50). The word *kindle*, in translated from the original Hebrew word *Yatsath*, and it means to burn or set on fire. Those who are reserved for destruction by devils are *kaput*, but those who see distinction are kindled. If you are not kindled, you can be stopped but if you are kindled you cannot be stopped. According to Jeremiah 21:13-14, the kindled or *burning-for-God* life is the unstoppable life. Even if the inhabitants dwell in rocks or hide in valleys, the kindled life moves against all opposition without constraint.

In Matthew 3:11-12, John the Baptist told the people of his time that "...*he* (Jesus) *shall baptize you with the Holy Ghost, and with fire: Whose fan is in his hand, and he will throughly purge his floor and gather his wheat into the garner but he will burn up the chaff with unquenchable fire.*" The child of God is called to be a kindler of God's fire that cannot be quenched. God is the one "*who maketh his angels spirits, and his ministers a flame of fire*" (Hebrews 1:7). In whatever atmosphere a kindled believer is found, he or she will burn bright notwithstanding the opposition

ROADS, ROOMS, AND RESEARCH

My late father, General (Dr). Sam Momah, died just as he lived – venerated and celebrated. In his 20 years after retirement, he set up a chain of companies, employed hundreds of employees and established monumental structures that were sure to outlast him. He had been awarded some of the highest accolades of the nation, in his capacity as a former minister of Science and Technology, and a few years before he died he had a major street in the capital, Abuja, named after him.

Towards the end of his life, he had sat down to establish the Sam Momah Foundation (SMF) as a tool to rejuvenate the reading culture in Nigeria's teeming youths. As an author who had penned over twelve critically acclaimed books, he wanted the reading environment he enjoyed as a youth replicated for the modern day youth.

As a result, the SMF launched the Sam Momah Library in his erstwhile former office location, and partnered with the Federal Governement to build Sam Momah reading rooms across all the Federal Government colleges in Nigeria (numbering about 105). He was passionate about education, and alongside the nation's Ivory towers, a Sam Momah Chair for Civil Engineering is in the works.

My father was the proverbial goldfish, with no where to hide. He was courted by government, curried by politicians, accessible to family, and without any airs around him. He epitomized the *city set on a hill* model espoused by Jesus in Matthew 5, and for which my Dad was "...*the light of the world (as a) city that is set on an hill cannot be hid. Neither do men light a candle, and put it under a bushel, but on a candlestick; and it giveth light unto all that are in the house*" (Matthew 5:14-15).

Prayer: Fire of the God of Elijah overshadow my life, in Jesus name!

Until you Change your Mind,
no body will Mind you!

- BISHOP DAVID IBEYIOME
(SALVATION MINSITRIES, PORT
HARCOURT, NIGERIA)

CHAPTER FORTY-FOUR

COMMUNION

*"...if we walk in the **light**, as he is in the light, we have fellowship one with another, and the **blood** of Jesus Christ his Son cleanseth us from all sin:"* (1 John 1:7)

If you ignore the body and the blood of the Lord Jesus Christ, you ignore the power of the communion that is able to remove burdensome living from your life. The Holy Communion elements represent the body and blood of the Lord Jesus Christ. He said, in Matthew 26:26-28, to his disciples *"...take, eat; this is my body and he took the cup, and gave thanks, and gave it to them, saying, Drink ye all of it; For this is my blood of the new testament, which is shed for many for the remission of sins."*

That is why there are things you will never overcome until you partake in the body and blood of the Lord Jesus Christ. In Revelation 12:11, the Bible says *"...they overcame him by the blood of the Lamb, and by the word of their testimony; and they loved not their lives unto the death."*

The Holy Communion must not just be a tradition to you, but a revelation for it to birth the life of God in you. Until the two disciples on the road of Emmaus took part in the Holy Communion, they were in darkness but when they partook of the body of the Jesus Christ, they saw Jesus and their darkness became light (see Luke 24:15-27).

There is a level of light you will never experience until you partake in the Blood and Body of the Lord Jesus Christ This is corroborated further by the Elder John. In 1 John 1:5-7, he said *"this then is the message which we have heard of him, and declare unto you, that God is **light**, and in him is no darkness at all. If we say that we have fellowship with him, and walk in darkness, we lie, and do not the truth: But if we walk in the light, as he is in the light, we have fellowship one with another, and the **blood of Jesus** Christ his Son cleanseth us from all sin."*

The *Sine Qua Non* for a combustible life is fellowship with Him who is the everlasting burnings and devouring fire (Isaiah 33:14). For that to happen, the middle wall of partipation must be pulled down by the Blood of Jesus.

In Ephesians 2:13-15, Apostle Paul says *"...now in Christ Jesus ye who sometimes were far off are made nigh by the blood of Christ for he is our peace, who hath made both one, and hath broken down the middle wall of partition between us having abolished in his flesh the enmity, even the law of commandments contained in ordinances; for to make in himself of twain one new man, so making peace."*

LIFE, NOT LITURGY!

The communion was the only thing that touched and opened the eyes of these two disciples (Cleopas *and Co.*) to the reality of Christ's resurrection (Luke 24:15-27). These two men had seen Lazarus raised from the dead, a tree wither in under twenty-four hours, the woman with the issue of blood totally healed instantly, Jairus daughter raised from the dead, the widow of Nain's son raised back to life, the paraytic take up his bed and walk, the deaf hear, the blind see, and heard Jesus preach the beatitudes.

They had heard the greatest sermons ever preached, and seen the greatest miracles ever demonstrated, but were still slow of heart to believe (see Luke 24:25)! In Luke 24:15-16, the Bible explains why. It says, *"...it came to pass, that, while they communed together and reasoned, Jesus himself drew near, and went with them but their eyes were holden that they should not know him."*

There was a spiritual force holding back their eyes from beholding the truth. In Luke 24:30-31, Jesus *"...sat at meat with them,...took bread,...blessed it,...brake* (it), *and gave to them. And their eyes were opened, and they knew him; and he vanished out of their sight."* The life that the greatest sermons, miracles and divine visitations could not reveal in 42 months, the Holy Communion birthed in seconds.

The communion is not liturgy, as some propagate it to be, but the life of God enshrouded in elements of bread and wine. In John 6:53-56, Jesus said *"...verily, verily, I say unto you, except ye eat the flesh of the Son of man, and drink his blood, ye have no life in you. Whoso eateth my flesh, and drinketh my blood, hath eternal life; and I will raise him up at the last day. For my flesh is meat indeed, and my blood is drink indeed. He that eateth my flesh, and drinketh my blood, dwelleth in me, and I in him."*

GARMENTS ROLLED IN BLOOD

In Hebrews 2:14-15, the writer of Hebrews declares that *"...as the children are partakers of flesh and blood, he also himself likewise took part of the same; that through death he might destroy him that had the power of death, that is, the devil and deliver them who through fear of death were all their lifetime subject to bondage."*

Don't take the blood for granted. It is not some old wives tale or fable but the most potent force on the earth today. People blurt out *the blood of Jesus* or *I plead the blood* at the slightest infringement of their solitude. But it is not a label or a lip balm to assuage some frayed nerves, but a potent destroyer of devils!

The two men on the road to Emmaus did a return six hour journey against their normal custom, because when the blood of Jesus comes it is like a supernatural tonic. It opens eyes, quickens bodies, and stimulates understanding. In Hebrews 10:19-22, the Bible says *"having therefore, brethren, boldness to enter into the holiest by the **blood of Jesus**, by a new and living way, which he hath consecrated for us, through* *the veil, that is to say, his flesh; And having an high priest over the house of God; Let us draw near with a true heart in full assurance of faith…."*

Where ever the blood and body of Jesus is available, a new and living way will be made accessible! The death of Jesus created access for those in the holy place and outer court to enter the Holy of holies, according to Matthew 27:51. It did this through the shed blood of Jesus on God's throne.

This blood removes restrictions and releases revelations for the Church: In Hebrews 4:4-6, the writer says since *"…we have a great high priest, that is passed into the heavens, Jesus the Son of God, let us hold fast our profession. For we have not an high priest which cannot be touched with the feeling of our infirmities; but was in all points tempted like as we are, yet without sin. Let us therefore come boldly unto the throne of grace, that we may obtain mercy, and find grace to help in time of need."*

You don't get the lights that lightens, except you partake of the blood of Jesus. In Isaiah 9:2-5, the prophet Isaiah says *"the people that walked in darkness have seen a great light: they that dwell in the land of the shadow of death, upon them hath the light shined… For every battle of the warrior is with confused noise, and garments **rolled in blood**; but this shall be with burning and fuel of fire."* Before there is brightness, there must blood shed and without sacrifice shining is impossible!

CAR THEFT IN LAGOS

I was attending Mountain of Fire and Miracles Ministries in my internship year while working as an intern at the military hospital, Yaba, Lagos, Nigeria. One night on my way back from evening Church service, I met armed robbers at the reception of the guest house in action.

On that fateful morning, I had heard God's gentle whisper tell me *"I will cover you"* and even though I had three menacing, revolver handling men around me I had no fear. The cold noose of the gun was struck to my temple and I was ordered to give them my car keys and other valuables I had. They took all my cash, my watch and even my gold rimmed glasses.

They asked me to lead them to my car hoping to make it a get away car, but on arriving at my car, they couldn't find the car keys. There was pitch darkness (as a result of interrupted power supply), and search as they could they couldn't find the car keys.

They eventually intercepted another innocent car driver, and drove away with his car. On their departure, I found the keys right where they had been looking for it and subsequently heard that the car they had apprehended was found abandoned in a neighboring country more than 300 kms away.

God had covered my car keys from them in fulfillment of His word to me, that morning. I had refused to give heed to frightened light, and as a result God intervened on my behalf. Halleluyah

Prayer: Any strangers in the closed places of my life, depart in Jesus name!

The Prayer of the Saints is the Solution in the Deepest Darkness, and the Path through the roughest Sea.

- Tobe Momah M.D.

CHAPTER FORTY-FIVE

CRY

"And when they cried unto the Lord, he put darkness between you and the Egyptians, and brought the sea upon them, and covered them; and your eyes have seen what I have done in Egypt: and ye dwelt in the wilderness a long season" (Joshua 24:7).

The prelude to shining is always burning! Until John the Baptist manifested as a burning light, his shining in the wilderness in Jordan was opacified. In John 5:35, Jesus described John the Baptist as *"...a burning and a shining light, (they)...were willing for a season to rejoice in his light."*

There is, however, no effective burning without a cry unto the Lord. In John 1:23, John the Baptist describes himself as *"...the voice of one **crying** in the wilderness, Make straight the way of the Lord...."* He first started crying, before he became a burning and a shining light. **The secret to true shining is the secret place.**

In Psalm 91:1-6, the Psalmist said *"he that dwelleth in the **secret place** of the most High shall abide under the shadow of the Almighty* (and as a result)...*He shall deliver thee from the snare of the fowler,...from the noisome pestilence,...cover thee with his feathers,...*(so) *you shalt not be afraid for the terror by night; nor for the arrow that flieth by day nor for the pestilence that **walketh in darkness**...;"*

There are pestilences that operate under the cover of darkness, and only a crying believer can overcome them. **The beginning of a closed destiny is a cryless mouth.** That is why, in Psalm 81:10, the Psalmist said "*...open thy mouth wide, and I will fill it*" and in Jeremiah 33:3, God says "*call unto me, and I will answer thee, and show thee great and mighty things, which thou knowest not.*"

When Joshua recalled the secret to God attacking the Egyptians with darkness, in Joshua 24:7, and giving the Israelites light and safety he attributed it to a cry (see Joshua 24:7). There is power in a cry, and even moreso a Godly cry.

PERSISTENCE IN PRAYER

One of the debacles of prayer is the lack of persistence among those who practice it. Too many stop their future shine and burning because their cry waned too soon, and the oil on their prayer alter dried up. They began with zest, but their zeal ebbed when faced with the magnitiude of their opposition.

This pattern is exemplified in Luke 14:28-30, where Jesus asked "*...which of you, intending to build a tower, sitteth not down first, and counteth the cost, whether he have sufficient to finish it? Lest haply, after he hath laid the foundation, and is not able to finish it, all that behold it begin to mock him, Saying, This man began to build, and was not able to finish.*"

The secret to the lamp that never goes out on the altar of prayer is a heart with a cry! The Samuel's, who say "*... God forbid that I should sin against the Lord in ceasing to pray for you...*" (1 Samuel 12:23) will have open visions and burning altars but the Eli's who rather than pray say "*...it is the Lord: let him do what seemeth him good*" (1 Samuel 3:18) will preside over an altar where "*...the lamp of God went out in the temple of the Lord, where the ark of God was,...*" (1 Samuel 3:3).

It takes persistence to be perfected, and a cry to God to become combustible! In 1 Peter 5:8-10, Apostle Peter adjures the Church to "*be sober* (and) *vigilant because your adversary the devil, as a roaring lion, walketh about, seeking whom he may devour: Whom* **resist stedfast** *in the faith, knowing that the same afflictions are accomplished in your brethren that are in the world. But the God of all grace, who hath called us unto his eternal glory by Christ Jesus, after that ye have suffered a while, make you perfect, stablish, strengthen, settle you."*

The same word, resist, is used in James 4:7 where apostle James advises the Church to *"submit yourselves therefore to God.* **Resist** *the devil, and he will flee from you."* The word resist is from the Greek Word *anthistémi,* and it is a **military** term that means to strongly withstand an opponent firmly. If there is no resistance, there is no fleeing of darkness.

In Isaiah 42:13-16, the prophet said *"the Lord* shall go forth as a mighty man, he shall stir up jealousy like a man of war: he shall **cry,** *yea, roar; he shall prevail against his enemies. I have long time holden my peace; I have been still, and refrained myself: now will I* **cry** *like a travailing woman; I will destroy and devour at once. I will make waste mountains and hills, and dry up all their herbs; and I will make the rivers islands, and I will dry up the pools. And I will bring the blind by a way that they knew not; I will lead them in paths that they have not known: I will make* **darkness light** *before them...."*

Where ever the cry unto God emanates from, the life of God and the light that defeats darkness manifests! God cannot tolerate darkness, and his tool for combating it and commanding combustion is the cry. In Ephesians 6:12, apostle Paul advises the Church to "... *wrestle not against flesh and blood, but against principalities, against powers, against the* **rulers of the darkness** *of this world, against spiritual wickedness in high places. Wherefore take unto you the whole armour of God, that ye may be able to withstand in the evil day, and having done all, to stand"* (Ephesians 6:12-13).

Commanding your Closed Places

It is in closed places that darkness thrives! It is within its walls that evil is contrived, and cruelty exhibited (Psalm 74:20). To discomfit the darkness, and paralyze it work, light is essential. This light is, however, based on the command of a cry from a Christian, and not a wimper from a wavering whiner.

In Psalm 18:33-45, the Psalmist acknowledges the power of a cry to overcome the enemies in a closed place. He states that God *"...maketh my feet like hinds' feet, and setteth me upon my high places. He teacheth my hands to war, so that a bow of steel is broken by mine arms* (and) *hast also given me the shield of thy salvation....*(so that) ***as soon as they hear of me***, *they shall obey me: the strangers shall submit themselves unto me.* ***The strangers shall fade away, and be afraid out of their close places.***"

The devil does not budge to logic, lies or lamentation. He answers only to light, and that light is heralded by a command! In 2 Corinthians 4:6, Apostle Paul said *"...God...commanded the light to shine out of darkness,* (and so it) *hath shined in our hearts, to give the light of the knowledge of the glory of God in the face of Jesus Christ."* Without a command, or cry, light is hidden and glory is silent! Use prayer and God will use you. Until the hand of God is upon you, with the strengthening power of the Holy Spirit, light is fractitious and prayer brittle.

In Psalm 77:1-19, the Psalmist acknowledged the power of a cry. He said, *"I* ***cried*** *unto God with my voice, even unto God with my voice; and he gave ear unto me. In the day of my trouble I sought the Lord: my sore ran in the night, and ceased not: my soul refused to be comforted. I remembered God, and was troubled:...The clouds poured out water: the skies sent out a sound: thine arrows also went abroad. The voice of thy thunder was in the heaven: the* ***lightnings lightened*** *the world: the earth trembled and shook. Thy way is in the sea, and thy path in the great waters, and thy footsteps are not known."*

IDAHOSA'S LEGACY

Archbishop Benson Idahosa (1938 – 1998) was a famous evangelist, Apostle and Pastor of the Church of God Mission (CGM) International with headquarters in Benin, Nigeria. He started in a corner, and rose to preach to more blacks and whites than any black man or woman alive in his time. He travelled to more than 160 countries, and at his death had established more than five thousand branches of the Church of God Mission globally.

He began his ministry with a well publicized turf war with the dreaded Ogboni cult of Benin city. Before the Archbishop arose, they believed they owned the city of Benin and its environs. It was common place then to see dead bodies at different corners of the street, but when the Archbishop arose he decreed a stop to all these fetish practices. He believed, according to Revelation 11:15, that "*the kingdoms of this world had become the kingdoms of his Lord, and His Christ*" and he was the owner – not just occupier - of the land.

This public affront to the traditions and customs of the great historical city of Benin rubbed many the wrong way. To them it was normal to hang corpses of dead birds, animals and humans at street corners as a human sacrifice to the gods of the land, but to Idahaosa it was an anathema. He challenged the witches to an open contest, and on national television threathened to kill the head of the witch coven in his city with his words if he confessed to being a wizard. The wizard quickly back tracked his confession and asked to be let off that day.

It was, also, on television that Idahosa unilaterally abolished the killings of human beings and offering of sacrifices in Benin City. He pronounced a death sentence on any unrepentant witches and wizards and openly declared war on the Ogboni cult. He declared Benin a Christian city, and refused to allow her host a world conference of witches which led the government of the day refuse visas to these visiting witches and eventually led to the cancellation of the conference.

In reply, these enemies of God sent Idahosa several death threats and actually attacked him physically, through hired assassins, thrice without success. By the time of his death, he had transformed Benin from a high tempo witch craft coven to a city in revival with the gospel of Jesus Christ. He established the first private University in Nigeria there, and opened hospitals and schools to the teeming millions who were formerly without access to these amenities.

Today, his legacy still lives on in the CGM Church network, schools, hospitals, and proteges of his ministry that have carried the torch of the gospel of revival to different nations of the earth. His towering influence in Nigerian Pentecostalism enabled several pivotal collaborations between overseas ministries such as Kenneth Copeland, Oral Roberts, Kenneth Hagin, and T.L Osborne to take place. He was, as described by his biographer – Ruthanne Garlock - a man with fire in his bones and a catalyst for the Last days Great awakening in Africa and beyond.

Prayer: Baptize me with fire in my bones that I cannot forbear speaking your word, in Jesus name!

You cannot catch fire
following a Cold leader!

- Tobe Momah M.D.

CHAPTER FORTY-SIX

CONVERSATIONS

*"Out of his mouth go **burning lamps**, and sparks of fire leap out. Out of his nostrils goeth smoke, as out of a seething pot or caldron. His breath kindleth coals, and a **flame** goeth out of his **mouth**"* (Job 41:19-21).

One of the greatest commanders of combustion is the conversation between believers. In Malachi 3:16, the prophet Malachi said *"...they that feared the Lord **spake often one to another:** and the Lord* hearkened, and heard it, and a book of remembrance was written before him for them that feared the *Lord, and that thought upon his name."*

The aftermath of these conversations was the igniting of flames. In Malachi 4:1, the prophet said *"...the day cometh, that shall **burn** as an oven; and all the proud, yea, and all that do wickedly, shall be stubble: and the day that cometh shall **burn** them up, saith the Lord* of hosts, that it shall leave them neither root nor branch."

The words of your mouth make your life flammable or fireproof! In Luke 12:35, the Bible says *"let your loins be **girded** about, and your lights **burning**."* The word *girded* is the Greek word *perizonnumi* and it means active work, or speaking words that fasten upon oneself. The result of speaking right words is a burning life.

When Apostle Paul wanted to cause a combustion flame to be ignited in the Ephesian Church, he counselled them to "*let no corrupt communication proceed out of your mouth, but that which is good to the use of edifying, that it may minister grace unto the hearers. And grieve not the Holy Spirit of God, whereby ye are sealed unto the day of redemption*" (Ephesians 4:29-30).

The Holy Spirit is the source of the combustion flame, but wrong words can snuff out His flame. In Isaiah 33:14-16, the prophet Isaiah asked "*who among us shall dwell with the devouring fire? who among us shall dwell with everlasting burnings* (but) *he that walketh righteously, and **speaketh uprightly**; he that despiseth the gain of oppressions, that shaketh his hands from holding of bribes, **that stoppeth his ears from hearing of blood, and shutteth his eyes from seeing evil**; He shall dwell on high: his place of defence shall be the munitions of rocks: bread shall be given him; his waters shall be sure.*"Your environment truly determines your element!

JOB'S JAMBOREE

Job was the wealthiest man in the east (Job 1:3), and while going through a trial of affliction his friend Eliphaz counsel led him to "*…decree a thing, and it shall be established unto thee: and the **light shall shine** upon thy ways* (so that) *when men are cast down,…thou shalt say there is lifting up and he shall save the humble person.*"

True light follows your words. If these words are combustible, there will be a consumption of every chaff and a deliverance of any debris. The words of the Lord are combustible words; in Job 41:18-19, the Lord is described as He who "*out of his mouth go **burning lamps**, and sparks of fire leap out. Out of his nostrils goeth smoke, as out of a seething pot or caldron. His breath kindleth coals, and a **flame** goeth out of his **mouth***" (Job 41:19-21).

On the way from Emmaus, the two disciples (Cleopas and co), testified saying "*did not our heart burn within us, while he talked with us by the way, and while he opened to us the scriptures?*" (Luke 24:32). You can't have interviews and instructions from the everlasting burnings and consuming fire and remain fire proof. His word is the secret to the flames of fire in your life (see Proverbs 26:20).

In Isaiah 8:11-12, the Lord warns the Church "...*with a strong hand, instruct*(ing)...(her) *not* (to) *walk in the way of this people, saying, say ye not, a confederacy, to all them to whom this people shall say, a confederacy; neither fear ye their fear, nor be afraid.*" The reason why the Lord was so stringent about their words is because it had significant spiritual impact later on.

In Isaiah 8:20,22, the Lord says "...*if they speak not according to this word, it is because there is **no light** in them....And they shall look unto the earth; and behold trouble and darkness, dimness of anguish; and they shall be **driven to darkness**.*" Those who speak right words radiate like a flame, but those who speak wrong words wither in the dark.

FIERY WORDS OR WEARYING WORDS?

Many believers speak wearying words, instead of fiery words and still wonder why their lives are not combustible. In Malachi 2:17, the Lord God said to the people of Israel that *"ye have wearied the Lord* with your words. Yet ye say, wherein have we wearied him? When ye say, every one that doeth evil is good in the sight of the *Lord, and he delighteth in them; or, where is the God of judgment?"*

Their words weary everyone, including God, and extinguish fire in the lives of the believer. These words are contrary to what is expected which are fiery words. In Jeremiah 23:28-29, God says "*the prophet that hath a dream, let him tell a dream; and he that hath my word, let him speak my word faithfully. What is the chaff to the wheat? saith the Lord. Is not my word like as a **fire**? saith the Lord; and like a hammer that breaketh the rock in pieces?*"

The words the believer should speak are fiery words, not wearying words! When God appeared to Job, He answered him "...*out of the whirlwind, and said, who is this that darkeneth counsel by words without knowledge?*" (Job 38:1-2). It is possible to darken counsel with words that are without knowledge, and consequently weary the hearers.

When God wants to "...*make the horn of David to bud* (and)... *ordain a lamp for his anointed*" (Psalm 132:17), He asks "...*thy children* (to) *keep...covenant and...testimony that I shall* **teach** *them* (so that He) *abundantly bless*(es) *her provision,...satisfy*(ies) *her poor with bread,* (and)...*clothe her priests with salvation: and her saints shall shout aloud for joy*" (Psalm 132:12-16).

Those that are taught by the Lord will carry a lamp of combustion wherever they go, and those who "...*return* (to Him will),...*stand before* (Him)...*and if* (they) *take forth the precious from the vile, thou shalt be as my mouth...And I will make thee unto this people a* **fenced brasen** *wall*" (Jeremiah 15:19-20). Your portion is to be a fiery wall that no enemy can penetrate, but it starts with been a mouthpiece for God!

BROKEN SILENCE, AND BREAKTHROUGH SOLUTIONS!

Jason and Ann Beiler (of Annie pretzels fame) were youth pastors at a local Church in Pennsylvania, USA when the greatest tragedy of their lives took place. Their second daughter was crushed under a tractor driven by Ann's sister, and died immediately. Their grieving process was abrupt, and none of them had any time to speak to anyone about their inner hurts.

With no one to open up to, Ann reached out to her pastor. In her vulnerable state, he took advantage of her and therein started a six year intimate relationship with the senior pastor of the Church. After fifteen other women in the Church – including two of her sisters and daughter – reported being abused by the senior pastor, Ann confessed to her husband. Jason, expecting him to divorce her.

Instead Jason told her "Hon, I want you to be happy, and I knew that you weren't happy, but I thought it was because Angie died. I'll do whatever it takes for you to be happy. If you need to go away, if you need to find another place, then just tell me, don't leave a note on the dresser in the middle of the night, but just tell me, and then I'll help you find a place and I'll help you pack your bags, and we'll do it together," but he said, "I just want you to know that if you go, you have to take the girls with you."

The fact that Jason trusted her with the girls broke her. She was determined then to make her relationship with Jason work and she financially supported him when he decided to go into a new profession by opening a pretzel shop. After tinkering with the menu a bit, she developed a recipe for pretzels that was much sought after and withing 15 years had thousands of branches and more than a billion dollars in revenue.

She credits the power of confession with saving her life, marriage and family. As a result, she started Broken Silence in 2018 with a mission of teaching and equipping women about living a lifestyle of confession that leads to freedom. Today, she and her husband live in Soldano, Texas and have two daughters and six grandchildren. She spoke out the truth of God's word and became a combustion commander in her generation.

Prayer: Touch my lips with the coals from your altar, and speak through me O Lord in Jesus name.

The tragedy of our time is not unanswered prayers or unoffered prayers, but unoffered lives!

- TOBE MOMAH M.D.

CHAPTER FORTY-SEVEN

CIRCUMSPECT

"Wherefore he saith, Awake thou that sleepest, and arise from the dead, and Christ shall give thee light. See then that ye walk **circumspectly**, *not as fools, but as wise, redeeming the time, because the days are evil. Wherefore be ye not unwise, but understanding what the will of the Lord is. And be not drunk with wine, wherein is excess; but be filled with the Spirit"* (Ephesians 5:14-18).

The word *circumspect* is the Greek word *akribos* which means to be extremely accurate, and very exact, because it was researched down to the finest details. It is the secret to an awakened life that shines and burns bright with the fire of the Holy Ghost. Especially in these last days, the need to be accurate and exact is not a choice but a command if you want to escape the evil days coming upon the world.

In Ephesians 5:14-18, the Lord said *"awake thou that sleepest, and arise from the dead, and Christ shall give thee* **light.** *See then that ye walk* **circumspectly**, *not as fools, but as* **wise**, *redeeming the time, because the days are evil. Wherefore be ye not unwise, but understanding what the will of the Lord is. And be not drunk with wine, wherein is excess; but be* **filled with the Spirit.**"

When you are filled with the Spirit, you will be aflame for the Lord. In Isaiah 10:16-18, the prophet Isaiah says *"...under his glory he shall kindle a burning like the burning of a fire and the light of Israel shall be for a fire, and his Holy One for a flame: and it shall burn and devour his thorns and his briers in one day and shall consume the glory of his forest, and of his fruitful field, both soul and body: and they shall be as when a standard-bearer fainteth"* (Isaiah 10:16-18).

What turns a fire into a flame is exactness! It is in you following His light and abiding under His glory, that burning flames emerge. As long as the Israelites stayed under the cover of the pillar of fire by night and the cloud of glory by day (Exodus 40:36-37), they were preserved from evil (Exodus 14:24). They, however, had to be exact in His directions to remain combustible (see Numbers 9:16-19).

DYING BESIDE YOUR WELL!

In Genesis 21, the story of Hagar and Ishamel and their near death experience is shared. It says, after Abraham sent her and her son away, they were dying from thirst and the mother "...*cast the child under one of the shrubs and she went, and sat her down over against him a good way off, as it were a bow shot: for she said, Let me not see the death of the child. And she sat over against him, and lift up her voice, and wept"* (Genesis 21:15-16).

Weeping, however, did not solve her problem. She needed perception, not pity and explanations not emotions. In Genesis 21:18-19, therefore, the angel said to her *"arise, lift up the lad, and hold him in thine hand; for I will make him a great nation. And God opened her eyes, and she saw a well of water; and she went, and filled the bottle with water, and gave the lad drink."*

Without revelation, Hagar and Ishamel would have died beside their well of nourishment. The indispensability of wisdom in the last days is explained in Isaiah 33:6. It says *"wisdom and knowledge shall be the stability of thy times, and strength of salvation* (with) *the fear of the Lord* is his treasure." Those who are guided by the Lord of lights will avoid the repercussions of darkness. It is those who walk in wisdom or are circumspect that shine like the sun. In Daniel 12:3, the Bible says "...*they that be* **wise** *shall* **shine** *as the* **brightness of the firmament**;...."

Without wisdom, many would be brightly inflamed and combustible believers would be shriveled and nondescript. In Ephesians 1:17-19, the apostle Paul prays "...*the God of our Lord Jesus Christ, the Father of glory, may give unto you the spirit of wisdom and revelation in the knowledge of him: The eyes of your understanding being **enlightened**; that ye may know what is the hope of his calling, and what the riches of the glory of his inheritance in the saints, and what is the exceeding greatness of his power to us-ward who believe, according to the working of his **mighty power**.*"

BURNING, BUT NOT BURNT OUT!

There is a scourge of burnt out believers in the secular and spiritual spheres today. More than 70% of pastors would change jobs if they had a choice, and more than 60% of physicians in America endorse feeling burnt out presently. In general, more than 50% of United States report feelings of burnt out including emotional and physical exhaustion that is brought upon by long periods of constant unrelenting stress.[1]

When you are burnt out, instead of burning for Jesus, it leaves an individual chaffed and with the smell of smoke upon that individual. Such people are incapable of providing leadership to a community. When Shadrach, Meshach and Abednego went into the fire for refusing to bow down to the idol in Daniel 3, they came out without "...*hair of their head singed or their coats changed or the smell of fire...on them*" (Daniel 3:27).

They became even more prominent rulers in Israel after that experience. According to Daniel 3:30, *"the king promoted Shadrach, Meshach, and Abednego, in the province of Babylon"* because they went into the evil iron furnace of Nebuchadnezzar with the everlasting burnings (Isaiah 33:14), and so Nebuchadnezzar's fire had no effect on them.

Many of these *burnt out* ones do not dwell with the everlasting burnings, and so remain victims of oppressions from satanic wickednesses. It is either you burn for God, or be burnt out and become a vestige of yesteryears. To the combustible, God says "...*fear not for I have redeemed thee,* (and)...*have called thee by thy name* (for) *thou art mine. When thou passest through the waters, I will be with thee; and through the rivers, they shall not overflow thee: when thou walkest through the fire, thou shalt not be burned; neither shall the flame kindle upon thee*" (Isaiah 43:1-2).

BORN IN THE FIRE, I REFUSE TO DIE IN THE SMOKE!

Mae Taylor Roberts was in the maiden meeting that heralded the birth of the Assemblies of God in 1914. As an eye witness to the outpouring of the Holy Spirit upon that motley group of individuals, that went on to shake the world, she cried out one day to God despondent about her spiritual state.

She said to the Lord, "*I was born in the Fire, and I cannot be content in the smoke.*" She wanted to get the substance, and not just the shadow. She was not content warming pews, and making up numbers but she wanted to be a catalyst for change.

She was tired of a lameduck Christianity that was of no value to her environment. She had tasted its fire, and did not want ash heap Christianity. She wanted to judge herself, before she was judged by fire in the last days (1 Corinthians 3:14-15).

Out of that cry came a spiritual re birth that made Mae Taylor Roberts a song composer, preacher, and a more active part of the Assemblies of God USA. She shared the experience of her spiritual journey in the weekly Pentecostal Assembly of God magazine, and composed a song called "Meeting in the air" that is still sung today.

Prayer: I (put your name here), arise and shine because my light has come and the glory of God has risen upon me!

1. Jack Kelly. Indeed Study Shows That Worker Burnout Is At Frighteningly High Levels: Here Is What You Need To Do Now. *Forbes*. April 2021

*Sustainability of impact depends
on Sensitivity to the Holy Spirit!*

– BISHOP OYEDEPO
(PRESIDENT LIVING FAITH CHURCH)

CHAPTER FORTY-EIGHT

CARPE DIEM

"Verily I say unto you, among them that are born of women there hath not risen a greater than John the Baptist: notwithstanding he that is least in the kingdom of heaven is greater than he. And from the days of John the Baptist until now the kingdom of heaven suffereth violence, and the violent take it by force" (Matthew 11:12).

The Latin word *Carpe diem* was first used by Horace in his work, *Odes*, as *carpe diem quam minimum credula postero* in 23BC and is translated literally as *enjoy the day, and pluck the day when it is ripe. Today's generation of writers have, however, popularized Carpe Diem as a phrase that means seize the moment.*

It means to be decisive in one's actions, and enjoy life while one can. It connotes a meaning similar to what Jesus said in Matthew 11:12, when he said *"…the kingdom of heaven suffereth violence, and the violent take it by force."*

Delay is dangerous in the portals of power, and finishers are unfailingly few as a result. Too many abandon what they should have instead accelerated and by the time they send it out it is too late to get it back.

John the Baptist was, according to Jesus, "...*Elias, which was for to come*" (Matthew 11:14), and is a symbol of the fire of the Holy Ghost. Like John the Baptist, he had an unorthodox ministry, that rattled organizations, and the set order of doing things (see 1 Kings 18:12 and Luke 3:19). He upturned the status-quo, and broke protocols but the signature of his ministry was fire (1 Kings 18:38).

SEIZE THE MOMENT!

The reason why John the Baptist was likened to Elijah was because he seized the moment. Rather than dilly-dally, delay, and double-guess himself, John the Baptist stepped out of the comfort of the priesthood into a wilderness ministry where he captivated the nation with his message of uprightness and truth (Luke 3:2-18 and Matthew 3:1-7).

The Bible describes John the Baptist as a custodian of the "...*the kingdom of heaven* (that) *suffereth violence, and* (so has to)...*take it by force*" (Matthew 11:12). The phrase *take it by force* is the Hebrew word *Harpazo* and it means to seize on, claim for one's self eagerly, snatch away or carry off by force.

Without seizing the moment, or enjoying a *Carpe diem* moment, the fire that Elijah and John the Baptist symbolized would have been lost. It (the fire) so touched the people in Elijah's day that they did not need a preacher, but repented readily and even helped Elijah kill all four hundread and fifty prophets of Baal (I Kings 18:39-40).

In the case of John the Baptist, he was described as a "...*burning and a shining light...*" (John 5:35) by Jesus, and as a result of his ministry "...*the people were in expectation, and all men mused in their hearts of John, whether he were the Christ, or not*" (Luke 3:15). In addition, Matthew records that "*then went out to him Jerusalem, and all Judaea, and all the region round about Jordan, and were baptized of him in Jordan, confessing their sins*" (Matthew 3:5-6).

No man of fiery impact makes a difference without seizing the moment, or taking it by force! Historically, Nero is chided for fiddling while Rome burnt. That is too much of a similar story in today's Church. Rather than make a stake for what we believe, too many in the Church champion alternative options and as a result lose the flame of their glory.

IF DARKNESS CAN BE FELT, LIGHT CAN BE KNOWN!

In Exodus 10:21-23, God spoke to Moses saying "...*stretch out thine hand toward heaven, that there may be darkness over the land of Egypt, even darkness which may be felt. And Moses stretched forth his hand toward heaven; and there was a thick darkness in all the land of Egypt three days: They saw not one another, neither rose any from his place for three days: but all the children of Israel had light in their dwellings.*"

The same way darkness can be felt, is the same way light can be known! It is not felt, like darkness above, but known as an inner witness in the spirit realm. That moment of deep knowing is a *Carpe Diem* moment. It is described in Isaiah 64:7, as follows. It says, "... *there is none that calleth upon thy name, that stirreth up himself to take hold of thee: for thou hast hid thy face from us, and hast consumed us, because of our iniquities.*"

If they had stirred up themselves to take hold of God, their combustion and the consuming of their enemies would have taken place rapidly. It says, in Isaiah 64:1-2, that "...*that thou wouldest rend the heavens, that thou wouldest come down, that the mountains might flow down at thy presence, as when the **melting fire** burneth, the fire causeth the waters to boil, to make thy name known to thine adversaries, that the nations may tremble at thy presence!*"

The impact of a *Carpe diem* (moment by moment) lifestyle is a combustible life where Gods infinite presence makes all the difference. For example, in Deuteronomy 33:1-3, the Bible states that "*the Lord* came from Sinai, and rose up from Seir unto them; he **shined forth** *from mount Paran, and he came with ten thousands of saints: from his right hand went a fiery law for them. Yea, he loved the people; all his saints are in thy hand: and they sat down at thy feet; every one shall receive of thy words.*"

As long as the saints are in His hands, and under His guidance, the Light will shine and the fire burn. When man is in charge, and self reigns, "...*they grope in the dark without light, and he maketh them to stagger like a drunken man*" (Job 12:25). In addition, apostle Paul adjures the Church to "...*walk not as other Gentiles walk, in the vanity of their mind, having the understanding darkened, being alienated from the life of God through the ignorance that is in them, because of the blindness of their heart*" (Ephesians 4:17-18).

DADDY, BONNY CAMP, AND *DIVINE INTELLIGENTSIA*

In 1990, one of the bloodiest coups that ever took place in Nigeria occurred and my father – then Col. Sam Momah – was in the center of it. As the Director of Army Works, my father was stationed at the Bonny Camp military outpost, and periodically shuttled between Ibadan (where my mother and siblings were living pending accomodation allocation to him in Lagos).

While in Bonny Camp, Victoria Island Lagos my father lodged at the exclusive officers' guest house in Bonny camp and on the day of the coup he was torn between travelling to Ibadan and staying back in Bonny Camp to do some work. After leaving the decision for late, he left for Ibadan (a two hour journey) late at night and arrived about midnight.

On waking up the next day, he was shocked to hear martial music on the radio. Apparently, there had been a military coup by a section of the Nigerian army (led by Major Gideon Orkar), and Bonny camp, Victoria Island had been the epicenter of the confrontation between loyalist forces and the dissidents. Where my father would have slept as riddled with bullets, and several officers in that complex were killed that morning.

My Dad hurridly returned to his post, and was told by his military intelligentsia friends tha he narrowly escaped death as the dissidents targeted the guest house and even deployed a bomb to gain entrance. It was a miracle, to them, that my Dad escaped just at the knick of time. Even though, his properties in the guest house were irreparably damaged, he knew he was blessed just to be alive.

He never stopped thanking God, and telling all that cared to listen that a *Carpe diem* decision to travel that night saved him from almost certain harm. He called those moments his *God-brain* moments, and taught him to be mre sensitive aand alert to the Holy Spirit when ever he told him to do anything.

Prayer: Father, Give me a God-brain that makes me think your thoughts always in Jesus name!

No matter how many Birds
fly over and around the Sun,
it cannot diminish its shine!

- TOBE MOMAH M.D.

CHAPTER FORTY-NINE

CHRIST

*"That Christ should suffer, and that he should be the first that should rise from the dead, and should **shew light** unto the people, and to the Gentiles"* (Acts 26:23)

Jesus Christ is the light of the world, and just like the Father is a devouring fire (Isaiah 30:27), an everlasting burning (see Isaiah 33:14) and a consuming fire (Hebrews 12:29) so is Jesus Christ (John 1:1). In Malachi 3:2-3, He is described as the *"... refiner's fire... (who)...sits as a refiner and purifier of silver: (for)...he shall purify the sons of Levi, and purge them as gold and silver, that they may offer unto the Lord* an offering in righteousness."

When a man or woman encounters this refiner's fire, he or she becomes a commander of combustion who brings offerings that glorify God and transforms lives. In Ephesians 5:8, the apostle Paul attributes the believers' fire to the presence of the Lord Jesus Christ. He said, *"Let no man deceive you with vain words: for because of these things cometh the wrath of God upon the children of disobedience. Be not ye therefore partakers with them. For ye were sometimes darkness, but now are ye **light in the Lord:** walk as children of light"* (Ephesians 5:6-8).

Jesus came to baptize the believer with unquenchable fire, according to Matthew 3:11-12. In that verse, John the Baptist said *"...he that cometh after me is mightier than I, whose shoes I am not worthy to bear: he shall baptize you with the Holy Ghost, and with fire: Whose fan is in his hand, and he will throughly purge his floor, and gather his wheat into the garner; but he will burn up the chaff with* **unquenchable fire.***"*

God's combustible presence is not just a purifier, but a catalyst for combustion. Jesus is not just the light of the world, but an arch combustioner too! In Hebrews 1:7, the writer of Hebrews says, God makes *"…his ministers flames of fire"* and in Psalm 104:4, the Psalmist said God *"…maketh…his ministers a flaming fire."*

It takes only one touch from Christ to make one combustible. In a world filled with disillusionment and discouragement, a believer who is a follower of Christ will burn and shine and as he or she does, they *give people permission to shine theirs.* In Isaiah 9:8, the prophet Isaiah says *"the Lord sent a word into Jacob, and it hath lighted upon Israel."*

LIGHT OUT OF DARKNESS

In Deuteronomy 9:1-3, the pathway from smouldering to shining, from fireproof to flammable, from dimness to distinction, and from waning to widespread flame is shown. It is, simply put, the presence of the Lord God Almighty, Jesus Christ, and the Holy Spirit with us wherever we go.

It says *"hear, O Israel: Thou art to pass over Jordan this day, to go in to possess nations greater and mightier than thyself, cities great and fenced up to heaven, a people great and tall, the children of the Anakims, whom thou knowest, and of whom thou hast heard say, Who can stand before the children of Anak! Understand therefore this day, that the Lord* thy God is he which goeth over before thee; as a **consuming fire** *he shall destroy them, and he shall bring them down before thy face: so shalt thou drive them out, and destroy them quickly, as the Lord* hath said unto thee."

Without the Lord on our side, it is an ardous task but when Christ is in us (as He promised in Matthew 28:19-20), it is possible. He said, in Colossians 1:26-27 that this *"…mystery which hath been hid from ages and from generations* (is)…*now…made manifest to his saints…whom God would make known what is the riches of the glory* *of this mystery among the Gentiles; which **is Christ in you, the hope of glory**.*"

The devils chief weapon, in these last days, is ignorance. His goal is to make the Church think God has forsaken the earth (see Zephaniah 1:12, Ezekiel 8:12, and Ezekiel 9:9), and so make her attempt to fight him alone. This vicious lie is been perpetrated across all quarters, and has led to the Church being defeated over and over again. The truth is "…*God is with us and no one can be against us*" (Romans 8:31).

God does not abandon His own in the dark but brings them out of the dark into the light. In Psalm 37:5-6, the Psalmist says *"commit thy way unto the Lord; trust also in him; and he shall bring it to pass. And he shall bring forth thy righteousness as the light, and thy judgment as the noonday."* In Psalm 43:3, he adds that God "…*sends out…light and…truth…*(to) *lead me* (and)…*bring me unto thy holy hill, and to thy tabernacles.*"

The Power of the Honeycomb

In 1 Samuel 14:27, the story of Jonathan and the honeycomb is shared. It says, "*Jonathan heard not when his father charged the people with the oath* (not to eat) (and)…*he put forth the end of the rod that was in his hand, and dipped it in an honeycomb, and put his hand to his mouth; and his eyes were enlightened.*"

When Jonathan tasted the honey, his countenance brightened and his eyes were enlightened. He later reprimanded his father, King Saul, for "…*trouble*(ing) *the land* (as)…*mine eyes have been enlightened, because I tasted a little of this honey. How much more, if haply the people had eaten freely to day of the spoil of their enemies which they found?*" (1 Samuel 14:29-30).

Honey is compared to the word of God, in Ezekiel 3:1-4. It says, "…*son of man, eat that thou findest; eat this roll, and go speak unto the house of Israel. So I opened my mouth, and he caused me to eat that roll. And he said unto me, Son of man, cause thy belly to eat, and fill thy bowels with this roll that I give thee. Then did I eat it; and it was in my mouth as honey for sweetness and he said unto me, Son of man, go, get thee unto the house of Israel, and speak with my words unto them."*

Honey is the revelation of the word, which is Jesus Christ (according to John 1:1), to those who eat it. **It is the word that brightens one's life and without it, commanding combustion is impossible.** Any man or woman who pays attention to the word will be a person marked out for distinction and the devouring flames of His presence.

In Proverbs 26:20, the wise man said *"where no wood is, there the fire goeth out:..."* The wood, in the above verse, is from the Hebrew word *ets* which means building or structural support. The Word of God is the Church's greatest builder and support structure (see Acts 20:32), and the chief tool for combustion. Take away the word of God, and surely the fire will go out!

MY PERSONAL CONVERSION STORY

In 1989, while walking on the corridors of my High school I was approached by my classmate, Akin Mabogunje, to surrender my liufe to Christ. I had grown up in Church, and had been a committed Church attender and actually loved reading the Bible. I was not an avid sinner, but I knew I had many shortcomings in my life – including lust which at that age and time in high school was so pervasive.

After hearing the message of salvation, and why everyone – including the so called goody two-shoes like myself – needed it, I knelt down on the corridor of my High school (King's Colllege, Lagos) and surrendered my life to Jesus Christ.

It was the start of something momentous, as the Bible opened up to me like never before and I began to have divine encounters with the supernatural. The Bible was not just a story book anymore, but a roadmap for living. I saw a heart conversion, with the lusts of the world giving way to the love for God and His people.

I proceeded on to College, and graduated with stellar grades after serving as a two-time Vice President of the Christian Union campus fellowship on campus. I met men and women of God like Austin

Ukachi, Uma Ukpai, Emma Kure, Edith Nwosu, Emma Ogidiolu, Chris Nwajiagwu, Chris Akosa, Alfred Itiowe, Paul Enenche, Paul Nwachukwu, D.K Olukoya, Emmah Isong, and several others who inspired me on my journey.

Today, as the superintendent of a ministry (Faith and Power Ministries) and an academic physician (associate professor at University of Mississippi Medical Center), I look back and unequivocally state that it was worth it all. The Bible aptly asks, "... *who hath despised the day of small things?...*" (Zechariah 4:10) and in Job 8:7 answers that "...*though thy beginning was small, yet thy latter end should greatly increase*" (Job 8:7). That truly has been my story!

Prayer: Help me Lord never to despise my small beginnings, O Lord, in Jesus name!

PART VIII

Conclusions

When you second-guess God,
you down-size your miracle!

- Tobe Momah M.D.

CHAPTER FIFTY

LET THERE BE LIGHT

*"This I say therefore, and testify in the Lord, that ye henceforth walk not as other Gentiles walk, in the vanity of their mind, Having the understanding **darkened**, being alienated from the life of God through the ignorance that is in them, because of the **blindness** of their heart: Who being past feeling have given themselves over unto lasciviousness, to work all uncleanness with greediness. But ye have not so **learned** Christ"* (Ephesians 4:17-20)

The last days Church is akin to the Israelite's exodus from Egypt. In 1 Corinthians 10:9-12, the apostle Paul warned them saying *"neither let us tempt Christ, as some of them also tempted, and were destroyed of serpents. Neither murmur ye, as some of them also murmured, and were destroyed of the destroyer. Now all these things happened unto them for examples: and they are written for our admonition, **upon whom the ends of the world are come.** Wherefore let him that thinketh he standeth take heed lest he fall."*

Theirs' was, however, no ordinary journey. It was a journey filled with signs and wonders, and a signature moment for God to demonstrate His power to the nations around them. God has earmarked the last day Church as His divine spectacle to advertise the gospel to the nations in the last days (see Micah 4:2 and Isaiah 60:3).

In Micah 7:15-17, God says *"according to the days of thy coming out of the land of Egypt will I shew unto him **marvelous** things. The nations shall see and be confounded at all their might: they shall lay their hand upon their mouth, their ears shall be deaf. They shall lick the dust like a serpent, they shall move out of their holes like worms of the earth: they shall be afraid of the Lord* our God, and shall fear because of thee."

The word marvelous, in the original Hebrew, is the word *pala* and it means to be extraordinary, special, and all surpassing. That is who the last days Church is called to be. That picture is, in Acts 13:17, collaborated further. It says, *"the God of this people of Israel chose our fathers, and exalted the people when they dwelt as strangers in the land of Egypt, and with an **high arm** brought he them out of it."*

The Church of the last days is the Church of the high arm of God! Whatever has been exhibited is nothing compared to what will be shown in these last days. The God who brought the Israelites out of Egypt in power will also bring the Church out of this world in power. He said, in Deuteronomy 4:37, that *"...because he loved thy fathers, therefore he chose their seed after them, and brought thee out in his sight with his **mighty power out of Egypt.**"*

God values an assertive initiative or a *high arm* attitude at the onset, because that is how the world will get our message about a living Christ. **It is the assertive Church that will be the ascending Church on the day of the rapture!** In Numbers 33:3, Moses said *"... they departed from Rameses in the first month, on the fifteenth day of the first month; on the morrow after the passover the children of Israel went out with an **high hand** in the sight of all the Egyptians."*

SUBSTANCE VERSUS SHADOWS

Now is the time for the Church to be like candles in the night that light up the night with her radiance. In the midst of so much upheavel, division, strife, and turmoil only a Church that manifests the substance of her faith (light), instead of casting shadows (darkness), will bring the Messiah back.

In 1 Timothy 4:1-2, the apostle Paul warns that "...*the Spirit speaketh expressly, that in the latter times some shall depart from the faith, giving heed to seducing spirits, and doctrines of devils; speaking lies in hypocrisy; having their conscience seared with a hot iron.*" In Luke 21:16-17, Jesus adds that in the last days "...*ye shall be betrayed both by parents, and brethren, and kinsfolks, and friends; and some of you shall they cause to be put to death. And ye shall be hated of all men for my name's sake.*"

There will be a powerplay between popularity with people and passion for God in the last days. Those who commit to love God passionately will walk in His light, but those who seek to please men will be overwhelmed with darkness. In Psalm 36:7-9, the Psalmist said "how *excellent is thy lovingkindness, O God! therefore the children of men put their trust under the shadow of thy wings. They shall be abundantly satisfied with the fatness of thy house; and thou shalt make them drink of the river of thy pleasures. For with thee is the fountain of life: in thy light shall we see light.*"

There is one shadow that never grows dark, and that is the shadow of the Alnmighty! Under that shadow, brightness and light are common place because in His shadow is the substance called light! In Ephesians 4:17-18, Paul adjures the Church to "...*walk not as other Gentiles walk, in the vanity of their mind, having the understanding* **darkened,** *being alienated from the life of God through the ignorance that is in them, because of the blindness of their heart.*"

The vanity of the mind is likened to the shadow, while the life of God is the substance (in Ephesians 4:17-18). Do you want a *substantial* life, or do you want to live forever in the shadows? When Jesus came, He chose to replace the shadows of existence with the substance of life. He said, in Matthew 4:16, that "*the people which sat in* **darkness saw great light***; and to them which sat in the region and* **shadow of death light is sprung up.***"

He (Jesus) is the secret to a light filled with substance and devoid of shadows of death and darkness. He asks, in Isaiah 29:17-

18, that "*Is it not yet a very little while, and Lebanon shall be turned into a fruitful field, and the fruitful field shall be esteemed as a forest? And in that day shall the deaf hear the words of the book, and the eyes of the blind shall see out of obscurity, and **out of darkness?**"*

Your best days are ahead of you, if you embrace the light of His glorious gospel (2 Corinthians 4:4). He (God) is the one who "... *revealeth the deep and secret things: he knoweth what is in the darkness, and the light dwelleth with him*" (Daniel 2:22). If they ignore Him, however, they will become "...*vain in their imaginations, (so that)... their foolish heart* (is) *darkened* (and) *professing themselves to be wise, they became fools*" (Rom 1:21-22).

LEARN TO BE A LION

The nature of a lion is to be a ferocious carnivore. It is born with everything it needs to hunt successfully, including clawed hands and feet, large canine fangs, strong jaws to grab the prey by the neck, and an uncanny ability to climb trees vertically or swim for an animal that size.

In spite of all these attributes, only 20% of lions survive to their second birthday, and less than 40% to their first birthday.1 Majority die in their first year of life, and the most common causes of death are starvation, animal attacks, and abandonment.

Even though a lion has everything, in vivo, needed to succeed as a predator they still struggle to survive. In Ezekiel 19:5-6, the Bible tells us that "...*when she (the lioness) saw that she had waited, and her hope was lost, then she took another of her whelps, and made him a young lion. And he went up and down among the lions,...became a young lion, and **learned** to catch the prey, and devoured men.*"

It is impossible to live like a lion without first learning to be a lion. You can look like a lion, roar like a lion, but until you start learning what it takes to be alion you will never live like a lion. The days of beginnings are the days of learning, and this book is designed to unleash the lion in you but first you must learn.

The power of a victorious mind starts with a consciousness of who you are. It will fail when you are ignorant. In 2 Timothy 3:13-15, apostle Paul advises the last days Church saying *"...evil men and seducers shall wax worse and worse, deceiving, and being deceived. But continue thou in the things which thou hast learned and hast been assured of, knowing of whom thou hast **learned** them;...that the man of God may be perfect, thoroughly furnished unto all good works."*

My prayer is that this book feeds the lion within you, and unleashes the lion of the tribe of Judea through you. A learner is a leader, and if Jesus could first learn before accomplishing His global mission (Hebrews 5:8) how much more you and I? The penalty for not learning, however, is *"...having the understanding darkened, (and) being alienated from the life of God through the ignorance that is in them, because of the blindness of their heart...but ye have not so **learned** Christ"* (Ephesians 4:18,20).

MY FINAL EXAMS STARTED WITH MY FIRST!

I had reading colleagues during my medical school years, and I would always tell them, after a grueling exam, that I expected an A grade from that exam. They would be confused, as they couldn't reconcile my position at near bottom of the class then with my expectations of getting top grades and graduating at the top of the class.

I spent adequate time studying but never compromised with my fellowship/ Church time or prayer time. On the day before our final exam to be a qualified medical doctor, I was in the Wednesday night prayer meeting/Bible study praising and praying to God while my colleagues read.

At the meeting, the leader of the sisters' fellowship was noted to be sick and I volunteered to take her to the emergency room (ER) of my teaching hospital that night. I was expected to take the final exams the next day, and as part of the (oral) exams, I was expected to identify a medical condition strictly by talking and examining a previously unknown patient.

While waiting for my sisters' coordinator to be attended to in the ER, I got busy talking with a middle aged male patient in the ER. This pleasant patient opened up about his health challenges, and how he was in the ER for protracted heart failure secondary to a valvular abnormality. Eventually, after the sisters co-ordinator (Ofoamaka) had seen the ER physician I took her back to her hostel.

When I arrived for the exam the next morning, I was pleasantly surprised to see the gentleman I had seen in the ER the night before as my clinical patient for the exam. Feigning ignorance of him, or his health conditions, I examined him with precision and accuracy. I gave the diagnosis, and the examiner said that I had done wonderfully well and so had passed the exams in flying colors.

While my reading mates were tortured waiting for the results of the exam, I relocated to my Dad's house in Abuja confident of my success in the exams. Eventually, after the results were released, I found out I had graduated at the top echelons of my class with the first batch of successful candidates.

Some of my colleagues who had mocked me when I stated my future sucess from the beginning, unfortunately had to repeat their classes and await another exam in another six months. The scriptures that said, "...*behold, there are last which shall be first, and there are first which shall be last*" (Luke 13:30) had been confirmed through my life. Selah

Prayer: Light of the world, light your life in my life in Jesus name.

CONTACTS

This ministry, Faith and Power Ministries, is dedicated to showing the power of God once again to this generation. It is dedicated to ushering in the last days' glory of God and, in the course of doing so, turning lives around for the kingdom of God.

Our email is tobemomah@yahoo.com. We can be contacted via email or via our websites www.tobemomah.com or on www.faithandpowerministries.org. I currently reside in West Monroe, Louisiana and can be reached at P.O Box 550 West Monroe, Louisiana 71294 U.S.A.

OTHER BOOKS BY THE AUTHOR

1. **Tobe Momah**. A General and a gentleman (*biography of General Sam Momah*) –Spectrum books 2003
2. **Tobe Momah.** Between the systems, soul and spirit of man (*a Christian doctors view on sickness and its source*) – Xulon press 2007
3. **Tobe Momah**. Building lasting relationships (a Manual for the complete home) – Xulon press 2006
4. **Tobe Momah.** Metrobiology – *A Study of life in the city* 1ST ed (a Doctor`s Daily Devotional) – Xulon Press 2008
5. **Tobe Momah.** Pregnancy: Pitfalls, Pearls and principles – Westbow Press 2011

6. **Tobe Momah.** Ultimate Harvest: Five F.A.C.T.S on Fruitfulness and how to grow the American Church again – Westbow Press 2012

7. **Tobe Momah.** From Edginess to Eagerness...*taking the Church back to willing service* Westbow Press 2012

8. **Tobe Momah.** Fear no Evil...*by hating evil* – Westbow Press 2013

9. **Tobe Momah.** Fear no Evil...by hating evil: A daily devotional – Westbow Press 2013

10. **Tobe Momah.** HEALING LIVES......*Stories of encouragement and achievement in the midst of sickness* – Westbow Press 2014

11. **Tobe Momah.** STEPS to the altar...*why a chosen generation is living ashamed at the altar* – Westbow Press 2014

12. **Tobe Momah.** Stay In Tune (S.I.T)...*Challenging an always going but Godless culture!* – Advanced Global Publishing 2015

13. **Tobe Momah.** Stay In Tune (S.I.T)...*Living daily in His presence* (A 366-day Devotional) – Advanced Global Publishing 2015

14. **Tobe Momah.** The Death Knell called Depression. Advanced Global Publishing – 2015

15. **Tobe Momah.** Heirs not Helper...*Raising a generation of plunderers, who are not just pleaders.* Advanced Global Publishing – 2015

16. **Tobe Momah.** Loyalty Legends...*living a life of abundance through the anointing.* Westbow Press (2017)

17. **Tobe Momah.** HEALING LIVES (II)...*Stories of encouragement and achievement in the midst of sickness* – Westbow Press (2017)

18. **Tobe Momah.** The Spirit of Acceleration...*rekindling the hope of those sick at heart!* – Christian Faith Publishers (2019)

19. **Tobe Momah**. Gracing Favor...*Two leaved gates of unprecedented greatness*. West point Press (2022).

20. **Tobe Momah.** Assertive Initiative...*the light that darkness cannot comprehend*. West point press (2022).

ABOUT THE AUTHOR

Tobe Momah MD, currently serves as the Vision Co-coordinator of Faith and Power Ministries, a 501c3 organization, with a prayer ministry in Jackson, Mississippi, and Monroe, Louisiana that is focused on building a prayer hedge over these two states and her surrounding environs. In pursuit of his God given vision to *"show His strength to this generation, and His power to all shall come..."* (Psalm 71:18), faith and Power Ministries airs Miracle radio on WNPR 99.1 Mississippi every Wednesday (6:30am – 7am) weekly and *"Health and Wellness with Dr. Tobe"* television programs daily on KMCT 39 Monroe, Louisiana.

This is beside the twice monthly Holy Ghost Night meetings, that hold on the second and last Fridays of each month in Jackson, MS and Monroe LA respectively (between 11pm and 4 am). The ministry also organizes an annual medical missions and through these missions (which have occurred annually between 2012 and 2021), thousands have been saved, healed, and delivered.

Dr Tobe Momah is core faculty and associate professor of Family Medicine at the University of Mississippi Medical Center (UMMC), Jackson USA since arriving Mississippi in 2017. He trained at the University of Nigeria, College of Medicine, Enugu Nigeria - where he served as two time vice president of the Christian Union campus fellowship - and the University of London, School of Hygiene and tropical medicine where he obtained his medical degree in Medicine/ surgery and his Master's in medical parasitology/tropical medicine respectively.

Tobe Momah has more than forty scientific publications and nineteen books in print. He attended the family medicine residency at The Brooklyn Hospital center, Weill Cornell Hospital system in New York, and has worked in the private, public and community health sphere prior to entering the academia at UMMC. He has traveled extensively to African nations, including Sierra Leone, Nigeria, Ethiopia, Mozambique on medical missions and provides free medical health care to the residents of that area who require medical help. He is board certified in Family Medicine and obesity Medicine and serves as an associate Pastor at Miracle Temple Evangelistic Church, Jackson MS.

He is married to Rita Momah (a public health specialist) and they are blessed with a set of twins Kingsley and Gloria. They make their home in the Madison, Ms area.